THE STRUCTURE OF POWER IN NORTH CHINA DURING THE FIVE DYNASTIES

THE STRUCTURE OF POWER IN NORTH CHINA DURING THE FIVE DYNASTIES

by

WANG GUNGWU

STANFORD UNIVERSITY PRESS
STANFORD, CALIFORNIA

STANFORD UNIVERSITY PRESS
Stanford, California

Printed in the United States of America
First published in 1963 by the University of Malaya Press
Paperback edition first published in 1967
by Stanford University Press
L.C. 67-26649

To my father

Preface

Leading scholars in China and Japan have during the last three decades opened a new era in research work on the T'ang and Sung dynasties. I owe an immense debt of gratitude to them and to their numerous studies which have contributed so much to our understanding of these periods. For this difficult period of transition between the two dynasties, I am specially grateful for a number of articles by Professor Y. Sudō and his colleagues and students in Japan. My conclusions, however, are my own and I hope that errors in interpretation will not be laid at the door of these scholars.

This study was originally submitted as a thesis for the degree of Ph. D. at the University of London and the research for this work was done in London and Cambridge in 1955-1957. At these centres, I received the ungrudging help of both Professor D. C. Twitchett and Professor E. G. Pulleyblank. For their personal attention and their great patience with my efforts to look at Chinese history afresh, I am indeed grateful. At London, I also received much encouragement from Professor D. G. E. Hall whose sympathy gave me the courage to turn from the history of South-east Asia to that of China when the material available made that necessary. And, I must mention Mr. E. Lust of the Chinese library of the School of Oriental and African Studies and Dr. M. Scott of the Chinese library of the University of Cambridge, whose kind help made my work easier and more pleasant.

There are many others to whom I owe a great deal. I should mention Professor C. N. Parkinson, Professor E. T. Stokes and the late Mr. Ian Macgregor who, each in his own way, taught me to love history; also, my friend and fellow-student, Dr. Wong Lin Ken, who read my manuscript and offered me valuable criticism. Also, the research was made possible by the generosity of the

British Council and the China Society in London. For their support, I am indeed grateful.

It is not possible to say how much I owe to my wife. At every stage of my research and writing, she has given me encouragement and help, and the final work is, in many ways, as much hers as mine.

WANG GUNGWU

London, 1961

Contents

Maps

Note: In Maps II–VI the names of prefectures in each region are given. Names of provincial capitals are underlined.

List of Rulers, Late T'ang to Early Sung

T'ANG

Li Yen (Hsi-tsung), 874-888
Li Chieh (Chao-tsung), 888-904
Li Tso (Chao-hsüan-ti), 904-907

LIANG

Chu Wên (T'ai-tsu), 907-912
Chu Yu-kuei (Ying-wang), 912-913
Chu Yu-chên (Mo-ti), 913-923

LATER T'ANG

Li Ts'un-hsü (Chuang-tsung), 923,926
Li Ssŭ-yüan (Ming-tsung), 926-933
Li Ts'ung-hou (Min-ti), 933-934
Li Ts'ung-k'o (Lu-wang), 934-937

CHIN

Shih Ching-t'ang (Kao-tsu), 937-942
Shih Ch'ung-kuei (Ch'u-ti), 942-946

Interregnum: *KHITAN LIAO* Yeh-lü
Tê-kuang (T'ai-tsung), 946-947

HAN

Liu Chih-yüan (Kao-tsu), 947-948
Liu Ch'êng-yu (Yin-ti), 948-950

CHOU

Kuo Wei (T'ai-tsu), 951-954
Ch'ai Jung (Shih-tsung), 954-959
Ch'ai Tsung-hsün (Kung-ti), 959-960

SUNG

Chao K'uang-yin (T'ai-tsu), 960-976
Chao K'uang-i (T'ai-tsung), 976-998

Abbreviations

CTS	*Chiu T'ang Shu*
CWTS	*Chiu Wu-tai Shih*
HTS	*Hsin T'ang Shu*
HWTS	*Hsin Wu-tai Shih*
K'ao-i	*Tzŭ-chih T'ung-chien K'ao-i*
SPPY	*Ssŭ-pu Pei-yao*
SS	*Sung Shih*
TCTC	*Tzŭ-chih T'ung-chien*
TFYK	*Ts'ê-fu Yüan-kuei*
TSCC	*Ts'ung-shu Chi-ch'êng*
WTHY	*Wu-tai Hui-yao*

In this study, Chinese dates are abbreviated in the following way: 4th/926 refers to the fourth month of 926. When the day of the month is important, it is placed first as a cardinal number, e.g. 21/4th/926 refers to the twenty-first day of the fourth month of 926.

THE STRUCTURE OF POWER IN NORTH CHINA DURING THE FIVE DYNASTIES

CHAPTER ONE

Introduction

In the history of China, the T'ang and Sung dynasties have often been mentioned together, the first as a period of vigorous growth and brilliant achievements and the second as one of literary and artistic maturity. It is rarely noted that between these two great dynasties was the period of the Wu-tai (Five Dynasties). From the following table, the reason for this neglect is clear:

T'ang dynasty, 618-907

Wu-tai, 907-960

Five Dynasties	*Ten Kingdoms*	
Liang, 907-923	Wu Nan T'ang	(Kiangsu, Anhwei, Kiangsi)
T'ang, 923-937	Wu-Yüeh	(Chekiang)
	Min	(Fukien)
Chin, 937-946	Nan Han	(Kwangtung and Kwangsi)
(Interregnum: Khitan Liao, 946-947)	Ch'u	(Hunan)
	Early Shu Later Shu	(Szechuan)
Han, 947-950	Nan P'ing	(Hupei)
Chou, 951-960	Pei Han	(Shansi, after 950)

Sung dynasty, 960-1279
Northern, 960-1126
Southern, 1126-1279

Following after almost 300 years of T'ang and coming before more than 300 years of Sung, the Wu-tai period was too short and confusing to be considered either interesting or significant.

Traditional Chinese historians have been content to find one main topic of interest in the fifty-three years from the fall of the T'ang to the foundation of the Sung. The topic concerned the problem of how the T'ang mandate was passed on to the Sung. It gave rise to arguments about dynastic legitimacy and the respective status of the five dynasties of North China and the various 'dynasties' to the south and west, but it did not stimulate much interest in the history of the period itself. This neglect was largely due to the fragmented state of the old empire. In a period of division, there was no centre of authority and therefore no integral subject for study. Also, although the five dynasties in North China were important as the precursors of the Sung and the bearers of the Mandate of Heaven, they each survived for so short a period that the historians, accustomed to studying history by dynastic period, were driven to conclude that there was little to say about them as there was no time for anything important to have happened.

It is now widely recognized that many significant issues in Chinese history have been obscured by the traditional dynastic approach. The weakness of this approach is particularly remarkable in periods of disunity and periods of frequent dynastic change. The Wu-tai was a period of the greatest disunity and the most frequent dynastic changes. In the Chinese mind, it was a unique example of the anarchy and moral confusion which inevitably followed the breakdown of the Confucian state. Hence there was probing inquiry into the reasons for the failure of the T'ang central government and uncritical praise of Sung reunification. The intervening years of lawlessness and disorder were fitted into a preconceived pattern as a warning and example to future statesmen.

It may well be that the Wu-tai period will always be known as one of moral and political disintegration. Such a classification, however, will not do justice to the two generations of men who lived through the difficult years. Nor will it help us to understand how the social and political framework survived and developed through the dynastic changes, and how the enduring traditions of the Chinese were transmitted to a new era. What is necessary is a new exploration of this transitional period free from Confucian preconceptions. The exploration may lead to several 'interpretations' and numerous fresh distortions before we settle on a clearer picture. But nothing surely can equal the judgements of the tough-minded Confucian historians both in severity and lack of sympathy.

The present study is an attempt to explain some of the features of the Wu-tai period in the light of the movement of events, the changes in political institutions and the ever shifting decisions of the many men in positions of power.[1] It concentrates on the evolution of a new structure of power from the last years of the Huang Ch'ao rebellion, 875-884, when the T'ang empire had all but disintegrated, to the Khitan invasion in 946-947. During this period of 60 years, the distribution of power went through a fundamental change. The system of military governors known as the *chieh-tu shih* which had undermined the authority of the T'ang dynasty was made obsolete. Independent provincial power was broken down and a new type of imperial government emerged.

This new type of government has never been fully examined. It has always appeared that the victory of the Confucian state under the Sung dynasty was merely the re-establishment of the T'ang system with a few modifications. The modifications were supposed to include greater centralization under the bureaucrats and the re-establishment of an even more Confucian government. This study shows that the changes during the Wu-tai period led to a central government which succeeded not because it rejected the *chieh-tu shih* system and returned to T'ang institutions but because it had incorporated the basic features of the *chieh-tu shih* system itself. This development came about firstly because the emperors of the Wu-tai up to the Khitan invasion had all been powerful *chieh-tu shih* themselves and thus brought to the new imperial courts those aspects of provincial government which they had found effective. Also, the emperors were able to create new

[1] My historical study of the period contrasts sharply with the sociological method used by Professor W. Eberhard. In a series of articles on the Wu-tai and in his *Conquerors and Rulers, social forces in Medieval China*, Professor Eberhard has explored the rich material of the *Chiu Wu-tai Shih* in order to clarify his theory of the 'gentry' society and to pursue his ideas on foreign conquests of China. He has not been interested in Wu-tai history itself and has made no attempt to help us understand the developments during this period. His contribution towards theoretical controversy has been valuable, but it is necessary to remind students of 9th and 10th century history that much work has still to be done on historical principles. The static analysis of one source, however rich, which Professor Eberhard has made, cannot be recommended.

centres of power at the court and to absorb other provincial personnel, both civil and military, into these centres. The two main features were the Palace Commissions through which the *chieh-tu shih* retainers exercised great influence and the Emperor's Personal Army which served the emperor in the same way that the *ya-ping* (governor's private army) had served their *chieh-tu shih*.

This study attempts to show that the transition from the T'ang to the Sung can better be understood in terms of the important changes during the first half of the Wu-tai period. It rejects the traditional view that each dynasty can be explained through the actions of its founders, that is, that the strength and weaknesses of the Sung can be understood by merely examining the decisions of T'ai-tsu, T'ai-tsung and their ministers. Certainly, with the Wu-tai, the changes were more fundamental than have been noted. It is not possible to understand fully the success of the Sung without first recognizing the complex and painful process which produced the government the Sung emperors eventually inherited.

It will be noted that this is not a study of all the five Wu-tai dynasties. The work begins with the Huang Ch'ao rebellion and ends with the Khitan invasion. It covers the last twenty years of the T'ang, the dynasties of Liang, Later T'ang and Chin and the beginning of the Han dynasty in 947. The 60 years studied here comprise merely one segment of the long history of the decline and re-establishment of a centralized empire.

It is not our task to reject the traditional dynastic periods, according to which the T'ang ended in 907 and the Sung began in 960. The dynastic periods have their own uses. But in terms of power and conquest rather than morality and legitimacy, a more significant division can be found in the year 755 when T'ang central power suffered a setback from which it never recovered, and in the year 979 when the Sung dynasty reunited under strong central rule the greater part of the territories of the T'ang empire. Between the years 755 and 979, one group after another, with the exception of the Sung founders, attempted without success to rebuild the stricken empire. A crucial point was reached in 884 when the T'ang empire survived only in name after the Huang

Ch'ao rebels were driven out of the capital, Ch'ang-an. At this time, central power was at its weakest.

During the 130 years from 755 to 884, two periods may be discerned, a period of apparent recovery from 755 to 820 and one of gradual but unmistakable decline until the catastrophic uprisings of 875-884. As for the 95 years from 884 to 979, it is more difficult to discern different periods of development. Certainly the first 40 years are striking as a period when two equally powerful rivals fought each other for the right to succeed the T'ang dynasty. On the one hand, there was Chu Wen and the remnants of the Huang Ch'ao rebels, on the other, there were the Sha-t'o Turks, bearing the T'ang imperial surname, in alliance with the Chinese forces of independent Ho-pei.[2] Until 923, the struggle was bitter and Chu Wen and his sons ruled uneasily as the Liang emperors and successors of the T'ang. In 923, the alliance of Sha-t'o Turks and Ho-pei Chinese won and the later struggles were fought between rivals within the alliance until Sung T'ai-tsu defeated the Sha-t'o ruler of Pei Han (Shansi) in 979.

From the point of view of the contenders for power it may be convenient to distinguish between the struggles of different groups in 884-923 and those within one group in 923-979. But in this study of the power structure, such a division would be meaningless. There was no significant change in the institutions where power was held and exercised. The T'ang 'restoration' in 923-926 revived features of T'ang government which had already been proved ineffectual. And after 926, it was found necessary to re-introduce military and administrative changes which Chu Wen had experimented with in 907-912. These were the basic features of the *chieh-tu shih* system which, in the following 20 years, transformed the nature of imperial government. By 947, the court had become an enlarged *chieh-tu shih* establishment dominated by the Emperor's Army (as the *ya-chün*) and the palace commissioners (as the *ch'in-li*) and made respectable by the bureaucrats and literati (as the *p'an-kuan*, *shu-chi* and *t'ui-kuan*). And outside the

[2] See Appendix, 'The Alliance of Ho-tung and Ho-pei in Wu-tai history', where I show briefly how this alliance came about and how it was meaningful for the rest of the Wu-tai, especially in the period 926-960.

court the Khitan invasion had broken the 190-year old independence of Ho-pei and exhausted the resources of most of the other provinces. The reconstruction of North China could start afresh. From then on, the *chieh-tu shih* system was no longer a threat to central power; what remained of it had become a part of imperial government itself.

CHAPTER TWO

The Military Governors and the T'ang Court 883-904

During the first half of the 8th century, a number of senior frontier commands were created for the defence of the northern and western borders of the T'ang empire. By 755, there were ten such commands, the commanders being known as *chieh-tu shih*, variously translated as 'regional commander', 'commissaire impérial au commandement d'une région' and 'military governor'.[1] Although the powers of the *chieh-tu shih* were primarily military, the commanders were later given more control over administrative matters. In time, the court conferred upon them several other titles which gave each of them full control of at least one prefecture and supervisory powers over many others. These additional titles also gave them special fiscal rights as well as rights over the local militia and the prefectural garrisons. In this way, they became in fact *governors* with military responsibilities. For this reason, the system of *chieh-tu shih* which became a dominant institution during the second half of the T'ang dynasty is here referred to as the system of military governors.

The military governors were first appointed for the specific purpose of defending the frontiers. There was initially no change in the administrative and fiscal system and the main administrative unit was still the prefecture over which a military governor was allowed only the right of inspection. But the rebellion of An Lu-

[1] The term *chieh-tu shih* has been translated in recent studies as 'Military Governor' (E. G. Pulleyblank, *The Background of the Rebellion of An Lu-shan*); as '*commissaire impérial au commandement d'une région*' (R. des Rotours, *Traité des Fonctionnaires*); as 'Regional Commander' (E. O. Reischauer, *Ennin's Diary*); and as 'Legate' (Howard S. Levy, *Biography of Huang Ch'ao*). Detailed discussions of the origin of the title are found in Pulleyblank, *op. cit.*, n. 32, pp. 149-152, also n. 13, pp. 106-109; and des Rotours, *op. cit.*, pp. 656-657, n. 1 and 2.

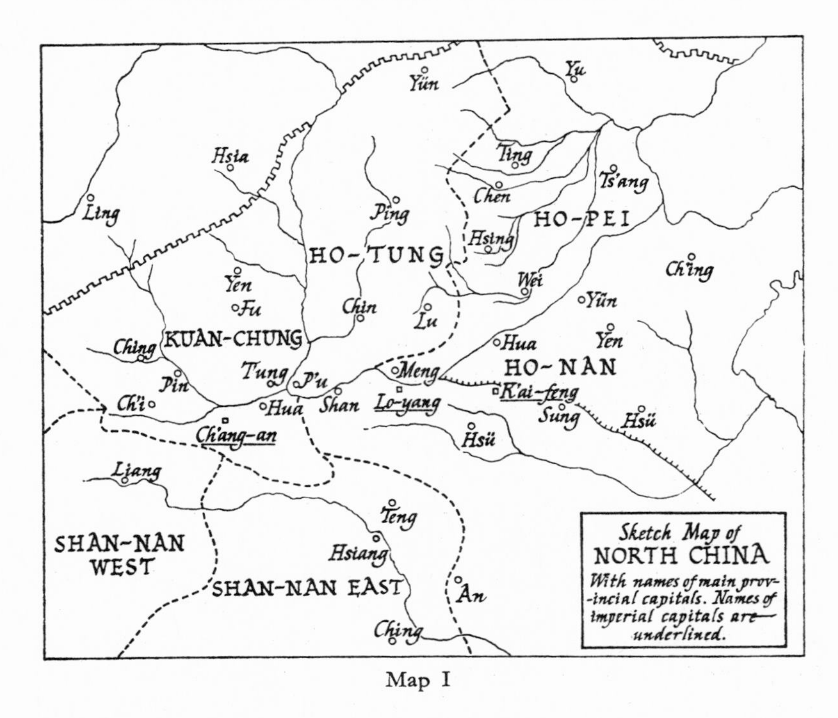

Map I

shan and his successors (755-763) brought great changes to the system. During the rebellion, several new military governors were appointed by both the central and rebel governments. When the rebellion was checked by the surrender of most of the rebel generals, the T'ang court appointed three of these generals to be governors of new provinces created from the larger provinces in the Ho-pei and Ho-nan region. Other governors were appointed to protect the metropolitan province of Kuan-chung as well as the key economic areas of the Yangtse basin. After the rebellion, the court was forced to concede to the governors greater control over the prefectures in their provinces. Most of them had large private armies which dominated the prefectural garrisons, and some even began to appoint their own prefects.

The details of the long struggle for control between the T'ang court through its loyal governors, and the ex-rebels who became increasingly independent, are outside the scope of this study.

Briefly, the struggle which lasted for over a century was unresolved, although several important battles were won by the court from time to time. The victories were gained partly by force, but more often by compromise and diplomacy, and by playing off the rebellious governors against one another. Another important factor was the policy of reducing the size of provinces in order to weaken the power of the governors. The emperor Hsien-tsung (806-820) was especially successful in carrying out this policy. By the end of his reign, the number of provinces in the Ho-pei region had increased from three in 762 to six and in the Ho-nan region from five to nine. Some of the governors were further weakened by the return of military authority to the prefects in each of their provinces. This meant that many of the governors had their powers reduced and limited to the prefectures in which their provincial capitals were situated. But the Ho-pei provinces which were in the hands of hereditary governors were unaffected by this policy and these governors continued to appoint their own prefects.[2] After 820, there were at least five such provinces, and although these were reduced to three by 845, the court never succeeded in regaining control over the greater part of the Ho-pei region.

Several imperial victories were won in the years 806-845. They were won chiefly by units of the reorganized imperial armies and the provincial armies bordering on the recalcitrant provinces. The older militia (*fu-ping*) system had long been abandoned and new professional armies were recruited at the capital and locally in the provinces. The palace armies had been expanded and under

[2] The clearest contemporary account of this was that by the ex-rebel officer and governor of Ts'ang, Wu Ch'ung-yin, in 819, preserved in his biography in *CTS* 161 (also in *TCTC* 241, Yüan-ho 14 (819)/4/*ping-yin*): 'I believe that the reason why the Ho-pei provinces have been able to resist the court is briefly this—it was because the prefects had been deprived of their office and the garrison officers allowed to take over military affairs. If the prefects were each given his share of authority and had charge of the garrison, then how can the governors revolt with one prefecture, even if they were as crafty as (An) Lu-shan and (Shih) Ssŭ-ming?'

As a result of this memorial, an edict ordering a reform of this practice was issued on the 19/4th/819. In Ho-pei, however, the reforms were effective only in Ts'ang province under Wu Ch'ung-yin himself.

the eunuchs the Shên-ts'ê (Divine Strategy) Army had become the largest and most privileged. In the provinces, the loyal governors were ordered to build up and maintain armies not only for local defence and garrisoning the frontiers, but also for augmenting any expeditionary army against rebellious governors. Both these developments had important consequences. The new palace armies gave the eunuchs the power to challenge that of the bureaucrats, and the struggle was one of the chief features of ninth-century T'ang history.[3] The eunuchs could directly influence imperial succession, and through the emperors they supported obtained further powers and privileges. They also had control over the provinces either by getting generals of the Shên-ts'ê Army appointed as governors or by appointing eunuchs to supervise the governors.[4]

As for the new provincial armies, there were several kinds. There were the armies which the independent governors had built up out of the remnants of An Lu-shan's army and further expanded with fresh recruitment in their provinces. These governors had encouraged professionalism, something not found before outside the imperial capital, and their strength as well as their weakness stemmed from the use of these hereditary officers.[5] The development of this kind of army forced the T'ang court to station permanent armies in the neighbouring provinces. It also

[3] Ch'ên Yin-k'o, *T'ang-tai Chêng-chih Shih Shu-lun Kao*, pp. 104-127.

[4] This system of eunuch supervision was known as the *chien-chün* system. There was an older *chien-chün* system which became ineffective by the beginning of Hsüan-tsung's reign. E. G. Pulleyblank, p. 74 (and p. 155, n. 55), calling them 'controllers', says eunuchs were first appointed *chien-chün* 'about 737 or perhaps earlier'. But this institution became important only after the An Lu-shan rebellion, when eunuchs began to take over more military responsibilities.

[5] Military families, often of non-Chinese origins, produced the high officers who either supported the governing family and its heirs or elected a governor among themselves whenever they thought it necessary. A measure of their power is the number of governors they killed or removed when these governors tried to return to the imperial fold. Also significant is the number of times court-chosen governors were refused entry or driven off by them.

A brief survey of the changes in leadership, mutinies and internal struggles in these provinces may be found in *T'ang Fang-chên Nien-piao*. Also see *CTS* 141-143 and 180 and *HTS* 210-213 for the biographies of the independent governors.

forced the court to encourage the same kind of professionalism and hereditary military class. Thus on both sides of a long but fluid frontier, similar types of armies were established. By the middle of the 9th century only the loyalties of the governors and the commanders distinguished the armies built up by the court from those of the independent governors.

There were two other kinds of armies which were also significant. The first of these were frontier garrisons which included units of the palace and other provincial armies. An important feature in these frontier garrisons was the presence of tribesmen whose loyalty could never be taken for granted. The second type were the smaller armies south of the Yangtse which were not large enough to justify the appointment of military governors to supervise them. They were based chiefly on local militia and were in the charge of Inspectors (*kuan-ch'a shih*). Sometimes these armies also included units from provincial armies in the north. Although they were adequate for defence against local banditry, they were helpless against any large rebellion or invasion. Any such danger would require the despatch of northern armies.[6]

After 820, governors began to be appointed at regular intervals to several provinces in the Ho-nan and Ho-tung regions. The new governors were a mixture of bureaucrats, generals of the imperial armies and surrendered rebels. In 845, regular appointments could be made to all but three provinces in Ho-pei.[7] From 845 to

[6] The use of tribesmen was not limited to frontier provinces. They were used in small numbers, for example, south of the Yangtse, for suppressing the rebellion in Yüeh (Chê-tung) province in 860; *TCTC* 250, Hsien-t'ung 1 (860)/4th month. In 869 large numbers were brought in to suppress the $Hsü_2$ rebellion. These included three tribes of Sha-t'o Turks, and tribes of T'u-yü-hun, Ta-tan (Tartar) and Ch'i-pi; *TCTC* 251, Hsien-t'ung 9(868)/11th month.

The importance of the smaller armies of South China is the effect they had on the north. Whenever there was serious trouble, northern armies had to be sent to deal with it. The most important examples are the An-nan troubles which began in 858 and led to the Nan Chao invasion of 862-866, and the rebellion of Ch'iu Fu in Yüeh province in 859-860. See *TCTC* 250, Hsien-t'ung 1 (860)/6th month; and *TCTC* 250, Hsien-t'ung 3 (862)/2nd month, ff. for the An-nan invasions.

[7] *T'ang Fang-chên Nien-piao* shows that before 820, almost all the governors of Ho-pei, Ho-tung and eastern Ho-nan held office for more than five years,

the outbreak of the Huang Ch'ao rebellion in 875, the governors were predominantly important bureaucrats. Table I, p. 12, for

TABLE I[8]

Year	*No. of governors known*	*Aristocratic or literati origins*		*Military of rebel origins*		*Unclassified*
	(a)	(b)	(c) Not certain	(d)	(e) Not certain	(f)
845	25	16	(2)	6	(1)	—
855	26	24	(1)	1	—	—
865	22	18	—	3	(1)	—
875	25	12	(2)	7	(2)	2

the years 845, 855, 865 and 875 shows the trend of the appointments for twenty-eight provinces north of the Yangtse (the three independent provinces of Ho-pei are not included).

This trend can be a rough gauge of conditions prevailing. There was a relatively peaceful period from 845 to 860 during which the number of bureaucrat governors rose to twenty-four, followed by risings, mutinies and a tribal invasion in the following period from 860 to 875 when the number was halved. It is interesting to note that there was only one non-bureaucrat governor in 855. He was T'ien Mou, the son of a rebel governor who had surrendered and, in 855, was the governor of $Hsü_2$ province for the second time. He had been called in to control the mutinous provincial

and that most of them did so till their death. After 820, they were considerably fewer. The notable exceptions, apart from the 'three governments of Ho-pei' were the governors of Lu, Ting and $Hsü_2$. Of these, $Hsü_2$ province accepted regular court appointments after 832, Ting after 838 and Lu after 844; see *TCTC* 244, T'ai-ho 5 (832)/3/*hsin-ch'ou* and *hsin-yu*; 246, K'ai-ch'êng 3 (838)/9/*jên-shên* to 11/*chia-hsü*; and 247, Hui-ch'ang 3 (843)/4/*hsin-wei* to 248, Hui-ch'ang 4 (844)/9/*wu-ch'ên*.

[8] This table has been drawn up from the *T'ang Fang-chên Nien-piao* and the *HTS*, 71-75, tables of the families of Chief Ministers.

In 845, the three provinces for which we have no information were Hsia, Yen and Ts'ang. The two governors of 'uncertain', but probably bureaucrat, origins in column (c) were those of $Hsü_3$ (Li Chih-fang) and P'u (Wei Kung-fu). The one 'uncertain' in (e) was the governor of Shuo-fang (Ho Ch'ing-ch'ao).

army in the one clearly restless area in the empire at that time.[9]

No attempt is made here to survey the events leading to the Huang Ch'ao rebellion in 875. But in order to understand what the rebellion did to the T'ang empire, it is necessary to describe briefly the relationship between a governor and the court on the eve of it. At this time, the court could rely on most of the governors it appointed and depended on them for the control of the provincial armies. Appointed by the court to help each of the governors in their duties were the eunuch Army Supervisor (*chien-chün*), the governor's Military Deputy (*hsing-chün ssŭ-ma*) and their assistants. On arrival at the provincial capital, the governor could recommend someone to be commander of the army (*tu-chih ping-ma shih*) though he probably always accepted the commander who was already there. He then selected men from the army for a residential garrison, or *ya-chün*, a kind of 'governor's guards'. The strength of this *ya-chün* varied considerably, but there were always an administrator in charge (*tu ya-ya*), an officer in command (*ya-nei*

In 855, the two provinces not included were Fu (in Kuan-nei) and Mêng (Ho-yang). The 'uncertain' one in (c) was the governor of Liang (Shan-nan West) (Wei Yu-i).

In 865, six provinces have been left out. These were Fu, Hsia, Ch'ing, Mêng, Shan and Ngo. The one 'uncertain' in (e) was the governor of Chên-wu (Kao Hung).

In 875, the three provinces left out were Hsia, Yen and Ts'ang. Two of the governors are not classified because there is no clue even to their probable origins. These were Lu Yung of Shan and Ts'ui Chi-k'ang of Ting. The two 'uncertain' in (c) were the governors of Pin (Li K'an) and Hua (Li T'ung). The two in (e) were those of Shuo-fang (T'ang Hung-fu) and Yün (Hsüeh Ch'ung).

There is no difficulty in classifying the governors of literati origins and those who had been rebels. But there is some doubt whether a man who had started his career in the imperial armies might not have been of aristocratic origins. In the examples above, however, emphasis is placed on aristocratic origins, and only military men of probably obscure origins have been placed in column (d) with those of rebel origins.

[9] The governor of Hsü$_2$ province in 855 was T'ien Mou, and it was this province which gave continuous trouble throughout this thirty-year period. In 5th/849, the army mutinied. It mutinied again after T'ien Mou left, in 4th/859; and after his death, in 7th/862. Biography of T'ien Mou in *CTS* 141 and *HTS* 148; also see *TCTC* 248, Ta-chung 3 (849)/5th month; 249, Ta-chung 13 (859)/4th month and 250, Hsien-t'ung 3(862)/7th month.

tu-chiang) and several officers (*ya-chiang, ya-hsiao*) and administrative officials (*ya-ya*).[10]

To help in general administration, the court appointed a number of bureaucrats as

fu-shih (Assistant Governor),
chieh-tu p'an-kuan (Governor's Administrator),
kuan-ch'a p'an-kuan (Inspector's Administrator),
chang shu-chi (Secretary),
kuan-ch'a chih-shih (Inspector's Secretary) and
t'ui-kuan (Law Administrator).

There were also the administrators and secretaries for the prefecture directly under the governor's control, and the magistrates of the counties in the prefecture. A governor could influence the appointment of all these subordinate officials if not actually select the men he wanted.[11]

The relationship between the governor and the prefects in his province varied from province to province. The court appointed the prefects and their staff independently, but they were clearly subject to the governor's supervision and control. Officially, the prefects could memorialize directly to the court, but they would normally hesitate to do so without consultation with their governor.

[10] On the various meaning of *ya*, see des Rotours, pp. 224-226, where he translates from the *Chung-kuo Ta Tzŭ-tien*. The *ya* here is the 'édifice servant à une administration', the 'bâtiment officiel' or even the 'palais (du commissaire impérial)'.

The provincial commander (*tu-chih ping-ma shih*) was helped by a Chief Discipline Officer (*tu yü-hou*) who was probably one of the officers of the residential garrison. Earlier in the T'ang, army affairs were administered by the governor's military deputy, but they were taken over by the *tu ya-ya* later on. The function of the deputy was much less important in the last decades of T'ang, especially when the governor was himself a military man; see *TFYK* 716, 13a-b.

[11] For further details of subordinate officials, see des Rotours, p. 656 ff. There are numerous references to governors recommending administrators and secretaries for both their prefectures and their provinces. Only assistant governors and military deputies seem to have been beyond the governors' own choice till after the Huang Ch'ao rebellion.

The classic example of a governor's choice of his highest officials is that of the governor of Ping (Ho-tung) in 880. The Chief Minister was appointed governor and brought with him his assistant governor, the governor's and inspector's administrators as well as the law administrator; *TCTC* 253, Kuang-ming 1 (880)/3/*hsin-wei*. This was, however, not the usual practice before 880.

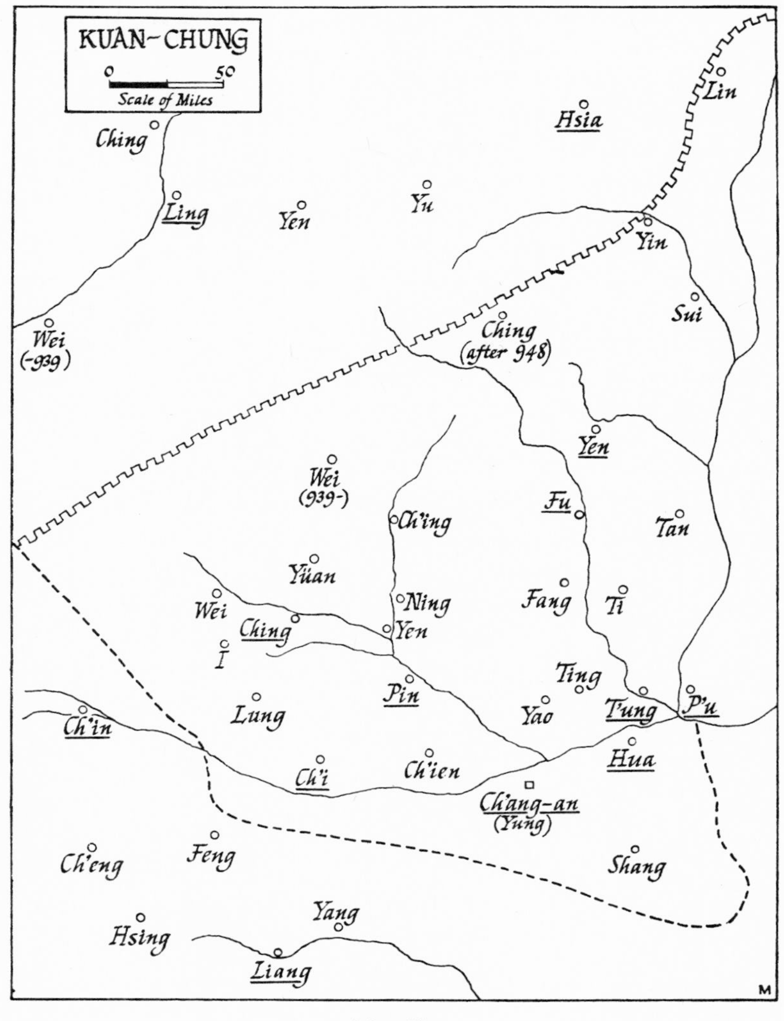

Map II

The prefects were mostly bureaucrats (except those in frontier prefectures) whose relationship with a bureaucrat governor was influenced by their ranks in the official hierarchy, and was therefore comparatively straightforward. But the officers of the provincial army probably had undue influence over those of the prefectural garrisons. This was because the provincial officers had a more permanent relationship with the prefectural troops than the bureaucrats who were regularly transferred.[12] With a governor of military and rebel origin, however, the prefects' relations were more complicated. They were allowed the control of their own garrisons, but an army-conscious governor who distrusted bureaucrat soldiers would prefer to have all units in his province under his command. Some of the governors created special garrisons with police and defence duties in strategic counties (*chên-chiang*) within the prefects' territories and either filled the garrisons with their own men or at least sent their officers to command them. Because of this, the prefects' military authority was often negligible.[13]

Many of the above features were changed in the decade after 875, chiefly owing to the ineffective attempts by the court to crush the Huang Ch'ao rebellion. A major factor in Huang Ch'ao's success was the discontent within the provincial armies. Since the P'ang Hsün mutiny, 868-869, was put down with the help of tribal cavalry from outside the Great Wall, this discontent seems to have grown. From 875 onwards, there was at least one mutiny every year. In 877, mutineers in two provinces, both within a hundred and fifty miles of Ch'ang-an, removed their governors. The most serious mutinies took place north of the Huang Ho in 878-880 when first the Sha-t'o Turks, the Ping provincial armies and local militia (in Shansi), and finally the reinforcements from

[12] This is borne out by the ease with which some officers of provincial garrisons took over the prefectures in their provinces after 880. Examples are, Ch'in Tsung-ch'üan's taking over of Ts'ai Chou (*CTS* 200 B and *HTS* 225), Shih P'u taking Su Chou after proclaiming himself governor at Hsü$_2$ (*CTS* 182; *HTS* 188 and *CWTS* 13), Chu Hsüan in Yün province (*CWTS* 13) and Wang Ching-wu in Ch'ing province (*HTS* 187). Also *TCTC* 254, Kuang-ming 1 (880)/11/*hsin-wei*; Chung-ho 1 (881)/8/*chi-ch'ou*; 255, Chung-ho 2 (882)/8th and 10th months as well as *K'ao-i*.

[13] The *chên* (garrisons) in des Rotours, pp. 737-743 and *T'ang Liu Tien* 30, were those along the frontiers in early T'ang. K. Hino, in the last two parts of his long article, 'Tōdai hanchin no bakko to chinsō', *Tōyō Gakuho*, XXVII (1939-40) pp. 153-212 and 311-350, has collected a great deal of evidence of their function later in the T'ang and shows how much the power of the independent governor depended on the use of such garrisons.

Lu province rose against their governors or their commanders and killed them.[14] Although the causes of these mutinies were independent of Huang Ch'ao's rebellion, the mutinies affected it in two ways. Firstly, the court was forced to send to the north most of its reserves from the Eastern Capital and Mêng province (in the Ho-nan Region) at a critical time and thus forfeited a line of defence east of the vital T'ung-kuan Pass. The result was that when Huang Ch'ao broke through the defences on the Huai river from the south in 880, he could march straight to T'ung-kuan. This shortage of reserves, together with the lenient treatment of mutineers, also aggravated the falling morale of the other provincial armies. There were many incidents to show the court's inability to control these troops. For example, when the governor of Yün province died in 879, an officer of the castle garrison seized power for a few days. Later in the same year, the army defending Ching Chou on the Yangtse went out of control. Part of it returned north as bandit gangs to pillage the canal area, and even managed to engage the provincial armies there till the middle of 880.[15]

This discontent was not limited to the lower ranks of the army. The reasons given by the governor of Hsiang in 879 for not destroying the rebels reflect the extent of discontent among the highest officers. As the governor is recorded to have said, 'The empire is wont to be ungrateful. In times of crisis, it nurtures its officers and is not niggardly in its rewards. When the affairs are settled, it rejects them or even punishes them. It is better to leave the bandits there as an investment for our wealth and position'.[16] More critical for the empire was the attitude of the commander of the imperial armies himself. He felt the same way about 'leaving

[14] The confusion in Ping province after the Sha-t'o Turks killed the defence commissioner at Shuo Chou lasted three years. In *TCTC* 253, a chronology is established after the careful sifting of the most conflicting material (*K'ao-i*, after Ch'ien-fu 5(878)/2/*chia-hsü*). All other sources for these events are relatively inadequate.

[15] *TCTC* 253, Ch'ien-fu 6 (879)/11th month, *K'ao-i*, argues for the bandit origins of the leader, Liu Han-hung. On the trouble the gangs caused, see *TCTC* 253, Kuang-ming 1 (880)/5/*chia-tzŭ* and 6/*kêng-hsü*.

[16] *TCTC* 253, Ch'ien-fu 6 (879)/11th month. Cf. the views of another commander earlier on, see Howard S. Levy, *Biography of Huang Ch'ao*, pp. 11 and 20-21.

the bandits there as an investment', and when he decided to let Huang Ch'ao cross the Yangtse and reach the Huai river in 7th/880, all effective resistance came to an end.[17]

From then on, army officers began to take over in their provinces or prefectures, several of them submitting to Huang Ch'ao. Huang Ch'ao in his turn adopted the policy of 'indulgence'[18] which the T'ang court had employed before, and kept them on as governors. It would have taken him too long to capture all these provinces and he was eager to reach the imperial capital first. What he did was to leave units of his army behind and an army supervisor to report on each governor, and he was content merely to receive the financial support of the provinces.[19]

The chief redistribution of power took place after the fall of Ch'ang-an to Huang Ch'ao in 12th/880. There were now two emperors, Huang Ch'ao at Ch'ang-an and the boy Hsi-tsung at Ch'êng-tu (in modern Szechuan province). The court at Ch'êng-tu, after the initial losses following the escape there, found that it had

[17] The commander, Kao P'ien, has been defended in recent times in research following the recovery of the collection of memorials and letters by Ts'ui Chih-yüan, Kao P'ien's Korean secretary. The work, *Kuei-yüan Pi-kêng Chi* is discussed in note 27 with the article in defence of Kao P'ien by Chou Lien-k'uan. There was no defence of his letting Huang Ch'ao cross the Yangtse, however, except that Huang Ch'ao had a far larger army. In view of this, I follow the versions in *CTS* 182 and *HTS* 224 C (Kao P'ien's biography) and *TCTC* 253, Kuang-ming 1 (880)/7th month and *K'ao-i*.

[18] Des Rotours, p. 826, translates *ku-hsi chih chêng* as 'gouvernement par la tolérance' and continues with the *HTS* view on it, 'En effet, le gouvernement par la tolérance fut provoqué par l'arrogance des soldats, et l'arrogance des soldats tira son origine de l'organisation des commanderies militaires (*fang-tchen*). Plus la tolérance fut grande, et plus les soldats et les généraux se montrèrent tous arrogants.'

[19] Wang Ch'ung-jung, the mutiny leader who became governor of P'u, first accepted Huang Ch'ao's authority, and then killed the supervisor and his men. *CTS* 182 and *HTS* 187 have different accounts of his surrender to Huang Ch'ao; *TCTC* 254, Kuang-ming 1 (880)/11th month and 12/*jên-wu* provide a chronology; and 12/end of month, with detailed *K'ao-i*, describe his killing of the '*shih*' and his men. The *shih* were not 'envoys', as the governor had surrendered, but probably a short form for *chien-chün shih* (Army Supervisor) as in the case of $Hsü_3$ province where the *shih* was killed in 5th/881; *TCTC* 254, Chung-ho 1 (881)/5 after *chia-tzu*.

Huang Ch'ao's use of *chien-chün shih* can be seen in the case of Chu Wên, who had to kill the *shih* in 9th/882 before he could surrender; *CWTS* 1, 2b and *TCTC* 255, Chung-ho 2 (882)/9/*ping-hsü*.

retained enough of its authority in the provinces to begin a counter-attack on Ch'ang-an. This was almost successful. It was greatly helped by the defection of the 'governors' Huang Ch'ao had appointed. His control over them had been nominal, and the governors did to him what they had done earlier to the T'ang court.

From the military point of view, the most important of the defections was that of the governor of P'u province at the southern bend of the Huang Ho and within striking distance of Ch'ang-an. Together with his brother, the governor of Shan province east of T'ung-kuan pass, he provided the containment of Huang Ch'ao in the Wei valley and made his defeat easier.[20] By 882, Huang Ch'ao held only two prefectures and the metropolitan counties of Ch'ang-an. Then, later in that year, one of Huang Ch'ao's own generals, Chu Wên, surrendered with one of the two prefectures. The court was now eager for a quick victory and called in thousands of frontier horsemen under Li K'o-yung, the leader of the Sha-t'o Turks to help. In 4th/883, Ch'ang-an was recaptured.

The restoration of the T'ang court, however, was far from complete. The dynastic authority over the provinces had become weaker than ever. The court did directly control Ch'ang-an and the two provinces in Chien-nan (Szechuan) and could still rely on three of the eleven provinces in Ho-nan, three of the nine north of the Huang Ho, the two provinces of Shan-nan and at least four of the eleven on the Yangtse and along the Southern coasts.[21]

[20] The governor of P'u, according to *TCTC* 254, surrendered on the third day (*jên-wu*) of 12th/880 and for the next few weeks provided cash and supplies to Huang Ch'ao. But at the end of the month, he turned against the rebels and had to fight off rebel attacks. It is not, however, known when his brother took over Shan Chou and cut off Ch'ang-an from the eastern provinces (*T'ang Fang-chên Nien-piao* concludes this was sometime in 881). It was probably before the short re-capture of Ch'ang-an in 4th/881 when the rebel leaders who abandoned T'ung Chou and Hua Chou did not escape via the T'ung-kuan pass, but tried to escape south-eastwards via Têng Chou; *TCTC* 254, Chung-ho 1 (881)/4/*ting-hai*.

There is also the poem by Wei Chuang, *Ch'in-fu Yin* which raises problems of how the author left Ch'ang-an and what routes were open from that city; see the long discussion in Ch'ên Yin-K'o's latest study of the question in 'Ch'in-fu yin chiao-chien chiu-kao pu-chêng', *Lingnan Journal*, pp. 17-25.

[21] See Table II. The four southern provinces were those of Ngo, Jun (Chê-hsi), Fu (Fu-chien) and Kuang (Lingnan). These were separated from the

But the remainder, if not actually defiant or hostile, were in the hands of independent or army-appointed leaders. They were wooed by the court, and were given titles for paying lip-service to the empire.

The following table for 7th/883[22] shows what the problem was like in North China in the areas which concern this study of the Five Dynasties. Although all the Yangtse provinces were important to the court in its effort to unify the empire, only the three which had a direct bearing on the developments in the North have been included.

TABLE II[23]

Provinces	*Status, origins of governors, date appointed*
I. *Kuan-chung* (Shensi and areas to its north and west)	
1 Ch'ang-an	court-chosen,[24] bureaucrat, 883.
2 Ch'i	self-appointed, leader of mutiny, 881.
3 Pin	court-appointed, leader of defence against Huang Ch'ao, 881.

main route up the Yangtse into Szuchuan by provinces the loyalty of whose governors was doubtful, but tribute sent to Ch'êng-tu seems to have reached the court without great difficulty at this time.

[22] I have preferred the month 7th/883 to the month Ch'ang-an was recaptured in 4th/883 because it was the date Li K'o-yung, the Sha-t'o Turk leader, was appointed governor of Ping province. This was the last effective court appointment to the provinces in North China. The abandonment of this strategic province to the Turks makes the date a significant one.

[23] This table has been compiled from a number of sources, the chief of which was the *T'ang Fang-chên Nien-piao*, *passim*, and the biographies of the governors in *CTS* 142, 164, 175, 178, 180, 182, 187, 200 B; *HTS* 185-188, 210-212, 218, 221 A, 224 C, 225 C; *CWTS* 1, 13, 25, 54, 62. Also *TCTC* 255, passim.

The three governors with (?) after their status have no biographies in the *Histories* and only the briefest mentions in *TCTC* from which I have suggested that they were probably either court-chosen or court-appointed.

(19) Lo-yang did not become a province again until 888. Ts'ui An-ch'ien, a distinguished bureaucrat, had been appointed governor (viceroy) in 1st/883, but Lo-yang remained in the hands of rebels. (26) Ts'ai was, until 888, in fact the centre of a rebel 'empire' extending from Huai-nan to Lo-yang, but it was made a province again after Ch'in Tsung-chüan was crushed.

The governor of Wei (no. 14), Yo Yen-chên, was the leader of a mutiny, not against a governor chosen by the court, but against the hereditary Han family ruling since 870. He was the prefect of Ch'an under the previous governor. For more details about the governor of Yang (no. 32), see note 27.

[24] In the table, distinction is made between court-chosen, court-appointed

Provinces	*Status, origins of governors, date appointed*
4 Ching	court-appointed, provincial officer, 882.
5 Fu	court-chosen (?), 882.
6 Hsia	court-appointed, tribal leader and a prefect, 881.
7 Yen*	court-appointed, tribesman frontier officer (?), 883.
8 Hua*	appointed by brother, the governor of P'u, 883.

II. *Ho-tung* (Shansi and areas to its north)

9 P'u	self-appointed, leader of mutiny, 880.
10 Ping	court-appointed, leader of Sha-t'o Turks, 883.
11 Lu	self-appointed, leader of mutiny, 881.

* = new province

III. *Ho-pei* (Ho-pei and northern Shantung)

12 Yu	son of previous governor, 876.
13 Chên	son of previous governor, 883.
14 Wei	self-appointed, leader of mutiny, 881.
15 Ting	court-chosen, son of a governor, 879.
16 Ts'ang	court-chosen (?), 880.

IV. *Ho-nan* (Honan, Shantung and northern Anhwei and Chiangsu)

17 Shan	appointed by governor of P'u, 881.
18 Mêng	appointed by Huang Ch'ao, surrendered, then court-appointed, 881.
19 Lo-yang	(under control of Mêng governor).
20 Pien	court-chosen, ex-Huang Ch'ao general, 883.
21 Hua	court-chosen, bureaucrat, 882.
22 Yen	court-chosen, imperial officer, 879.
23 Yün	self-appointed after death of governor, provincial officer, 882.
24 Ch'ing	self-appointed, leader of mutiny, 882.
25 Hsü$_3$	self-appointed, leader of mutiny, 880.
26 Ts'ai	self-appointed, leader of mutiny, 881; (now supporting Huang Ch'ao).
27 Hsü$_2$	self-appointed, leader of mutiny, 881.

and self-appointed governors. Only when the court was able to choose the man it really wanted is a governor described as court-chosen, irrespective of whether the eunuchs or the bureaucrats were behind the choice. It is noted, though, if the eunuchs were clearly the backers of the man appointed. If the court had no choice but to honour the only strong man in the province, the governor is described as court-appointed. Those who had seized power and then received official confirmation because the court was in no position to deal with them are described as self-appointed.

Provinces	Status, origins of governors, date appointed
V. *Shan-nan* (Northern Hupei and southern Shensi)	
28 Hsiang	court-chosen, imperial officer, 879.
29 Liang	court-chosen, protégé of eunuchs and General of Imperial Guards, 880.
VI. *Chien-nan* (Szechuan)	
30 I	court-chosen, brother of leading eunuch and General of Imperial Guards, 880.
31 Tzŭ	court-chosen, protégé of eunuchs and General of Imperial Guards, 880.
VII. *The Yangtse provinces*	
32 Yang	court-chosen, ex-commander of imperial armies against Huang Ch'ao, 879.
33 Ngo	court-chosen, bureaucrat, 879.
34 Ching	court-appointed, provincial officer chosen by eunuch Supervisor, 882.

In the thirty-three provinces, the governors of thirteen were court-chosen, those of six court-appointed, and those of nine self-appointed. Of the court-chosen governors, three were bureaucrats and eight were professional soldiers of whom one had already turned away from the court. This compares poorly with the beginning of 880 when probably as many as twenty-nine governors were court-chosen. Of these, about half had been bureaucrats.[25] The contrast in 883 is obvious, especially where direct bureaucratic control of the provinces is concerned. Of the three bureaucrats who were left, two were replaced by the next year,[26] and the third was the governor of the imperial capital itself.

Briefly, comparing the period before and after the Huang Ch'ao rebellion, it may be said that the balance of power between the bureaucrats and the eunuchs which had dominated the history of the sixty years of T'ang rule prior to the rebellion was now upset

[25] *T'ang Fang-chên Nien-piao*, *passim*, for the beginning of 880, shows that there were at least twelve bureaucrat governors out of the twenty-six governors whose names were recorded.

[26] *TCTC* 255, Chung-ho 4(884)/3rd month, and 256, Chung-ho 4/10th month and end of the year.

by the resurgence of the military, whether imperial or rebel in origin. This shift of power led to the loss of central control over most of the empire and was eventually to create the most difficult problems of recovering control over the provinces. Some of these problems which the T'ang court bequeathed to the Five Dynasties form the subject of this study.

In the past, a policy of 'indulgence' towards the independent governors had been followed and this had always given the court time and opportunities to recover. This policy was followed again in 883, not only because it was the only thing the court could do, but also because there was hope that the policy might be made to work again. The situation in 883, however, was very different from any the court had faced before. A great number of provincial and rebel armies had elected governors and prefects whom the court could neither transfer nor dismiss. Larger areas were thus no longer directly subject to any central supervision. Even more important, the court-chosen governor of the important province of Yang (Huai-nan) was defiant and supported rebellions in several provinces south of the Yangtse.[27] This aggravated the rebellious

[27] The governor was Kao P'ien. As commander-in-chief of the imperial forces against Huang Ch'ao, he had let the rebel army cross the Yangtse in 7th/880 with disastrous consequences for the imperial armies. He then failed to send help after the fall of Ch'ang-an to Huang Ch'ao, and was replaced as commander-in-chief and salt and transport commissioner. This angered him. He stopped sending tribute to the emperor, then at Ch'êng-tu, and then sent an ex-rebel to take one province south of the Yangtse and encouraged the rebel officers of another to join him against the governor of Jun (Chê-hsi). This is the story in Kao P'ien's biography in *CTS* 182; and in *HTS*/224 C where he is placed in the section for *p'an-ch'ên* ('Rebel Officials'); and in *TCTC* 254, Chung-ho 1 (880)/1/*ting-ch'ou*, 5/*i-wei* and 9/*hsin-hai*, and Chung-ho 2 (882)/4th and 255, Chung-ho 2/5th month.

Recent research based on the *Kuei-yüan Pi-kêng Chi*, in 20 chüans, by Ts'ui Chih-yüan, has disputed this. This, a work by the Korean secretary of Kao P'ien in 880-884, consists chiefly of a collection of memorials and letters he wrote for Kao-P'ien during the four years. It was collected after the author had returned to his country and was presented to the king of Silla in 886. It seemed to have reached China in the Northern Sung and there was a copy of it in the imperial Ch'ung-wên Library. The editors of *HTS* seem to have seen it and it is likely that it was still in the Library when Ssŭ-ma Kuang compiled the *TCTC*. There is, however, no evidence that they consulted the work. In fact, in two *K'ao-i* passages in *TCTC* 253, Kuang-ming 1 (880)/7th month and 254, Chung-ho 2(882)/1/*hsin-hai*, works mentioned included

situation in South China which had partly been a hangover from Huang Ch'ao's long campaigns there in 878-880. But the loss to the

several early works on the period like *Ching-t'ing Lu* (驚聽錄), *Kuang-ling Yao-luan Chih* (廣陵妖亂志), *Hsü Pao-yün Lu* (續寶運錄), *T'ang-mo Chien-wên Lu* (唐末見聞錄), *T'ang-nien Pu-lu* (唐年補錄), *Pei-mêng So-yen* (北夢瑣言), P'i Kuang-yeh's *Chien-wên Lu* (皮光業，見聞錄), and the official works, *CTS*, the later Veritable Records (*shih-lu*) and *HTS*, but not the *Kuei-yüan Pi-kêng Chi*, although the events were controversial. On the other hand, in three damning passages in *TCTC* 254, Chung-ho 1/9/*hsin-hai* and Chung-ho 2/4th, and 255, Chung-ho 2/5th month, where Kao Pien's treachery and stupidity is exposed, no *K'ao-i* is provided as if the events were not controversial.

Chou Lien-k'uan in his special study in defence of Kao P'ien, 'T'ang Kao P'ien Chên-Huai shih-chi K'ao', *Lingnan Journal*, pp. 11-45, finds it incredible that Sung Min-ch'iu (compiler of the *Veritable Records*), Ssŭ-ma Kuang and Sung Ch'i (editor of the biographies in *HTS*) should reject the *Pi-kêng Chi* altogether as a reliable source. With extensive quotations from the work, he tries to prove that Kao P'ien has been sadly wronged by all the historians.

While valuing the *Pi-kêng Chi* as an important source for the years 880-884, I have not been convinced by Professor Chou that it contains material which redeems Kao P'ien. I agree that the *TCTC* has been unduly influenced by the *Kuang-ling Yao-luan Chih* to include all the sordid details of Kao P'ien's superstitious nature and the hocus-pocus of the fake Taoist Lü Yung-chih (254, Chung-ho 2 (882)/4th month), and that the *Yao-luan Chih* was written by someone hostile to Kao P'ien, possibly of Chê-hsi province, the governor of which was Kao P'ien's enemy. But the sanctimonious protests on Kao P'ien's behalf in the *Pi-kêng Chi* are also unsupported by any other source. They also have the disadvantage of being those carefully selected by Ts'ui Chih-yüan, who admits in his preface that in the four years of service, he had written 'more than ten thousand pieces, but after weeding out, (had preserved) not more than one or two in ten'. (*Pi-kêng Chi*, preface, 2a.) In presenting them to the king in order to win high office in Silla, he would be expected to preserve only those which showed himself and his previous master as loyal. There is probably an opposite bias in favour of Kao P'ien which must also be questioned.

Further, it is clear that Ts'ui Chih-yüan was not the only secretary to Kao P'ien. There was also the poet and historian Ku Yün who began to serve Kao P'ien before Ts'ui Chih-yüan and continued for another four years after the latter had returned to Silla. Professor Chou has noted this without considering the possibility that Ku Yün, the more senior in Kao P'ien's service, might not have written all the more important memorials and letters (see Professor Chou's article, pp. 32-33). The most revealing evidence against Kao P'ien has been the memorial of 5th/882 and the imperial edict answering it (both quoted in *CTS* 182 and summarized in *HTS* 224 C and *TCTC* 255, Chung-ho 2/5th month). The memorial, a vital document, was attributed to

imperial coffers owing to the imperfect control of these vital economic areas was irremediable. Furthermore, Huang Ch'ao had escaped into Ho-nan in search of another base for his activities. And before he was finally crushed, he had created another rebellion, that of Ch'in Tsung-ch'üan, the governor of Ts'ai province. And this rebellion did even more to isolate the court from the eastern half of the empire.[28]

Lastly, there was a stranglehold on Ch'ang-an from *within* the Wei valley. This was initially due to the loss of the capital in 880, but later on two mutiny leaders and an adventurous officer had taken over the three nearest provinces and, although they were not hostile, they were not chosen by the court and could not be removed except by force. This was a new situation in T'ang

Ku Yün (in *HTS* and *TCTC*). This has not been convincingly shown to be a forgery by Professor Chou. Who should want to forge two long documents like these? Would the editors of the *CTS* be so unsuspecting a little more than forty years after Ku Yün's death (he is said to have died about 894, and only about ten years afterwards, two historians of the late T'ang, Chia Wei and Chang Chao, were already beginning their studies)? Also, Ku Yün's many works (mentioned in Professor Chou's article, p. 32) were probably in circulation, and his contribution to the last *Veritable Records of Hsi-tsung* (873-888), with many famous figures like the Chief Minister Lu Hsi-shêng, the poet Ssŭ-k'ung T'u and the essayist Ch'ien I must make forgery in his name quite difficult.

I think Professor Chou (p. 24 and pp. 33-36) has made out a case for certain omissions in *CTS*, *HTS* and *TCTC*, but the reasons why Kao P'ien did not send help to Ch'ang-an in 881-882 given in Ts'ui Chih-yüan's memorials ('Jang kuan ch'ing chih-shih piao', *Pi-kêng Chi*, 2, 12b-15a) and several letters (the most important of which were the reply dated 4/7th/882 to commander Hsi, 'Ta Hsiang-yang Hsi Chiang-chün shu', ch. 11, 15a-17b; the letter calling for supplies, 'Kao-pao chu-tao chêng-ch'u kang-yün shu', ch. 11, 6a-7b; and the second letter to Chief Minister Hsiao Kou, 'Hsiao Kou hsiang-kung (ti-er)', ch. 10, 5a-6a) are not conclusive. They read like excuses for inaction, unless independent evidence can be found to show that Chou Pao, the governor of Jun, and Shih P'u, governor of $Hsü_2$, were the really treacherous ones who had joined forces to prevent Kao P'ien from leaving his province to save Ch'ang-an.

Pending a more thorough re-examination of the subject, I have retained the version in *CTS*, *HTS* and *TCTC*. Their editors have shown that many more sources were available to them than are to us today.

[28] Biography of Ch'in Tsung-ch'üan, *CTS* 200 C; *HTS* 225 C. And *TCTC* 256, Chung-ho 4(884)/end of the year and Kuang-ch'i 1(885)/6th-7th months; 257, Kuang-ch'i 3 (887)/4th month and 5/*hsin-ssŭ*.

history, for no emperor before Hsi-tsung had been so confined in his capital.[29]

When the recovery of Ch'ang-an was imminent early in 883, the court chose two men to be governors in Ho-nan; Wang To as governor of Hua province and Chu Wên as governor of Pien, both provinces situated to guard against the independent Ho-pei provinces and protect the Grand Canal. And three months after retaking Ch'ang-an, the court-chosen governor of Ping province was recalled and Li K'o-yung, the Sha-t'o Turk, was appointed to replace him. Apart from these three, the court could only confirm the appointments of mutiny leaders and ex-rebels and hope for continued support from previously chosen governors. The three appointments of Wang To, Chu Wên and Li K'o-yung constituted the court's first uncertain steps to regain control over its empire.

Wang To was a successful bureaucrat who had twice been a chief minister of the empire. He had also been twice the commander-in-chief of the expeditionary armies against Huang Ch'ao. The interesting point about his provincial appointment is that the old struggle between the eunuchs and the bureaucrats was probably responsible for it.[30] Wang To was not made governor to try and recover imperial control over the Eastern provinces. He was already quite old by that time, and was not in any case given control of the armies in Ho-nan which were still loyal to the court. Moreover, he was not appointed to the more important Pien province which he had governed before, but to Hua which, though important as a stronghold against the Ho-pei governors, was not vital for the control of the whole of Ho-nan.[31]

The second governor, Chu Wên, had a completely different background. He had been Huang Ch'ao's general and was prefect of T'ung Chou when he surrendered in 9th/882 to the imperial

[29] See Table II, nos. 2 and 3 and no. 9 (who also controlled nos. 8 and 17). The history of the twenty years after 883 was for the court largely the history of dealing with these three provinces.

[30] *TCTC* 255, Chung-ho 3(883)/1/*i-hai*; cf. *CTS* 164, 5a-6a.

[31] Wang To had been governor of Pien in 873-875 before he was called to court as a Chief Minister. There is, however, a record that Wang To was not very successful as governor in Ssŭ-k'ung T'u's biographical notice (*hsing-chuang*) of Wang Ning (*Wên-chi*, 7, 4a).

commander. He was the third son of an impoverished teacher. When his father died, he was brought up to be a family retainer or a manor steward in the household where his mother worked as a servant.[32] He became a village tough instead and probably

[32] There were two main sources for the life of Chu Wên. The Liang *Veritable Records* was compiled soon after 915 (and the supplementary *Ta-Liang Pien-i Lu* compiled a little later to augment it) by his followers during his son's reign. The *T'ang Biographies* (*T'ang Lieh-chuan*) was compiled about 930, after the fall of Liang, by Chang Chao (see *TCTC K'ao-i*, 28, 3b and 8a). They were the basis for all later information about Chu Wên in *CWTS*, *TFYK* and *TCTC*. Unfortunately, the *CWTS* chüans on Chu Wên have not been preserved and the present edition of *CWTS* has only a very few items from the original and mostly those concerning supernatural events. The remaining bulk of the seven chüans have been copied from the *TFYK* and *TCTC K'ao-i*.

From what remains about Chu Wên's early life, his origins seem obscure; *CWTS* 1, 1b-2a (the original, preserved in *Yung Lo Ta Tien*). But the *Pei-mêng So-yen* 17, 1a (followed in *HWTS* 1, 1a) says that his father was a 'teacher of the five classics' who died when he was a boy. This seems to be borne out by the fact that Chu Wên's elder sister married a member of the Yüan family, also of Sung Chou (in a neighbouring county), whose father was the administrator (*p'an-kuan*) of Hsü$_3$ province and whose grandfather was a deputy prefect (*shao-yin*) of Ch'êng-tu (*CWTS* 59, 7b, biography of Yüan Hsiang-hsien, Chu Wên's nephew). Chu Wên's father could not have been of too humble an origin if this could happen. It is also likely that the daughter was married off before his death, in which case he died about 864, or after (her son, Yüan Hsiang-hsien was born in 864).

At his death, he left three sons. His wife could either join the Yüan family with her daughter or return to what was possibly her mother-in-law's family, the Liu household of Hsü$_2$ Chou. Chu Wen's relations with the Liu family are not clear, but it is known that his father's mother was a Liu (*WTHY* 1, p. 7). As Hsiao hsien (蕭縣) in Hsü$_2$ Chou was only some forty miles from Chu Wên's T'ang-shan hsien (碭山縣) in Sung Chou, it is not unlikely that his grandmother was related to the Liu family of Hsiao hsien if not actually a member of it. If this was so, it explains why his mother brought the three boys to Hsiao hsien.

It would also confirm that Chu Wên's origins were not as obscure as is traditionally made out, for the Liu family was the leading family in the area (Liu families have been dominant in the Hsü$_2$ Chou area since Han times, the Han founder having come from it) and the master of the household, Liu T'ai, was the county magistrate (*CWTS* 108, 11a-b). It would further modify our understanding of his mother being a 'servant' (*yung-shih* 傭食 in *HWTS* 1, 1a and 13, 1a), working for their keep rather than as a menial, and explain how the description in *CWTS* 1, 1b, of 'depended for their livelihood' (*yang-chi yü* 養寄於) was not an euphemism. (*TCTC* 254, Kuang-ming 1 (880)/12/

formed his own small bandit gang in the neighbourhood. Some time in 876-877, he and his friends had joined Huang Ch'ao.[33] Chu Wên's surrender in 882 could have hardly been better timed as there was immediate relief to the imperial army. He was appointed governor of the new province of T'ung, became Grand General of the Imperial Guards and a deputy field commander soon afterwards. On 23/3rd/883, only six months after his surrender, he was appointed Military Governor of Pien province, the appointment to take effect after the fall of Ch'ang-an. This was four days before a crucial victory and half a month before the entry into Ch'ang-an. It was already known that Huang Ch'ao planned to escape east to Ho-nan via the Lan-t'ien pass. A reformed rebel with nothing to lose, and with a reputation among other rebels, was probably the man to win the battles still to be fought. A strong recommendation must have come from the P'u governor, Wang Ch'ung-jung, one of the chief architects of the expected victory. He knew of Chu Wên's background and of his experience of the provinces astride the all-important canal route from the south-eastern granaries. Chu Wên could be expected to understand both local banditry and the rebel armies that remained with Huang Ch'ao. Further, he had sought the patronage of Wang Ch'ung-jung, and had quickly

jên-ch'ên, uses the word 'depend' (*i* 依).) Also, Chu Wên and his brothers were not treated as servants, but probably expected to be useful members of the family with responsibilities in the manor.

[33] It is not clear when Chu Wên joined Huang Ch'ao. In 875-876, numerous gangs operated in the region between the Huai and the Yellow rivers, on both sides of the Pien canal. When Huang Ch'ao came west from the Shantung coast in 8th/876, many of these probably joined him, including Chu Wên's gang. If not then, he could have joined Huang Ch'ao in 7th/877 when the latter was actually besieging the armies of the imperial commander-in-chief at Sung Chou (north-west of $Hsü_2$); or at the latest, a few months later, in 2nd/878, when Huang Ch'ao took over the leadership after Wang Hsien-chih's death and regrouped his army at Po Chou (west of $Hsü_2$). After this, the rebels crossed south of the river—Chu Wên was certainly with them by then. He had joined with his elder brother who died at Kuang Chou. See *TCTC* 252, Ch'ien-fu 3 (876)/8th month to 253, Ch'ien-fu 5 (878)/2nd month and *K'ao-i*.

Howard S. Levy, *Biography of Huang Ch'ao*, p. 77, n. 162, says Chu Wên joined Huang Ch'ao in 877. This was based on an unconfirmed account in *HWTS* 1, 2a.

taken to calling his patron 'uncle' because his own mother was of the Wang clan. Now, as a 'nephew', he could have asked Wang Ch'ung-jung to press the appointment for him.[34]

The third appointment was again different in its background. Li K'o-yung was not a common rebel but a Turkish aristocrat, son of the hereditary chieftain of the Sha-t'o tribe. His father was an imperial commissioner for three Turkish tribes and the prefect of Shuo Chou. As a boy he had followed his father south to help put down the P'ang Hsün mutiny (869), and when his father was rewarded that year with the imperial surname, he became a member of the imperial family (in the branch of Prince Chêng).[35]

After a stay at Ch'ang-an Li K'o-yung had returned north to be a border officer, and by 877 had become the deputy commissioner of a Turkish garrison. The next year, he led a tribal revolt which developed into a border war. For two years he caused such consternation in Ping province that the court sent six governors in succession to crush his tribal army, but without any success. The seventh governor, a Chief Minister and a former governor of the province, was finally sent with a hand-picked team of officials to deal with him. Reinforcements which could be ill-afforded were brought from the Eastern capital. Eventually in 6th/880, Li K'o-yung was defected, chiefly because he was betrayed by some of his officers. Six months afterwards, Huang Ch'ao captured Ch'ang-an. Li K'o-yung was granted a pardon and invited to join the imperial forces againt the rebels. After considerable bargaining which gained him the governorship of a newly created province, he went south. In 4th/883, the rebels were dislodged and he led the imperial armies into Ch'ang-an.[36]

[34] On Chu Wên calling Wang Ch'ung-jung 'uncle' (*chiu* 舅), see *TCTC* 255, Chung-ho 2 (882)/9/*ping-hsü*. His mother's biography in *CWTS* is mostly lost (see *CWTS* 11, 1a), but there are preserved two passages which confirm that her surname was Wang; also *Pei-mêng So-yen*, 17, 1a-b, and *HWTS* 13, 1a-b.

[35] *CWTS* 25, 1b; and HTS 218, 3a.

[36] Details of his first mutiny in *TCTC* 253, Ch'ien-fu 5(878)/1/*kêng-hsü*, ff. and *K'ao-i*. Also *CWTS* 25, 3a-4a.

Concerning the six governors who failed, *TCTC* 253, Ch'ien-fu 5(878)/5/*ting-ssŭ*, 7/*chi-hai*, 12th month; Ch'ien-fu 6 (879)/2/*hsin-wei*, 5/*hsin-mao*, 8/*chia-tzŭ*, intercalary 10/*ting-hai*, 11/*kêng-ch'en*; Kuang-ming 1 (800)/2/*kêng-hsü*.

Li K'o-yung's interest in Ping province had dated from 878. That he demanded his appointment as its governor was likely. The demand could be forcibly backed by the presence at Ch'ang-an of thousands of the best horsemen in the empire feasting daily in triumph for three months. Unable to fob them off with titles and to recompense them sufficiently from the strained imperial coffers, the court came round to appointing their leader governor of Ping. It had no illusions about their trustworthiness, nor could it find fault with the present governor who probably argued strongly against his old enemy. The court could only hope to use Li K'o-yung against other enemies at some future date.[37]

These three appointments, so disparate in nature, were no part of any great plan to recover the empire. The three men were unlikely partners and their ability to co-operate with one another was soon put to a test in Ho-nan. The fight against Huang Ch'ao went on for another year. Wang To was completely ineffective from the start and Chu Wên could not cope with the rebels alone. Li K'o-yung had to be called south again and, together with Chu Wên, succeeded in defeating Huang Ch'ao. This seemed to have been the success the court needed. With the help of these two men, it could hope to recover its authority over the rest of Ho-nan and the valuable Huai-nan (Lower Yangtse) region.

But the triumph was short-lived. A quarrel soon occurred between the two governors and a hasty attempt was made by Chu Wên to massacre Li K'o-yung and his bodyguards on the night of 14/5th/884.[38] The court was then asked by both men to

Li K'o-yung's eventual defeat, in *CWTS* 25, 4a-b; *TCTC* 253, Kuang-ming 1(880)/3/*hsin-wei*, 6/*kêng-tzŭ*, and 7/*wu-ch'ên*. His re-instatement, in *CWTS* 25, 4b-6a; *TCTC* 254, Chung-ho 1(881)/2/*ping-shên* and 3rd month, 5/*chia-tzŭ*, 6/*wu-hsü*; 255, Chung-ho 2(882)/10th and 12th month.

The new province created for him consisted of Tai and Hsin Chou cut out of the large Ping province.

[37] The chronology of Li K'o-yung's rewards in 5th/883 and 7th/883 is studied in *TCTC* 255, Chung-ho 3(883)/7th month, *K'ao-i*. Both *CWTS* 25, 6b-7a and *TCTC* 255, Chung-ho 3(883)/5th month say how much he was feared by the other imperial officers at Ch'ang-an.

[38] *CWTS* 1, 4a-b (from *TFYK* 187, the wording of one part is exactly the same as the text preserved in quotation in *TCTC* 255, Chung-ho 4 (884)/5/*chia-hsü*, *K'ao-i*). Also *CWTS* 25, 8a-9a; *CTS* 19 B, 17a-b; *HTS* 218, 4 b; and *TCTC* 255, *op. cit.* *TCTC* follows *CWTS* 1, 4a-b, for the reasons for Chu

arbitrate on the incident, and when it was unwilling to investigate the matter, it merely gained the mistrust of Li K'o-yung and the contempt of Chu Wên. Chu Wên's act of treachery was not merely historically important as the beginning of the struggle with Li K'o-yung which was to last for forty years through two generations. It had immediate consequences for imperial power in North China. The Ho-nan and Ho-tung regions were now separated by this rivalry, never to co-operate again for the empire. The two governors were left to extend their power in their respective regions. They gathered around themselves territories and resources to oppose each other, and thus built up two centres of power.

An indirect result of this quarrel was the danger to the empire from the new rebellion led by Ch'in Tsung-ch'üan. Had the two continued their co-operation in Ho-nan, they might have prevented the rebellion from being as successful as it was during the next three years. Instead, Chu Wên was left virtually alone to deal with these rebels. If any single event could be said to have blasted all hopes of an imperial restoration, it was probably this quarrel. It had reduced to nothing the court's first steps to regain control. The withdrawal of the tribal cavalry and the Ping provincial army from Ho-nan exposed the Eastern Capital to the rebels and Ch'ang-an was almost completely cut off from Ho-nan until 6th/887. During these years of isolation, Chu Wên survived to defeat the rebels and, by so doing, attained a position of authority in Ho-nan. His loyalty was then so valuable to the court that he was given a free hand and even encouraged to gain further control over the other provinces in the region.

The court still had nominal administrative control over several provinces. It selected the staff of the governors including the chief administrator, legal and financial experts, various secretaries and assistants. These officials, however, were inclined to develop loyalty for their respective governors. Each governor depended

Wên's action, and argues in *K'ao-i* why this version was preferred to those in *CWTS* 25, 8a-9a and the *Liang T'ai-tsu Pien-i Lu*. The eighteenth-century re-compiler of the *CWTS*, Shao Chin-han, argues that *TCTC* was wrong to prefer the version in 1, 4a-b, and should have followed that in 25, 8a-9a (see commentary in *CWTS* 25, 8a).

on them for efficient administration and was careful to keep them contented. Once they were appointed, the governor would keep those who were efficient and recommend their re-appointment. The officials could remain indefinitely so long as the same governor was still in office. They could be promoted and receive increases in salary without being moved from their posts. Since this was so in most provinces, the officials themselves saw no advantage in leaving unless it was for a promotion to the court. After some time, each governor acquired a team of administrators on whom he could depend without fear of interference from the court. The court's administrative control over the provinces was thus steadily weakened until it merely provided the governors, from time to time, with administrators chosen from some of its ablest officials.[39]

In two other ways, the court was forced to give in to the governors. Firstly, they lost direct control over the various prefectures. The appointment of most of the prefects, county magistrates and their immediate staff was still the prerogative of the court. But this, too, had become merely a means of providing the governors with trained administrative personnel. The powers of these prefects and magistrates were restricted as the governors also appointed their own representatives to each prefectural capital and county town. Often, these representatives were backed by the local defence garrisons or were themselves the officers commanding them. In this way, the court-chosen officials tended to be indistinguishable from the governors' own employees. It was only a matter of time before many governors dispensed with court-chosen prefects and magistrates altogether, and recommended their own men for these

[39] This survey has been based on readings in the biographies of the main governors and the bureaucrats. Some of the details are brought out in the provincial government of Chu Wên in Chapter Three. The developments were not new, but chiefly an extension of the situation in Ho-pei to the rest of North China.

Apart from the administrators under Chu Wên at Pien, prominent examples of such administrators were Li Hsi-chi and I Kuang under Li K'o-yung at Ping (*CWTS* 60, 1a-4b and 55, 9b); Li Chü-ch'uan of Hua (*CTS* 190 B; 19a-b); Wang Ch'ao of Ch'i and Ts'ui Shan of Pin (*TCTC* 259, Ching-fu 2(893)/10th month), and Chêng Chun of Ching, Ma Yü of Yu and Li Shan-fu of Wei (*CWTS* 60, 4a-b).

posts. These men were usually their trusted personal officials or army commanders.[40]

The other loss to the court was in its direction of the military forces in the provinces. While it continued to send eunuch Army Supervisors (*chien-chün*) who were still expected to report on the loyalty of the governors, it was unable to back their admonitions and protests with strong imperial forces. In this way, the supervisors were rendered ineffectual. Instead, the governors could cultivate their friendship and use them for their own benefit. Palace intrigues could thus be better understood by officials in the provinces. The governors could, with the help of friendly eunuchs, participate in these intrigues or take sides more easily in any struggle at the court and thus influence and interfere with court decisions.[41] The appointment of military deputies (*hsing-chün ssu-ma*) by the court also became a contribution to the governor's already large team of trained officials. Not surprisingly, these deputies were not really allowed any authority over the armies which were either directly in the governor's hands or were under his personally selected commanders. In time, two officers became increasingly important and eventually transformed the structure of power in the empire. They were the chief commander of the provincial army and the administrator of the governor's guards. This development in Chu Wên's province will be studied in greater detail in the next chapter.

The court's spheres of control in the provinces were thus

[40] The information available for most of the provinces is limited, and I have drawn some conclusions from the few successful provinces like Pien and Ping in which these developments followed closely those in the three Ho-pei provinces of Yu, Chên and Wei. For details of Pien province, see Chapter Three, *passim*.

[41] Ever since Li Tê-yü removed eunuch supervisors from army commands in 843-844, the Army Supervisor has played a far smaller role. Thereafter, the Supervisor was only allowed ten guardsmen for every thousand men he supervised: *TCTC* 248, Hui-ch'ang 4(844)/8/*wu-shên*.

The most prominent example of Supervisors and ex-Supervisors who helped their governors was that of Han Ch'üan-hui, who became a military secretary to the emperor after being Supervisor to Li Mao-chên the governor of Ch'i. Later, Han Ch'üan-hui and Chang Yen-hung, then Supervisor to Li Mao-chên, were both made the Commanders of the Shên-ts'ê Army (*TCTC* 252, T'ien-fu 1(901)/1/*ping-wu*).

systematically reduced. Instead of only three independent governors in Ho-pei, there were now a score of others all over the country. The only way to control the warlordism was probably by officient diplomacy and intrigue and by playing off the governors against one another. The idea of re-uniting the empire by the assertion of power had to be abandoned and a dynastic duty was thus abrogated. The method of 'diplomacy' was already adopted when the newly appointed governors, Chu Wên and Li K'o-yung, urged the court to arbitrate in 5th/884 on Chu Wên's attempted murder of Li K'o-yung and were given an equivocal answer instead. The court pacified Li K'o-yung by making him the most powerful governor in North China while Chu Wên was satisfied that it had turned a blind eye to the whole affair.[42]

The court's relative success was not to be repeated. After its return to Ch'ang-an in 3rd/885, the proximity of three strong governors in the Wei valley itself made interference in court decisions by military pressure much easier and the use of 'diplomacy' much more difficult. The formula of the court against the provinces soon proved to be too simple to cope with the increasing difficulties to be faced. There developed political alignments within the court which were backed by powerful governors supporting one or another group. There were defensive alliances between the governors against either the court or other allied governors. The alignments became increasingly complicated, and a study of these alignments would be necessary before any of the stages of the various struggles can be clear. The limitations of our sources make the correct weighing of power both at the court and in the provinces almost impossible. The bias is too much in favour of the groups which survived into the Wu-tai (Five Dynasties) period. An outline of the chief conflicts at Ch'ang-an, however,

[42] *TCTC* 256, Chung-ho 4 (884)/7th-8th months. In *TCTC* 255, Chung-ho 4(884)/5/*chia-hsü*, Chu Wên's reply to Li K'o-yung's letter of protest ended with, 'I did not know of last night's treachery. The court had sent of its own accord a representative to plan it with Yang Yen-hung (the commander of the Pien provincial army). Now that (Yang) Yen-hung has suffered for his crime (he was killed by Chu Wên), I only hope that you will consider it sympathetically.'

has been attempted and the remainder of this chapter will deal with the events leading to the fall of the T'ang.

In 885, the emperor returned to Ch'ang-an with a new army of fifty-four regiments, each of a thousand men at full strength. This army was controlled by the eunuch T'ien Ling-tzŭ. When the army had to be paid and fed, the eunuch put pressure on the nearby governor of P'u to surrender the salt monopoly of the province. He soon found himself fighting against an alliance of the P'u governor and Li K'o-yung. The imperial forces were ignominiously defeated and the court, only nine months after its return, was forced to leave Ch'ang-an again.[43] This was an ominous indication of events still to come.

Some of the chief bureaucrats at this time disassociated themselves from T'ien Ling-tzŭ's actions. They remained at Ch'ang-an and invited the governors of Pin and Ch'i provinces (both neighbouring Ch'ang-an to the west) to settle the differences at the court. Eventually, the bureaucrats agreed with the governors to depose emperor Hsi-tsung. This was a significant break with the T'ang tradition. Now a new emperor was chosen by an anti-eunuch group. This event shows how an alliance of governors had already begun to dominate the intrigues of the court. The attempt to depose Hsi-tsung, however, did not succeed. This was largely because the alliance of the two western governors broke up at a crucial moment. A compromise was reached in the refugee court and the eunuch T'ien Ling-tzû was dismissed. In 12th/886, the court returned once more to Ch'ang-an.[44] But the situation in the provinces was hardly changed. The new governor of Pin was a provincial officer who had murdered the previous governor, and the governor of Ch'i could no more be trusted than before. The governor of P'u was still supported by Li K'o-yung, the man with the strongest army in the empire.

[43] *TCTC* 256, Kuang-ch'i 1(885)/Intercalary 3rd and 4th months; 8th month; and 10/*kuei-ch'ou* to 12/*i-hai*.

[44] The emperor had been restored, in fact, by the successful use of methods of diplomacy. More important than the victory was perhaps the loss of faith in the bureaucracy. Few of the leading figures in the court had followed the emperor in his flight and, when the coup failed, it was said that almost half of the chief bureaucrats were executed (*TCTC* 256, Kuang-ch'i 2 (886)/12/*chia-yin*).

It was clear that no group of governors could take over all power as long as there was jealousy and the possibility of betrayal among them. No governor was yet strong enough to do so alone, and none of the governors would allow any other to gain more power than he already had. If the court could encourage this vigilance in each of them while rebuilding the imperial armies, it could still hope to regain control over the empire eventually.

The chance soon came to use the armies. In 887, the Ch'i governor was attacked and killed, and Li Mao-chên, the commander who led the expeditionary army, was appointed in his place.[45] This appointment was a major gain for the court at that time but the political effects were to prove disastrous later on.

In 3rd/888, Chao-tsung succeeded to the throne after the death of his brother Hsi-tsung. He gave the bureaucrats more authority over the imperial armies and tried to get personal control of vital sections of the armies at the expense of the eunuchs who had placed him on the throne. Yang Fu-kuang, the leading eunuch, was finally forced by the emperor to leave Ch'ang-an, but he was able to leave with a section of the imperial armies personally loyal to him. He had in the course of years arranged to have his adopted sons appointed governors and prefects in the Chien-nan region (Szechuan). He now joined the ablest of them, Yang Shou-liang, the governor of Liang province (in northern Szechuan). The regiments which stayed behind with the emperor were too weak to give battle, so Li Mao-chên, the Ch'i governor, offered to help with his provincial army. Thus Yang Shou-liang and Li Mao-chên, two able ex-commanders of the imperial armies, now fought as rival governors, each with a section of these armies.[46]

In due course, other ex-commanders like Wang Chien of I

[45] *TCTC* 257, Kuang-ch'i 3(887)/6/*wu-shên* and 8/*jên-yin*.

[46] *TCTC* 258, Ta-shun 2(891)/8th month and 10/*i-yu*; 259, Ching-fu 1 (892)/1/*ping-yin* and 2/*wu-yin*; and 8/*hsin-ch'ou*. About this time, the imperial armies were so divided in their loyalty and so resentful of the eunuchs who had killed one of their commanders (Li Shun-chieh killed in 12th/891, *TCTC* 258, 12/*wu-tzŭ*), that in 4th/892 an officer brought more than a thousand cavalry troops to join the governor of Ch'i and greatly strengthened his army (*TCTC* 259, Ching-fu 1 (892)/4/*i-yu*). Biography of Li Mao-chên, *CWTS* 132, 1a-4b.

province (western Szechuan) and Han Chien of Hua (east of Ch'ang-an) also became involved.[47] The struggle of 891-894 was in fact a struggle between various sections of the imperial armies which ended in the removal of eunuch power and in the victory of the governors who had been ex-commanders. But when the imperial armies were drawn into the provinces to serve new governors, imperial power was really near its end.

The emperor for all his efforts had not succeeded in getting any more power for himself. By the middle of 893, he had become frightened even by the presence of army commanders at the capital and replaced several of them with imperial princes.[48] But his attempt to move Li Mao-chên from Ch'i province was unsuccessful and elicited from Li Mao-chên a memorial which clearly expressed the contempt the imperial commanders had for the throne. The memorial comments on the emperor and his court:[49]

> His highness in his noble position could not protect the life of his own uncle. With the respect of the empire he could not destroy (Yang)Fu-kuang, a mere eunuch . . . The court now only observes strength and weakness and does not value right and wrong . . . (It) exercises the law on those who have failed and offers rewards to those who succeed. . .

Li Mao-Chên then warns, 'The mood of the army changes easily and their horses are difficult to restrain except that they fear that your people will suffer the consequences.' And finally, he pointedly adds, 'I wonder when the imperial retinue leaves the capital where it would go.' The memorial had some blunt truths behind its rhetoric, and the imperial response was pathetic. Chao-tsung ordered the recruiting of several thousands of urban youths from Ch'ang-an to fill the greatly depleted fifty-four regiments of the imperial armies and sent them under imperial princes against Li Mao-chên. The latter routed the army without difficulty and threatened Ch'ang-an. The emperor was forced to consent to his

[47] For Wang Chien, *CTS* 19B-20B; and *TFYK* 223 (which now forms the biography in *CWTS* 136, 1a-5b). For Han Chien, *CWTS* 15, 1a-4a.

[48] *TCTC* 259, Ching-fu 2 (893)/Intercalary 5th and 6th month.

[49] *TCTC* 259, Ching-fu 2(893)/7 after *ting-hai*. On the emperor's inability to protect his uncle from the eunuch Yang Fu-kuang, see *TCTC* 258, Ta-shun 2(891)/after 8th/*kuei-ch'ou*.

demands, which included the execution of Chao-tsung's most trusted chief minister and four leading eunuchs.[50]

There was little that Chao-tsung could do about the governors. Neither could he trust the eunuchs and bureaucrats, most of whom had begun to patronize the governors after Li Mao-chên had brought about the death of their most prominent members in 893. In the following years, the struggle among the governors for influence in the court overshadowed all other developments.[51] With the help of the eunuchs and bureaucrats who had become the tools of the governors they patronized, the governors decided to test their strength in 895.

The governor of Ch'i, Li Mao-chên, was an ally of two other governors in the Kuan-chung region. Li K'o-yung was the ally of the other governor in the Ho-tung region (Shansi), Wang Hsing-yü. When Wang Hsing-yü died in 895, there was a dispute over the succession. His son appealed to the three governors of Kuan-chung to intervene on his behalf while his nephew turned to Li K'o-yung for help. The struggle between the two groups was swiftly settled. Li K'o-yung defeated the Kuan-chung governors, and forced them to withdraw support for the son and to accept his candidate, the nephew. The emperor, seeking a new

[50] *TCTC* 259, Ching-fu 2(893)/7th-8th months; 9/*i-hai* to *i-yu*; 10th month.

[51] The outstanding figure at the time was Ts'ui Chao-wei (*CTS* 179 and *HTS* 223) who acted as the 'eyes and ears' of the governors of Pin and Ch'i, and observed the Chief Minister Tu Jang-nêng in 893 so that 'what Jang-nêng said in the morning, the two governors were certain to know of in the evening' (*TCTC* 259, Ching-fu 2(893)/7th month). After the imperial defeat, he pressed for Tu Jang-nêng's execution on the governors' behalf.

'Thereafter, every move at the court had to be referred to Pin and Ch'i (governors) for a decision, and the Southern and Northern offices (the bureaucrats and the eunuchs respectively) frequently adhered to the two governors in order to get imperial favours' (*TCTC* 259, Ching-fu 2 (893)/10th month). Ts'ui Chao-wei, through his relative who was assistant governor of Pin, also helped the governor to influence the imperial choice of chief ministers (*TCTC* 260, Ch'ien-ning 2(895)/2nd-3rd months).

The struggle came to the open in 895 when the governors killed Ts'ui Chao-wei's rivals; then the emperor recalled two ex-chief ministers who were supported by Chu Wên; and Li K'o-yung blocked the favours to Ts'ui Chao-wei's protégé and tried to raise an ex-administrator of his province to power; *TCTC* 260, Ch'ien-ning 2(895)/5/*chia-tzŭ* and 6/*hsin-mao*.

equilibrium in power, pacified Li K'o-yung with rich rewards and sent him back to his province.[52]

The new position probably pleased Chao-tsung, for a third force had now been formed. In addition to the Kuan-chung and Ho-tung alliances, there was also the powerful governor in Ho-nan, Chu Wên, who decided to support the defeated candidate against his old enemy, Li K'o-yung.[53] Chao-tsung could now hope to use 'diplomacy' to maintain a new balance, for none of the groups was as yet strong enough to defy the others. The basic flaw in any equilibrium that could be achieved, however, was unremoved—there was no authority left behind the diplomatic moves. This was accentuated by the fact that all the three groups were trying to expand their power. For example, Li Mao-chên was not content with the four provinces in his control but made plans to take two others to his north. Li K'o-yung had extended his control over south eastern Ho-tung and two provinces in Ho-pei while Chu Wên was still fighting in eastern Ho-nan to add two more provinces to the four he already governed. It was only a matter of time before they turned against each other.

The first to do so were Chu Wên and Li K'o-yung. The bitterness between them upset the balance for which the court had hoped. While they were fully engaged in a bloody struggle for the Ho-pei provinces, Li Mao-chên was able to march to the capital for the second time to stop the emperor from strengthening the imperial armies. This time, the emperor's new armies showed even less

[52] The biography of Li Mao-chên, *CWTS* 132; of Wang Hsing-yü, *CTS* 175 and *HTS* 244 C; of Han Chien, *CWTS* 15; of Wang Kung the nephew and Wang K'o the son, *HTS* 187 and *CWTS* 14; and of Li K'o-yung, *CWTS* 25. Also *TCTC* 260, Ch'ien-ning 2(895)/3rd month; 5th month; 7/*ping-ch'ên*, ff.; till fall of Pin Chou in 11/*ting-mao* and withdrawal of Li K'o-yung in 12/*wu-hsü*.

[53] The growth of Chu Wên's power while the court was trying to regain power in the Wei valley was slow, having taken him already twelve years. But he did control at this time four provinces apart from his own.

He had begun to try and influence court decisions by recommending Chang Chün to be Chief Minister again in 2nd/896 (*TCTC* 260, Ch'ien-ning 3(896)/2nd month).

As his enemy, Li K'o-yung supported the governor of P'u against that of Shan; Chu Wên took the other side. Also, Shan was the only province left between him and the Wei valley. His influence at the court would ultimately depend on his control of it.

resistance, and the court was once again forced to move out of Ch'ang-an.[54]

The problem of where to move to marked the beginning of the final stage of the T'ang 'restoration'. There were no governors who could be trusted. There was no way open to Ho-nan (Honan) or to Chien-nan (Szechuan) and the governor of Shan-nan East (Hupei) was unreliable. The only route left was the precarious one of getting to Li K'o-yung's capital in Ho-tung through the country of Tangut tribesmen whose loyalty was already uncertain. There was also the danger of being stopped and captured by Li Mao-chên's army. So when Han Chien, the governor of the neighbouring Hua province, turned from his ally Li Mao-chên and offered to be host to the emperor, an offer dangerous to refuse, the emperor accepted.[55]

In doing so, Chao-tsung could only hope for temporary relief. The weakness of Han Chien was obvious to all. He had only two small prefectures in his province and was surrounded by enemies on all sides. His only advantage was his personal wealth and long defensive preparations. The court might have observed that he was in no position to depose the emperor. But the rift between him and Li Mao-chên was also dangerous. There was no longer an alliance to defend Kuan-chung from the governors in the east. It could only be hoped that the feud between Chu Wên and Li K'o-yung would continue indefinitely until they were both exhausted, while adjustments of power could be made in Kuan-chung.[56]

[54] *TCTC* 260, Ch'ien-ning 3(896)/6/*ping-yin* to 7/*ping-shên*.

[55] *TCTC* 260, Ch'ien-ning 3 (896)/7/*hsin-mao* to *chia-wu*. Han Chien's words to Chao-tsung have been recorded as:

'Right now, (Li) Mao-chên is not the only ambitious (*pa-hu* 跋扈 describes the flouting of authority, of the law) governor. If Your Highness leaves the capital to travel far in the border regions, I fear that once the retinue crosses the river, there will not be a day of return. Although the army of Hua Chou is now weak, it controls the area of the Passes (T'ung-kuan pass) and is also sufficient to defend itself. I have accumulated (supplies) and disciplined (the army) for already fifteen years (only twelve years at Hua Chou, since 884). It is not far from Ch'ang-an to the west. I hope Your Highness will come and plan for a restoration here.'

[56] Han Chien's fear of Chu Wên can be seen in his decision to recall the now pro-Chu Wên minister Ts'ui Yin (previously a supporter of the Kuan-chung

But the harm Han Chien could still do was underestimated. From 1st/897, he reduced the emperor to a mere puppet by disbanding his personal bodyguards, by removing all the princes from military commands and absorbing all their armies, and then by executing the ablest of the emperor's commanders. He also interfered with the emperor's choice of chief ministers and caused the officials he feared to be disgraced.[57] Within a few months, the emperor was stripped of everything he could use to defend himself. In 8th/897, all the imperial princes he had trained were murdered by Han Chien. What Han Chien's purpose was in thus completely enslaving the emperor is not clear. He could not expect to depose the emperor and found a new dynasty on the strength of two prefectures. Neither could he expect to keep the emperor with him indefinitely. Chu Wên had already won his main battles in Ho-nan. Li K'o-yung was preparing to ride south to 'save the emperor' and Li Mao-chên was urging that the emperor be returned to Ch'ang-an immediately.

If Han Chien had hoped to bargain with the emperor's person for his own survival against these strong rivals, it soon became evident that his survival depended on his sending the emperor back to Ch'ang-an. One of the chief ministers, Ts'ui Yin, had been persuading Chu Wên to rebuild the palaces of Lo-yang, the Eastern Capital, and take the emperor there. This was the most dangerous threat of all, and both Li K'o-yung and Li Mao-chên insisted that Han Chien release the emperor in order to place him farther from Chu Wên's reach. Han Chien had no alternative but to do so. He undertook the rebuilding of the palaces at Ch'ang-an (burnt by Li Mao-chên in 7th/896) and on 8th/898, sent Chao-tsung back.[58]

clique); *TCTC* 260, Ch'ien-ning 3(896)/9/*i-wei*. In fact, Chu Wên was still too busy in eastern Ho-nan where the stubborn resistance of the Yün and Yen governors was being helped by Li K'o-yung who sent several batches of cavalry to them, and himself harassed Chu Wên's northern provinces. *TCTC* 260, Ch'ien-ning 2(895)/1/*kuei-wei*; 4th month; 12th month; record the help Li K'o-yung sent. 260, Ch'ien-ning 3 (896)/intercalary 1st month and 6th month give accounts of his harassing Chu Wen.

[57] *TCTC* 61, Ch'ien-ning 4 (897)/1/*chia-shên* to *ting-hai*; and 8th month.

[58] Han Chien called for help to rebuild the palaces in 1st/898; *TCTC* 261, Kuang-hua 1(898)/1/*jên-ch'ên*. They were not ready till 8th/898; 261, 8/*chi-wei*.

The new situation had simplified matters. The three groups of power were reduced to two, with Chu Wên on one side and an uneasy alliance of Li K'o-yung, Li Mao-chên and Han Chien on the other. The issues, too, were simpler—whether the emperor should be at Ch'ang-an or at Lo-yang. In these circumstances, the old struggle between the eunuchs and the bureaucrats returned to the foreground. Once free from the oppressive limits of Han Chien's power, their leading members again took sides among the governors. As neither the eunuchs nor the bureaucrats had any armies of their own, their struggle depended on borrowed strength. The eunuchs sought the support of the Kuan-chung and Ho-tung clique, while Ts'ui Yin, the leading bureaucrat, found support from Chu Wên.[59] In this struggle the balance steadily shifted to Chu Wên's advantage.

The two important events which helped Chu Wên's extension of power were Li K'o-yung's loss of one of his provinces to Chu Wên and the mutinies in western Ho-nan by the T'ung-kuan Pass. The loss of his province exposed Li K'o-yung's capital to Chu Wên's attack. The mutinies in western Ho-nan brought Chu Wên to the gates of T'ung-kuan Pass and within easy striking distance of the capital.[60]

The shift in power was decisive at the court. Ts'ui Yin, with Chu Wên's support, was too powerful now to be moved. He used Chu Wên's influence to make the emperor kill a rival minister as well as the two eunuch commanders of the newly recruited imperial army. The other eunuchs were so frightened by this that they deposed the emperor five months later in 11th/900 and put up the heir-apparent instead. This was not done to oppose Chu Wên. In fact, they forged a letter from the deposed emperor offering

[59] For a year after 8th/898, the eunuchs were more powerful than the bureaucrats and Ts'ui Yin was forced out in 1st/899 (*TCTC* 261, Kuang-hua 2(899)/1/*ting-wei*). But the tide turned at the beginning of 900 when they failed to move Ts'ui Yin out to Ling-nan (*TCTC* 262, Kuang-hua 3(900)/2/*jên-wu* and 6/*ting-mao*). The events at court coincided closely with Chu Wên's successes at Lu Chou and Shan Chou, see note 60 below.

[60] For Lu province, *TCTC* 261, Kuang-hua 1(898)/12th month; Kuang-hua 2(899)/5/*chi-hai* to 8/*i-yu*. *TCTC* 262, T'ien-fu 1 (901)/3/*jên-tzŭ*.

For Shan province, *TCTC* 261, Kuang-hua 2 (899)/6/*ting-ch'ou*; 11th month.

Chu Wên the throne and a new dynastic line. They hoped that Chu Wên would accept them as part of the palace heritage and turn to them instead of the bureaucrats for help in the future. At the same time, they were so afraid of Chu Wên that they did not dare kill Ts'ui Yin, the one man who could have ruined their plans.

It was a desperate attempt, and the motives were so involved that no clear picture can now be drawn. The response of the three governors of Kuan-chung and Ho-tung is vague. The two in Kuan-chung seem to have supported the coup. What explanations the eunuchs gave them are not known. The governors certainly could not have agreed to the offer of the throne to Chu Wên. As for Chu Wên, he was tempted by the offer, but the fact that the eunuchs had planned the coup made him decide against it. The coup lasted less than two months. On the 1/1st/901, with Chu Wên's backing, Chao-tsung was restored.[61]

The last three years of Chao-tsung's reign were dominated by Chu Wên, and will be considered in the next chapter. The position of the other military governors and their relations with the court can be briefly described. A process of elimination by war and diplomacy among themselves had reduced the number of independent governors. By 904 there were, north of the Yangtse, eight governors who held more than one province, and only four others still independent. During these years, there was no more than a formal reference to the emperor, for example, when providing an excuse for attacking another governor and when asking for the confirmation of a satellite governor of a newly conquered province. The court was also sometimes approached

[61] *TCTC* 262, Kuang-hua 3 (900)/11/*kêng-yin*; 12/*wu-ch'ên* and *K'ao-i*, have the most detailed account. Biography of Li Chên, *CWTS* 18, 9b-11a; and Liang Annals, *CWTS* 2, 3b-4a (preserved in *TCTC K'ao-i* and restored from *TFYK* 187). Also *TCTC* 262, Kuang-hua 3(900)/12/*wu-ch'ên* and T'ien-fu 1 (901)/1/*i-yu*.

TCTC K'ao-i quotes the *T'ang Pu Chi* (唐補紀) giving a long story of how Chu Wên had known of the eunuchs' plans for deposing the emperor and turned against them only because of their treacherous attempt to use Ts'ui Yin against him (Ts'ui Yin was, in fact, Chu Wên's supporter at the time). This is not supported by any other source, and was rightly rejected, but it indicates the different contemporary understanding of the motives involved.

TABLE III[62]

Province (With date of submission or acquisition)	*Status and origins of governor and date of appointment*
I. *Territory under Chu Wên*	
a) *directly controlled by him or his men*	
20 Pien*	court-chosen, 883
21 Hua (886)*	(court-appointed, 890)
23 Yün (897)*	(court-appointed, 898)
9 P'u (901)*	(court-appointed, 901)
25 Hsü$_3$ (887)	appointed by Chu Wên, 904
18 Mêng (888)	appointed by Chu Wên, 903
19 Lo-yang (888)	appointed by Chu Wên, 904
27 Hsü$_2$ (893)	appointed by Chu Wên, 904
22 Yen (897)	appointed by Chu Wên, 903
(35 Hsing (898)**	appointed by Chu Wên, 903)
(26 Ts'ai (899)	reduced to prefecture of Hsü$_3$)
17 Shan (899)	self-appointed, 899; (surrendered)
8 Hua (901)	appointed by Chu Wên, 904
1 Yung (901)	appointed by Chu Wên, 904
24 Ch'ing (903)	son of previous governor, 899; (surrendered)
b) *satellite governors*	
13 Chên (900)	son of previous governor, 883; (submitted after siege)
14 Wei (891)	son of previous governor, 898; (submitted after defeat)
15 Ting (900)	uncle of previous governor, 900; (submitted after siege)
(36 Chin (901)**	self-appointed, 899; (submitted voluntarily))

[62] Like Table II, this has been compiled from *T'ang Fang-chên Nien-piao*, *passim*, and the biographies of the governors, chiefly in the *CWTS* 13-15, 17, 22-23, 25, 50, 63, 132, 134-136; *HTS* 186-187, 210-212; and *HWTS* 39. Also important was *TCTC* 264-265, *passim*.

There is some difficulty about deciding who were the governors of Fu (no. 5) and Yen (no. 7) in 904 and the four new governors under Wang Chien.

II. *The rest of North China*

a) *under Li K'o-yung*

10 Ping	court-appointed, 883
(37 Chên-wu (893)**	Li K'o-yung's brother, 903)

b) *under Liu Jên-kung*

12 Yu	appointed by Li K'oyung, 895; rebelled in 897
16 Ts'ang (898)	Liu Jên-kung's son, 898

c) *under Li Mao-chên*

2 Ch'i*	court-chosen, General of Imperial Guards, 887
4 Ching (899)*	(court-appointed, 899)
3 Pin (897)	Li Mao-chên's adopted son, 897
5 Fu (899)	probably also an adopted son, (?)
(38 Ch'in (890)**	Li Mao-chên's nephew, 903)

d) *under Li Ch'eng-ch'ing*

6 Hsia	nephew of previous governor, Tangut tribal leader, 896
7 Yen (889?)	uncle of Li Ch'êng-ch'ing, 897

e) *under Chao K'uang-ning*

28 Hsiang	son of previous governor who was an ex-Ts'ai rebel, 893
34 Ching (903)	Chao K'uang-ning's brother, 903

f) *under Wang Chien*

30 I	court-appointed, General of Imperial Guards, 891
31 Tzŭ (897)	a distant relative of Wang Chien, 897
29 Liang (902)	Wang Chien's adopted son, 903

(Wang Chien also controlled four new provinces created out of the above three. These were mostly under adopted sons)

g) *under two other governors*

32 Yang	self-appointed, prefectural officer, 892; (also held Hsüan and parts of Hang province, both south of the Yangtse)
33 Ngo	self-appointed, leader of mutiny, 886

* = provinces under Chu Wên (I, a) and Li Mao-chên (II, c) themselves
** = new province

to arrange truces and negotiations in order to gain time for those concerned.

Only a few governors had direct access to the capital where they could make their demands felt. These, too, were reduced in number as they fought among themselves. In 904, there were only three left, with great differences in strength and in the number of provinces ruled. They were Chu Wên, Li K'o-yung and Li Mao-chên. Table III for 904 may be contrasted with Table II for 883. The province numbers in Table II have been retained while four new provinces have been added.

The table shows how much stronger Chu Wên was compared with the others and why he was able, in 901, to march into the Wei valley to get the emperor away from Li Mao-chên. It also shows why he could move the emperor to Lo-yang in 904, and there murder him. The rise of Chu Wên between 883 and 904 is considered in detail in Chapter Three, in a study of the structure of a new central power.

CHAPTER THREE

The Growth of a Central Power 883-907

During the last twenty years of the T'ang dynasty, several military governors tried to build up by force a new source of authority. The most successful was Chu Wên, governor of Pien province, who eventually founded a new dynasty. His place in Chinese history has been a lowly one. Traditional Chinese historians have always made villains of the men who dethroned emperors of long and distinguished lines. In recent years, however, he has been castigated for different reasons. His crime was to have betrayed Huang Ch'ao by surrendering to the T'ang imperial army in 882.[1] This study does not attempt to dispute or confirm his allotted place in history. It is chiefly concerned with the way his power was built up and examines the prerequisites of power in this period.

Chu Wên's later success has made it possible for a comparatively detailed picture of his career to be drawn here. It is, however, impossible to determine if he had made any innovations in the organization of the Pien provincial government because few details have been preserved about the other provinces. Many features which appear to have been changes made by Chu Wên might have been modelled on developments made by other governors. It seems clear that the basic organization which Chu Wên had was common to all the governors in North China and the outline of this organization which follows is also intended to show the kind of opposition he had to face.

Pien province consisted of four prefectures south of the Grand Canal, two of which also controlled a large area north of it. In the

[1] Among the writings of early historians, the Sung historian Hung Mai's sympathy for Chu Wên was exceptional; *Jung-chai Sui-pi*, 1, 7b, and *Jung-chai San-pi*, 10, 2a-b. In a number of recent history text-books published in China, there have been hostile attitudes to Chu Wên when dealing with the Huang Ch'ao rebellion.

province, there were important stations and granaries which had been built to aid grain transportation along the Canal. But its importance was not only economic. Its strategic position had proved essential ever since 763 for the containment of the independent governors of Ho-pei and for the subjugation of rebel governors in Ho-nan. It had, therefore, one of the largest armies in the region, the Hsüan-wu Army. This was in the hands of professional soldiers and surrendered rebels who had been mutinous several times in the late eighth and early ninth centuries, but who had been loyal to the court-chosen governors since 824.[2] Most of the governors since then had been bureaucrats, but the last governor before Chu Wên was probably of military origins. Little is known of him except that he had brought men and supplies with him to recover Ch'ang-an in 883. He was undistinguished in the final campaigns there and his replacement did not affect the loyalty of the army remaining at Pien Chou.[3]

On 3/7th/883, Chu Wên entered the capital of Pien province as the new governor.[4] This was more than three months after his appointment and almost three months after the recovery of Ch'ang-an. The delay in his taking office was probably due to various duties, such as clearing the metropolitan area of all banditry and disciplining the mixed Chinese and tribal armies. It may also have been due to some bargaining about the number of men he was allowed to take with him to the province. The rebel army which had surrendered with him had been largely dispersed or absorbed into the imperial armies with which it had fought. When Chu Wên

[2] *T'ang Fang-chên Nien-piao*, chüan 2. Of the 29 governors of Pien in 59 years (824-883), at least 24 were bureaucrats. For troubles along the Grand Canal close to Pien Chou and Sung Chou, see Ch'üan Han-shêng, *T'ang Sung Ti-kuo yü Yün-ho*, pp. 77-92.

[3] K'ang Shih was called from Pien Chou to be a Vanguard Commander of the imperial armies attacking Ch'ang-an in 1st/882; *TCTC* 254, Chung-ho 2(882)/1/*hsin-wei*. He is not, however, named in the Report of Victory (*lu-pu* 露布) of 4th/883 where there is a long list of meritorious officers; *CTS* 200 B, 7a-8a.

[4] His appointment and early life and career have been considered in Chapter Two, notes 32 and 33.

finally left for Pien Chou, he had with him only a few hundred men and officers.[5]

The composition of this troop is not known. It is known, however, that it included a core of military retainers (*pu-ch'ü*) of at least eighty men,[6] the majority of whom had probably surrendered with him in 9th/882. But he seems to have recruited new military retainers in the following ten months (9th/882-7th/883), including a senior officer of another provincial army.[7] In the following table

[5] *TCTC* 255, Chung-ho 3 (883)/7/*ting-mao* and *CWTS* 1, 3b. According to the biography of Huang Ch'ao (*HTS* 225 C, translated by Howard S. Levy, pp. 36-37) and in the biographies of Wang Ch'ung-jung (*CTS* 182, 1a-b; *HTS* 187, 1b), it is clear that when Chu Wên surrendered he had a large army of thousands with him. The dispersal of these men is not recorded, but most of them probably came under Wang Ch'ung-jung when Chu Wên was made his deputy and probably remained with him after the Ch'ang-an victory.

There is no further mention of the sections of the Pien provincial army recorded earlier as having been called to the Wei valley under the governor, K'ang Shih (*TCTC* 254, Chung-ho 2 (882)/1/*hsin-wei*). It is doubtful if any of them was placed under Chu Wên at this stage. They might have returned earlier to Pien Chou when it became known that Huang Ch'ao had escaped into Ho-nan; or were among the 20,000 men left to defend Ch'ang-an (*TCTC* 255, Chung-ho 3(883)/4/*chia-ch'ên*).

[6] *CWTS* 19, 4b, says more than eighty men followed Chu Wen as *chung-chüan* (中涓) and names eight. In the biography of one of the eight in *CWTS* 59, 1a, he is called a *pu-ch'ü* (部曲). I have translated both as 'military retainer'. There were many similar terms in use in late T'ang, Wu-tai and early Sung periods like *ssŭ-yang* (廝養), *yüan-sui* (元隨), *ts'ung-jên* (從人) and others collected in Y. Sudō, 'Gōdai Ketsu-doshi no Yagun ni Kansuru itsu Kosatsu', *Tōyō Bunka Kenkyusha Kiyō*, pp. 47-62. Professor Sudō shows that in late T'ang and in the Wu-tai, *pu-ch'ü*, and several other terms, described both domestic servants and military retainers, including men who were soldiers and officers in the 'governor's guards' (*ya-chün*) of the provinces; pp. 4-5, 47-62 and 63-64. For more details about *pu-ch'ü*, see N. Niida, *Shina Mibunhō shi*, Tokyo, 1942, chapter 8, *passim*, especially pp. 865-885.

[7] This was P'ang Shih-ku; *CWTS* 21, 1a-2a. He was called a *chung-chüan*, a military retainer, but his early career is difficult to follow. The earliest record in which he was mentioned is the Report of Victory of 4th/883. He was then known as P'ang Ts'ung and was the commander of a regiment of the Hsü[2] provincial army; *CTS* 200 B, 7 b. It is not known how he came to join Chu Wên's ranks.

There seems no doubt that P'ang Ts'ung was the same man as P'ang Shih-ku. He did not have his name changed until 897; see the edict on changing his name by Chang Hsüan-yen in *Wên-yüan Ying-hua*, 457, 8a, 'Shou P'ang Ts'ung

are the men known to have come with Chu Wên, their biographies having been preserved because of the part they played in his early successes. Attention has not only been drawn to their social origins, but also, wherever possible, to their first connections with Chu Wên. An early supporter who joined him later at Pien Chou has also been included to complete the picture of the most trusted men in his new career. There is a significant predominance of the men who were already his retainer officers or were soon to be made so.

TABLE IV[8]

Name	Origins
1 Hu Chên*	a county minor official before he joined Huang Ch'ao; was Chu Wên's commander.
2 Ting Hui*	son of a rich farmer who gave up farming and formed his own gang; joined Huang Ch'ao after which he became one of Chu Wên's military retainers.
3 Chu Chên	origins obscure; a military retainer.
4 P'ang Shih-ku	origins obscure; officer of $Hsü_3$ provincial army, fought creditably against Huang Ch'ao; later a military retainer.
5 Têng Chi-yün	origins obscure; joined Huang Ch'ao; placed under Chu Wên as a military retainer.
6 Chang Ts'un-ching	origins obscure; possibly from Huang Ch'ao's gang
7 Liu K'ang-ngai	a farmer forced into Huang Ch'ao's army; surrendered with Chu Wên
8 Kuo Yen	a farmer forced into Huang Ch'ao's army; surrendered with Chu Wên.
9 Shih Shu-tsung*	origins obscure; possibly recruited after Chu Wên's surrender and then made a military retainer.
10 Hsü Huai-yü*	origins obscure; followed Chu Wên early; arrived later (884?) at Pien Chou.

* Signifies that he was later one of Chu Wên's military governors

wu-ning p'ing-nan chich-tu kai-ming shih-ku chih'. His biography in *CWTS* also says his original name was Ts'ung.

[8] Hu Chên's biography, *CWTS* 16, 6b. When Chu Wên surrendered, Hu Chên was the commander of the 'original troops' (*yüan-ts'ung* 元從) or the 'personal troops' (*ch'in-chiang* 親將); *TCTC* 255, Chung-ho 2(882)/9/*ping-*

Chu Wên's first problem was to win over the leaders of the professional Hsüan-wu army in Pien province and establish his own men in command of various units within it. There were two sections of this army, the main fighting force and the 'governor's guards', the *ya-chün*. The guards were a most important body of men. They were the governor's personal troops and bodyguards and the officers were also used to command units of the main army in battle. It was normal at this time for a governor to select his own men for the guards, especially men who were his military retainers. He had, however, also to consider re-employing the men whose place in the guards had been hereditary.

Chu Wên began by using his own officers. Of the men in the table above, Ting Hui (no. 2 in Table IV) was made his administrator (*tu ya-ya*) and Hu Chên (1) a commander (*ya-chiang*). He made

hsü. *TCTC op. cit.*, says he was one of those who advised Chu Wên to surrender. If he was the Hu Chên mentioned in the Report of Victory of 4th/883 (*CTS* 200B, 7b), he seems to have been given a command in the imperial armies after his surrender and before his going to Pien Chou.

Ting Hui's biography, *CWTS* 59, 1a-2a. Chu Chên's biography, *CWTS* 19, 4b-6a, in which is found the list of eight of Chu Wên's earliest retainers. Five of the eight have biographies in the *CWTS* and are in this table. Of the remaining three, only one is mentioned again as one of Chu Wên's top commanders in 902 (Li Hui, in *TCTC* 263, T'ien-fu 2(902)/6/*i-hai*, and *K'ao-i*, quotation from the *Liang T'ai-tsu Veritable Records*).

P'ang Shih-ku's biography, *CWTS* 21, 1a-2a (see note 6). Têng Chi-yün in *CWTS* 19, 8a-b, where he is said to have been attached (*li* 隸) to Chu Wên, 'under his banner' (*hui-hsia* 麾下). Y. Sudō, *Yagun*, p. 46, includes the phrase in his list about joining the *ya-chün* or being a military retainer. Chang Ts'un-ching's biography in *CWTS* 20, 7a-8a. Liu K'ang-ngai's in *CWTS* 21, 8b-9a, says that he was later 'taken into confidence' (*wei-i hsin-fu* 委以心腹), another phrase in Y. Sudō, *Yagun*, p. 46. Kuo Yen's biography in *CWTS* 21, 6a-7a.

Shih Shu-tsung's biography in *CWTS* 19, 1a-2b, says he was a native of a county in Pien Chou who enlisted in Chu Wên's army and was made a troop leader of five men (*wu-chang* 伍長) under P'ang Shih-ku. But his name is in the list of retainers in *CWTS* 19, 4b.

Hsü Huai-yü's biography in *CWTS* 21, 4b-6a, says, 'when young . . . followed Chu Wên when Chu Wên started his army (? *ch'i-chün* 起軍)'. I wonder whether *ch'i-chün* could have referred to Chu Wên's own gang formed before he joined Huang Ch'ao.

officers of his own men including his eldest son who was still a boy. The most important of these officers was Chu Chên (3) who was given special responsibilities of selection, training and reorganization, not only of the new guards, but also of the provincial army later on.[9] As for the hereditary officers, Chu Wên retained their services and also appointed their sons as guards officers. One of them was made an adjutant (*t'ung-tsan kuan*) and became a trusted adviser. There were also the sons of high-ranking officers of the main army who had already been given posts in the guards; for example, one of them was retained as an official assisting in reception.[10]

In the main army a similar policy was followed. The commanders seem to have been retained with a professional officer holding the highest command.[11] But the reorganization for a defensive war against the armies of Huang Ch'ao which were ravaging the countryside was left to Chu Wên's own officers. This task was entrusted to the guards officer Chu Chên who, in the course of the next few years,

[9] Ting Hui, in *CWTS* 59, 1a. Hu Chên is called a *ya-chiang* in *TCTC* 256 Kuang-ch'i 2(886)/11th month. Chu Wên's eldest son was Chu Yu-yü, biography in *CWTS* 12, 4b-5a. Chu Chên was given 'an important post' (*yu-chih* 右職) to control the guards (the *fu-shin* 腹心); *CWTS* 19, 4b. Another *ya-chiang* was Têng Chi-yün (no. 5 in Table IV); *CWTS* 19, 8a.

[10] Liu Han, *CWTS* 20, 2b-4a. The other guards officers were K'ou Yen-ch'ing biography in *CWTS* 20, 8a-9b; also *TFYK* 467, 21a-b; and Liu Ch'i, biography in *CWTS* 64, 8a-b.

A *t'ung-tsan kuan* (通贊官) seems to have been an officer in the guards in charge of information and conveying messages in and out of the governor's residence. Y. Sudō, in his 'Gōdai Ketsudoshi no Shihai Taisei', *Shigaku Zasshi*, no. 4, pp. 321-322, shows that the *t'ung-tsan kuan* was also called *t'ung-ying kuan* (通引官) and had his equivalents in the Wu-tai courts.

[11] This was probably Yang Yen-hung who was the commander in charge of the attempt to massacre the Sha-t'o Turks and their leader Li K'o-yung in 5th/884; *CWTS* 25, 8a-9a and *TCTC* 255, Chung-ho 4(884)/5/*chia-hsü*. In *CWTS* 19, 6b, Yang Yen-hung is said to have had a horseman bodyguard (a *ch'i-shih* 騎士) of his own, Li Ssŭ-an, who was later chosen by Chu Wên for his own use. Yang Yen-hung is also mentioned in *CWTS* 22, 8a-b, as a successful commander against Huang Ch'ao in 884.

was very effective in his selection of officers and in the training of soldiers. All the men recruited by the various officers as well as the men who had surrendered, T'ai-tsu (Chu Wên) put under (Chu) Chên. More than fifty officers who were selected by (Chu) Chên were all found suitable.[12]

The army was largely infantry. Chu Wên was dissatisfied with this after seeing how efficient the tribal cavalry under Li K'o-yung had been at the battle of Ch'ang-an. He ordered the formation of new cavalry units and the first five hundred horsemen were left in the command of a retainer officer, P'ang Shih-ku (4). Under him were placed other officers; for example, another retainer officer, Shih Shu-tsung (9) who was made a section leader. Other units were formed soon after, also under officers who had come with Chu Wên. Chang Ts'un-ching (6) was appointed a commander of the right flank and Kuo Yen (8) rose later to be a cavalry commander. Guards officers like Teng Chi-yün (5) were also given the command of the 'light cavalry'.[13] Other officers were selected locally. Chu Wên personally picked men for his guards at parades of the provincial Hsüan-wu Army. There was also the example of a man who came from a Pien Chou family which had produced high-ranking officers in the imperial armies.[14]

Chu Wên's military reputation had helped to awe the provincial officers and his later success as a commander in the field must have won him the army's loyalty. An important factor in his early

[12] *HWTS* 21, 6b, probably taken from an earlier source than the *CWTS*, like Chu Chên's biography in the *Liang Veritable Records*, or from the *CWTS* Basic Annals of Chu Wen, which has not been preserved. In Chu Chên's biography, *CWTS* 19, 4b, his work is summarized as 'selected and trained troops and controlled the retainers'.

[13] P'ang Shih-ku, *CWTS* 21, 1a; Shih Shu-tsung, *CWTS* 19, 1a. Chang Ts'un-ching, *CWTS* 20, 7a; and Kuo Yen, *CWTS* 21, 6a.

Têng Chi-yün, *CWTS* 19, 8a. Hsü Huai-yü was soon afterwards made a deputy commander of the 'personal following' (*ch'in-ts'ung* 親從), Chu Wên's personal troops; *CWTS* 21, 4b-5a. The six men are all in Table IV.

[14] Li Ssŭ-an was picked by Chu Wên at a parade; *CWTS* 19, 6b. Wang T'an's great-grandfather had been a defence commissioner (*fang-yü shih*) and his grandfather a garrison commander near Ch'ang-an. His father was a court official. But in 883, Wang T'an had already become a junior officer (*hsiao-chiang* 小將) in the Pien army; *CWTS* 22, 8a.

control of the army was certainly its reorganization under personally selected men whom he could trust, especially under the military retainers he had placed in the guards garrison.

Two imperial officials, the eunuch Army Supervisor (*chien-chün*) and the governor's Military Deputy (*hsing-chün ssŭ-ma*), were probably appointed at the same time as Chu Wên and sent to Pien Chou together with him. However, the Supervisor could not interfere with Chu Wên's authority when imperial power was negligible and when Chu Wên was unconcerned about good reports to the court. As for the Military Deputy sent with him, Chu Wên does not seem to have had him for long. When a neighbouring prefect was forced out of his office by an attacking rebel army and escaped to Pien Chou, Chu Wên made him the new Military Deputy.[15] This suggests that he was soon in a position to choose the man he wanted for the highest imperial appointment to his province.

Not much is known about Chu Wên's relations with the prefects in his province. It is probable that Sung Chou was so closely controlled by the Hsüan-wu Army that Chu Wên's success with the Army gave him easy domination over its prefect. The prefect of Po Chou asked for help a few months later when attacked by Huang Ch'ao and Chu Wên marched in to take over direct control. As for the prefect of Ying Chou, he had a strong army of his own which he used to support Chu Wên against the rebels in Ho-nan.

There is little information about the administrative officials of the province. Apart from the finance experts, they were comparatively unimportant at this time when the province was restricted in size and constantly attacked by rebels. Chu Wên's biography describes the conditions at Pien province when he took over in 883 thus:

> At that time, Pien and Sung had suffered from famines for successive years. The administration and the citizens were in difficulty. The coffers and the granaries were empty. Outside, there were attacks by large enemy forces, and inside, the arrogant army was difficult to control. Fighting increased day by day . . .[16]

[15] *CWTS* 1, 5b-6a (from *TFYK* 187), says this was in 886.

[16] *CWTS* 1, 3b (from *TFYK* 187); this was abridged in *TCTC* 255 Chung-ho 3(883)/7/*ting-mao*.

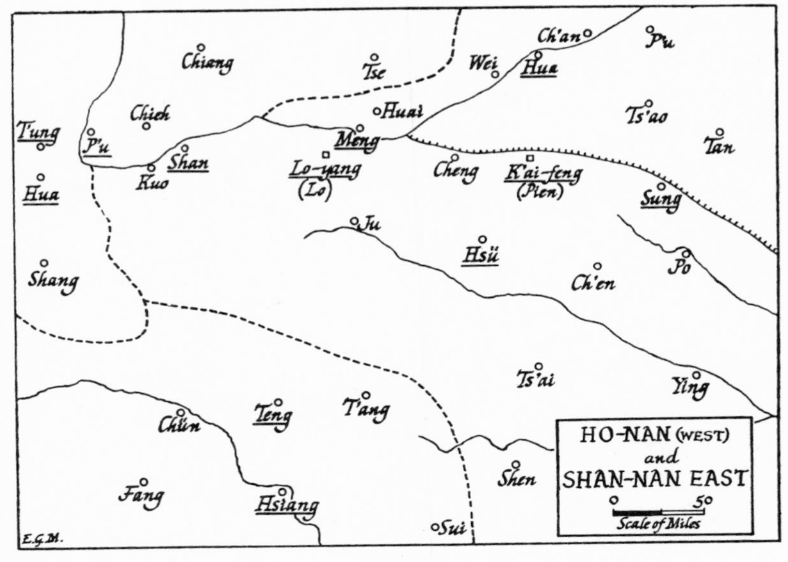

Map III

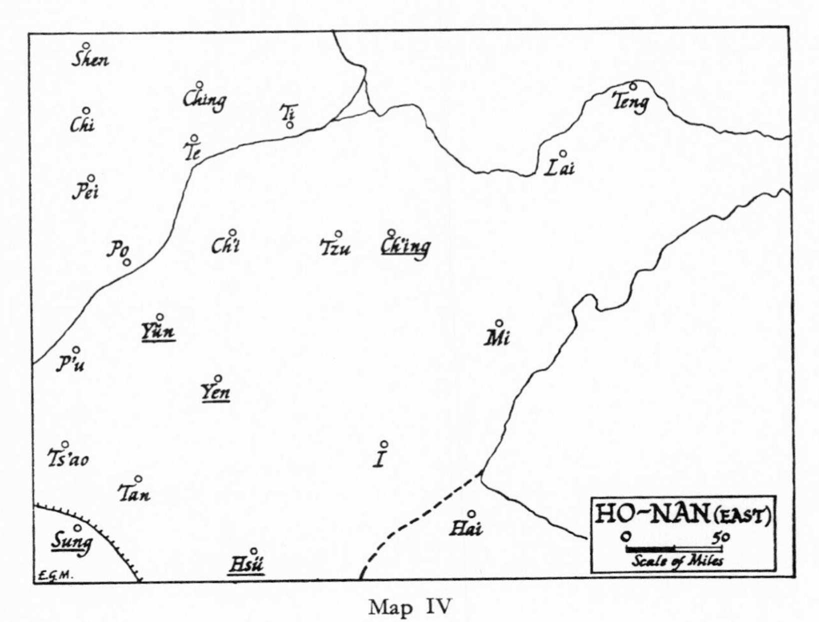

Map IV

Conditions may have been exaggerated a little in order to emphasize Chu Wên's success in overcoming his initial difficulties. But the dangers were there. The Huang Ch'ao armies had been attacking the countryside and were now supported by the armies of the governor of Ts'ai. Only the besieged garrison of a prefecture south of Pien Chou delayed the rebels from a major attack on Chu Wên's capital. That garrison's long resistance, in fact, broke the impact of Huang Ch'ao's armies on the whole area. Chu Wên was also helped by the resistance of other prefectures.[17] This time, none had submitted to Huang Ch'ao as they had done in 880. Huang Ch'ao's defeat at Ch'ang-an had discredited him and he was not a potential emperor any more. Also, the prefectures were no longer led by bureaucrats defending a disintegrating empire, but by garrison officers fighting to maintain their new positions which had recently been recognized by the restored T'ang dynasty.

Chu Wên's first success against Huang Ch'ao was in 12th/883. He had marched to save a county in Po Chou and as a result of the victory took over the prefectural capital. But though he directly controlled three of the four prefectural capitals of Pien province, he felt it was not possible to defeat Huang Ch'ao from these three walled cities. In 1st/884, he joined with the neighbouring governors to call in the governor of Ping, Li K'o-yung, and his nomad cavalry. In 4th-5th/884, the combined forces of the governors finally crushed the great rebel armies and Huang Ch'ao died in 6th/884.[18] During these few months, there occurred the events which turned the course of Chu Wên's career.

Firstly, there were the successive surrenders of several of his ex-comrades from Huang Ch'ao's army. They strengthened Chu Wên's forces considerably and provided him with some of his best officers. His previous comrades also provided him with a counter-weight against the professional section of the provincial

[17] For the defence of Ch'ên Chou, see biography of Chao Ch'iu, *CWTS* 14, 6a-7b. Other prefectures which resisted Huang Ch'ao were Ying Chou under the prefect Wang Ching-jao (*CWTS* 20, 4a-5a); Hsü$_3$ Chou which fell to the Ts'ai rebels only in 886; and Po Chou which was saved by Chu Wên at the end of 883.

[18] *HTS* 225 C, 8b-9a; *CWTS* 1, 4a; *TCTC* 255, Chung-ho 4(884)/2nd month; 256, Chung-ho 4/6/*ping-wu*.

army where any opposition to his leadership might have been found. It put him in a stronger position to decide on a policy of expansion and gave him a freer hand to direct the army where he chose. The other event, already discussed in the last chapter, was the attempt by Chu Wên to kill Li K'o-yung on the night of 14/5th/884. The event marked the end of hope for a genuine restoration of T'ang power and left him free to expand in Ho-nan without danger from the Sha-t'o Turks.

The rebels who surrendered provided Chu Wên's army with a second group of officers who owed personal loyalty to him. Together with those in Table IV, they formed the nucleus of his organization and were the men who helped him through the most difficult years of his governorship of Pien from 883-887. The following table gives some details of the ex-rebels who are known to have become Chu Wên's chief commanders and administrators. Most of them were military men of lowly origins who had had no previous connexions with him. Their surrender was expedient for him as well as for themselves. His trust in them seems to have been repaid by loyal service from every one of whom there is record. Included in the table is a twelfth man who had been a personal follower of Huang Ch'ao. His surrender to Chu Wên was delayed but nonetheless interesting.

The men named in the table were used in different ways by Chu Wên. The place each was given throws some light on his organization. Most of them had been officers who had surrendered with their troops, but it is not known whether they were allowed to keep their own men. The two who had surrendered earlier in 3rd/884, Li T'ang-pin (no. 1 in Table V) and Wang Ch'ien-yü (2), were sent to fight Huang Ch'ao and their quick success suggests that they were allowed to lead some of their own troops. At least two of the others, Li Tang (3) and Li Ch'ung-yin (9), were given full commands, one of a new cavalry unit and the other of the vanguard infantry. It is possible that the two were permitted to keep their own retainers. The remainder were divided between those who were appointed officers in the main army, serving either under Chu Wên himself or under his chief commander, and those who were taken into the governor's guards. Several of them were

TABLE V[19]

	Name	*Origins and place in Huang Ch'ao's army*
1	Li T'ang-pin	origins obscure; a brilliant officer.
2	Wang Ch'ien-yü	an ex-hunter turned bandit; probably served the imperial forces before joining Huang Ch'ao.
3	Li Tang	from an established family, travelled to Ch'ang-an where he was a friend of palace eunuchs; after Ch'ang-an fell, became Huang Ch'ao's military secretary.
4	Ko Ts'ung-chou*	probably from a wealthy family in the prefecture where the rebellion started; rose to be an officer.
5	Huo Ts'un	origins obscure; a commander.
6	Chang Kuei-pa*	from a family of county officials; a distinguished career with Huang Ch'ao and given title 'meritorious official' in 880.
7	Chang Kuei-hou*	cousin of the above; rank unknown.
8	Chang Kuei-pien	probably brother of no. 6; rank unknown.
9	Li Ch'ung-yin	origins obscure; an officer famed for bravery and Chu Wên's friend.
10	Chang Shên-ssŭ*	origins obscure; an officer.
11	Huang Wên-ching	origins obscure; probably an officer.
12	Hua Wên-ch'i*	son of farmer, started as retainer to Huang Ch'ao and after 880 was head of his attendant officers; escaped to Hua Chou after his death and was in Chu Wên's service possibly in 887.

* signifies that he was later one of Chu Wên's military governors.

[19] Li T'ang-pin's biography, *CWTS* 21, 7a-b. Wang Ch'ien-yü was also named in 21, 7a, as having surrendered with Li T'ang-pin. How this is to be reconciled with Wang Ch'ien-yü's biography in *CWTS* 21, 7b-8b, which says that he had been put in the Pien provincial army earlier on, I am not sure. I follow *TCTC* 255, Chung-ho 4(884)/3rd month in preferring the more unconscious comments in another man's biography.

Li Tang's biography, *CWTS* 19, 10a-b. Ko Ts'ung-chou's biography, *CWTS* 16, 1a-5a. Huo Ts'un's in *CWTS* 21, 2a-3b. Chang Kuei-pa and his cousin and brother have biographies in *CWTS* 16, 7a-11b (that Chang Kuei-hou was a cousin and not a brother is shown in the quotation from *Liang Kung-ch'en Lieh-chuan*, an early anonymous collection of biographies of Liang 'meritorious officials', in *TCTC* 255, Chung-ho 4(884)/5/*kuei-hai*, *K'ao-i*).

Li Ch'ung-yin's biography in *CWTS* 19, 10b-11a. Chang Shên-ssu's in *CWTS* 15, 12a-b. Huang Wên-ching's in *CWTS* 19, 8b-9b. Hua Wên-ch'i's biography in *CWTS* 90, 8a-9b, calls him a retainer (*chi-kang* 紀綱); this makes him the only personal follower of Huang Ch'ao known to have gained high office in the later dynasties. His biography in *HWTS* 47, 1a-b, shows that

soon given their own commands, but not all were given military duties. Chang Kuei-pien (8), for example, was a guards officer who was sent as an envoy to 'establish good relations with the areas close by'.[20]

In spite of these additions to his army, Chu Wên was still not strong enough to cope with the new rebellion in Ho-nan. After Huang Ch'ao's defeat, the rebel leadership was taken over by Ch'in Tsung-chüan. The rebels attacked with success in all directions. In 885-886, they captured Lo-yang, the Eastern Capital, and Chêng Chou, and began at the end of 886 to lay seige to Pien Chou. These were anxious years for Chu Wên. He could not depend on the court for any military aid during this time for the emperor had again fled from Ch'ang-an and a usurper had been put on the throne. Left to defend himself alone, Chu Wên turned to his neighbouring provinces. There was no central authority to direct any of them to help him and he could only expect support from the governors and prefects whom he could persuade to form alliances with him.

The first alliance was made with the prefect of Ch'ên Chou in 885. This was the prefect whose defence had held down the Huang Ch'ao armies in 883-884. Chu Wên had then come to his help and in 885 had sealed this bond by marrying his daughter to the prefect's son. Chu Wên thus ensured that at least one prefecture stood

CWTS was wrong to say that he joined Chu Yu-yü (Chu Wên's son) at P'u Chou. The name should have been Chu Yü, the prefect appointed by the governor of Yün province (also mentioned in *TCTC* 257, Kuang-ch'i 3(887)/10/*ting-wei*). If Hua Wên-ch'i did not join Chu Wên when he first captured P'u Chou in 10th/887, he must have done so when P'u Chou was taken again in 11th/892, this time by Chu Yu-yü: *TCTC* 259, Ching-fu 1(892)/11/*i-wei*. Perhaps he came under Chu Yu-yü's command at this time—hence the different versions in the *CWTS* and the *HWTS*.

[20] Li T'ang-pin and Wang Ch'ien-yü; *CWTS* 21, 7a and 21, 8a. Li Tang and Li Ch'ung-yin; *CWTS* 19, 10b and 19, 11a.

Of the others, Ko Ts'ung-chou was put under Chu Wên himself, and distinguished himself by saving Chu Wên's life two months later; *CWTS* 16, 1a-b. Huo Ts'un was put under the chief commander before he was later given a command; *CWTS* 21, 2a. Chang Kuei-pa and his cousin, Chang Kuei-hou, were made officers in the provincial army; *CWTS* 16, 7a and 9a. So was Chang Shên-ssŭ; *CWTS* 15, 12a. Huang Wên-ching, however, was used in the guards; *CWTS* 19, 8b-9a.

Chang Kuei-pien, *CWTS* 16, 10b.

between Pien Chou and the rebel capital to the south. With this support to his south, Chu Wên was able to beat off two rebel attacks, and in 5th/886 he was able to send a cavalry commander to attack the rebel capital.[21] But this failed and the rebels began the siege of Pien Chou. All this time, Chu Wên received no help from the two remaining court-chosen governors in Ho-nan, one to his north and the other to his east. They were content to form alliances for their own defence with the governor of Yün (north-east of Pien) whose province lay between them. When Chu Wên was besieged, he too was forced to follow this course. Because the governor of Yün was of the same Chu clan, Chu Wên formed a 'fraternal' alliance with him early in 887 and asked him for substantial military support. This was given to Chu Wên and played an important part in the raising of the siege.[22]

More important for Chu Wên's military strength, however, were the additional armies he recruited in other provinces. An opportunity to recruit men arose when the provincial army of Hua (north of Pien province) mutinied in 11th/886. Both Chu Wên and the governor of Yün sent armies to take over with the excuse that the court-chosen governor of the province was a failure. The race to capture that provincial capital is evidence of the desperate conditions at the time. The procedures of gubernatorial succession were completely ignored. Whichever of the two attacking armies could take Hua Chou would have the use of a whole army.

Chu Wên sent his best troops under the chief commander himself, and by forced marches they arrived before the army from Yün province. The city was captured and Chu Wên appointed one of his own guards commanders to be the deputy governor (*chieh-tu liu-hou*). The Hua provincial army was reorganized by drawing some units of its officers and men into the Pien army and

[21] *CWTS* 1, 4b (from *TFYK* 187), and biography of the Ch'ên Chou prefect, Chao Ch'iu, *CWTS* 14, 5b-8a; also *TCTC* 256, Kuang-ch'i 1 (885)/8th month and Kuang-ch'i 2(886)/5/*kuei-ssŭ*.

[23] Chu Hsüan, the son of a local 'boss' in Sung Chou (in a county neighbouring that of Chu Wen) and from a 'powerful family' (*hao-yu* 豪右), had risen to be governor of Yün through service in the Ch'ing provincial army; *CTS* 182, 13b-14a; *CWTS* 13, 1a-3a. For the relations between the Yün and Yen governors, see also TCTC 256, Kuang-ch'i 2(886)/end of year.

leaving a few Pien officers in command of the rest.[23] A large part of the army had to be left behind at Hua because the Huang Ho had to be defended against the hostile armies of Ho-pei, and a strong army was needed to cover the northern approaches to Pien Chou. The main advantage was that Chu Wên now had reserves which he could use when necessary.

Two other efforts at recruiting outside his own territory were more immediately rewarding. One was directed at western Ho-nan. He sent his cavalry commander with several thousand men to fight their way through rebel-controlled areas to the west.[24] This force had to deal with a major bandit gang whose defeat provided many recruits. It then had to fight its way back with the few thousands recruits to Pien Chou. The task took about six months. Before this expedition to the west had returned, Chu Wên sent another to the east to recruit men in the comparatively wealthy and peaceful Ch'ing province (Shantung).[25] This large army had

[23] *CWTS* 19, 11a, says Li Ch'ung-yin was made a commander at Hua Chou; *CWTS* 22, 4b, says Niu Ts'un-chieh was a junior officer; while *CWTS* 21, 13a, mentions a tribesman in the Hua provincial army whose son, a guards officer, later led a section of the Hua army to follow Chu Wên to battle.

For the capture of Hua Chou in 886, see *CWTS* 1, 5b (from *TFYK* 187), followed in *TCTC* 256, Kuang-ch'i 2(886)/11th month, which rejects the chronology in *CTS* 19 B, 20b and *HTS* 9, 10a. The new deputy governor was Hu Chên (no. 1 in Table IV); *CWTS* 16, 6b.

[24] *CWTS* 21, 6a-b, biography of Kuo Yen the commander of the expedition. *CWTS* 16, 1b, biography of Ko Ts'ung-chou and *CWTS* 19, 11a, of Li Ch'ung-yin give a few details about the bandit gang under Huang Hua-tzŭ. Also *TCTC* 257, Kuang-ch'i 3(887)/4th month.

The expedition was supposed to have gone in summer and returned in winter. *TCTC* says vaguely that it began in 4th/887. I am inclined to put it in 886, a short while after 5th/886, when the same commander, Kuo Yen, made an unsuccessful attack on the Ts'ai capital. It is possible then for the expedition to have returned in winter shortly after another had been sent east early in 887. Chu Wên was therefore still in no position to counter-attack the rebels because some of his best men were away. In fact, *CWTS* 16, 1b, claims that Ko Ts'ung-chou went with both expeditions.

[25] *CWTS* 19, 5a-b, biography of Chu Chên, the chief commander. More details are given in *CWTS* 16, 1b, biography of Ko Ts'ung-chou; *CWTS* 20, 2b-3a, biography of Liu Han, the supervisor of the expedition; *CWTS* 21, 2a, biography of Huo Ts'un and *CWTS* 21, 7a, biography of Li T'ang-pin. Also in *CWTS* 1, 6a-b (from *TFYK* 187, with a short text also quoted in Hu San-shêng's commentary to *TCTC* 256, Kuang-ch'i 3(887)/2nd month), and *TCTC* *op. cit.* and 257, Kuang-ch'i 3(887)/4/*hsin-hai*.

to pass through Yen province where the governor tried to stop them. It also met with resistance from a neighbouring prefectural army and then from the Ch'ing provincial army. After three successive victories against these armies, the recruiting force reached deep into Ch'ing province and captured a county town. It had obtained men, horses and equipment after each of the three victories and now augmented these by enlisting men in the captured county. It is claimed that the army returned after being away for only two months with ten thousand recruits and one thousand horses.

This recruiting in other provinces gives some information about the strength of Chu Wên's army. While Chu Wên was not strong enough to defeat the rebels who besieged him in Pien Chou, he felt strong enough to send out two large recruiting parties. The plan was a shrewd one. By sending these men to live off the country away from his besieged capital, he not only stopped the drain on his granaries but also increased the size of his armies. This strategy and enterprise was well rewarded and he had in 4th/887 possibly as many as thirty thousand men to counter-attack his besiegers.[26]

In the 4th-5th/887, Chu Wên fought to break the siege. He called in the provincial army of Hua and received help from his 'brother' governors of Yün and Yen.[27] The rebels were finally

The figures are from *TCTC* 257, *op. cit.* No figures are given elsewhere except in *CWTS* 20, 2b-3a, where an even greater number of recruits, thirty thousand, is recorded. The *TCTC* figures seem far more probable.

[26] This is a very rough figure based first of all on *CWTS* 21, 6a, which says Chu Wên had only 'several tens of *lü* (旅)'. In the context, this was more likely to have been exaggeratedly small. If *lü* still meant roughly five hundred men, this would put the total figure as not less than ten thousand. From Chu Wên's ability to send a few thousand men each to the east and to the west at about the same time, I think the figure was probably nearer twenty thousand than ten. Then, even if the figure in *TCTC* 257, Kuang-ch'i 3(887)/4/*hsin-hai* of ten thousand new recruits from the east may be exaggerated, the additional recruits from the west might swell the total number of new men to ten thousand. The grand total would then be about thirty thousand.

[27] They were both 'brother' governors probably from the beginning of 887 when the governor of Yün's (Chu Hsüan) cousin, Chu Chin, captured Yen Chou from the court-chosen governor Ch'i K'o-jang by a trick. *TCTC* 256, Kuang-ch'i 2(886)/end of year, says that this was some time in 886, but *CWTS* 19, 5a-b and 16, 1b, both say that early in 887, Chu Wên's expedition to the east had to fight the army of the governor Ch'i K'o-jang.

TABLE VI[28]

A. *The conquest of Ho-nan*, 887-897

4th/888	Captured Mêng province and Lo-yang.
12th/888	Ts'ai rebels surrendered.
888-893	Attacks on Hsü$_2$ Chou; captured it in 4th/893.
895-897	Sieges from 895 led to fall of Yün Chou (1st/897) and Yen Chou (2nd/897).

B. *Expansion to the north and west*, 898-903

898-900	(Ho-pei)	Captured Hsing province; governors of Chên and Ting submitted.
898-899	(Ho-nan)	Captured Ts'ai Chou; Shan governor surrendered.
901	(Ho-tung)	Captured P'u province; Lu governor surrendered.
901-903	(Kuan-chung)	Captured Hua province and Ch'ang-an.
903	(Ho-nan)	Ch'ing governor surrendered.

C. *Failure against Huai-nan and elsewhere*, 887-905

887-890	Failed to take over Yang province.	
892-895	Lost four Huai-nan prefectures.	
11th/897	Grand attack badly defeated.	
903-905	Beat off attack from Yang, 4th/903; attack on Huai-nan failed in 1st/905.	
900	(Ho-pei)	Siege of Ts'ang Chou abandoned.
901-902	(Ho-tung)	Two sieges of Ping Chou beaten off by the Sha-t'o Turks.
901-903	(Kuan-chung)	Siege of Ch'i Chou abandoned.

D. *Chu Wên's relations with the imperial court*, 903-907

903	All eunuchs killed; Chu Wên's army filled palace.
904	Moved emperor to Lo-yang, 1st/904; murdered emperor, 8th/904.
905-906	Chu Wên made imperial Generalissimo; declined the throne several times, 905-906.
4th/907	Deposed boy emperor and founded Liang.

[28] The chronology for the events tabulated is based on *TCTC* 257-265. The brief notes after the dates are also largely based on the *TCTC* after comparisons with the *CWTS* 1-2 and *CTS* 20 A-B. The more important events which are mentioned later in the chapter are given detailed references when they occur.

driven off, and Chu Wên was ready to take the initiative to gain the leadership of the Ho-nan region.

The path to Chu Wên's final leadership was a difficult one. Although there were dissensions and jealousy among the other governors, the opposition to him was still extremely strong and it took him ten years to win the leadership he coveted. And it was to take another ten years before he could found the Liang dynasty. During that time, he had to dominate Ho-pei, capture the metropolitan area, reach one short stretch of the Yangtse and contain the Sha-t'o armies of Ho-tung. These stages of his progress from 887 to 907 are briefly tabulated in Table VI. They form the historical background to this study of his growing power.

The striking feature of Chu Wên's power was the way in which he built it up piecemeal and the time he took to do it. There were no dramatic successes, nothing comparable to An Lu-shan or Huang Ch'ao. The T'ang government had done enough to curb powerful governors by breaking up the provinces and Chu Wên had no popular support. He had to work within the framework of the *chieh-tu shih* system. This system had weakened the existing central government so that he and other governors could develop their own power. But it also put limitations on their ability to expand that power. As governor of a province in the heart of the empire, Chu Wên had no safe borders. He had to fight in every direction and yet could not be openly ambitious without the danger of his neighbours banding against him. He had first to build an army to 'conquer' the neighbouring provinces, then organize their defence under *chieh-tu shih* recommended by him without discarding his cloak of respectability as a court-chosen defender of the empire. It was a slow task which needed many adjustments in the provincial structure.

The growth in numbers of Chu Wên's army was matched by the growth, after 887, in the number of fronts he had to fight at the same time. It was not possible for him to lead all the battles. He had to send expeditionary armies under his leading officers and especially under Chu Chên, the chief commander. In the following years, he delegated so much responsibility to Chu Chên that he became powerful enough to challenge Chu Wên's authority.

Chu Wên had sent a guards official to supervise Chu Chên on the model of the imperial eunuch Supervisor, and later used him as an *ad hoc* supervisor. This was of no avail. Chu Chên found an excuse to kill the second-in-command and this threatened to spark off a major mutiny against Chu Wên. Although Chu Wên acted in time and had the chief commander executed, the danger was acute.[29]

A new chief commander was appointed after Chu Chên's execution, but this man was not given the same powers. Chu Wên was now more cautious and reorganized the army further. He had created several special regiments under selected officers and some of them now accompanied the chief commander to battle and shared the field commands. Chu Wên also made other officers commanders of expeditionary armies. In this way, no one commander could threaten his authority so dangerously again.[30]

Over the years, the Pien provincial army had been carefully transformed into Chu Wên's personal army. The details of the organization are not clear, but there is information about a few of the units which formed the core of this army. There was the *Yüan-ts'ung* cavalry consisting of his earliest followers. There were the *Hou-yüan* and the *T'ing-tzŭ* regiments, both concerned with the governor's office and residence and hence the defence of the governor's person. If they were not a part of the guards, they were probably part of the permanent army Chu Wên personally led, the *ch'in-chün* or the *ch'in-ts'ung* which later seems to have been known as the

[29] The earlier supervisor was Liu Han; *CWTS* 20, 2b-3a. The second-in-command was Li T'ang-pin; *CWTS* 19, 5b-6a. For the events leading to the final quarrel, see *CWTS* 19, 5b and 6a-b; *TCTC* 257, Kuang-ch'i 3 (887)/11th month and 258, Lung-chi 1(889)/6th-7th month; also *TFYK* 449, 13b.

[30] Apart from Kuo Yen who had been given commands before this (see note 25 above), there were expeditionary commanders like Huo Ts'un, Ting Hui and Chu Wên's eldest son Chu Yu-yü (*CWTS* 21, 2a-3b; 59, 1a-2a; and 12, 4b-5b). Later, other prominent commanders were Ko Ts'ung-chou, Chang Ts'un-ching and Chu Wên's adopted son Chu Yu-jang (*CWTS* 16, 1a-5a; 20, 7a-8a; and 19, 2b-3a).

There were also the two officers of Huang Ch'ao who had surrendered and been given unit commands, Li Tang and Li Ch'ung-yin. They were sent as expeditionary commanders in 890, but for having been defeated, they were both executed (*CWTS* 19, 10a-b and 10b-11a).

Ch'ang-chih Army.[31] There were also special regiments for reconnaisance, for defence against attacks from the rear and for border defence.[32]

The discipline of the army was rigorous. Chu Wên had the men tattooed so that deserters could not easily evade re-capture. In battle, the men in each section were held responsible for the safety of their officer. If he was killed, all the men were executed. This was not entirely effective and numerous bandit gangs were formed of deserters and men of defeated regiments who dared not return. But the methods must have been successful enough, for tattooing and mass punishments were continued throughout

[31] *yüan-ts'ung*, 元從; *CWTS* 22, 8b, biography of Hu Chên; 21, 8b-9a, biography of Liu K'ang-ngai; 19, 10a-b, biography of Li Tang; and 59, 7b-10a, biography of Yüan Hsiang-hsien.

hou-yüan, 後院; *CWTS* 19, 1a-2b, biography of Shih Shu-tsung.

t'ing-tzu, 廳子; *CWTS* 16, 8b-10b, biography of Chang Kuei-hou; 19, 8a-b, biography of Têng Chi-yün; 64, 2b-5a, biography of Wang Yen-ch'iu.

ch'in-chün or *ch'in-ts'ung*, 親軍, 親從; *CWTS* 21, 4b-6a, biography of Hsü Huai-yü.

ch'ang-chih 長直 was the first of the four armies turned into the Imperial Guards in 907; see *WTHY* 12, p. 156. Also see *CWTS* 20, 2b-4a, biography of Liu Han, and 20, 8a-9b, biography of K'ou Yen-ch'ing.

Another important unit was the Long Swords (*ch'ang-chien* 長劍) regiment created soon after Chu Wên went to Pien Chou. But I have not been able to place it in the central army or *chung-chün* (中軍); *CWTS* 19, 2b-3a, biography of Chu Yu-kung; 19, 3a-4b, biography of Wang Ch'ung-shih; 21, 4b-6a, biography of Hsü Huai-yü.

[32] Special reconnaissance or vanguard troops were the *t'a-pai* (踏白) and *k'ai-tao* (開道) regiments; *CWTS* 22, 8a-10b, biography of Wang T'an and 19, 6b-7b, biography of Li Ssŭ-an for *t'a-pai*; *CWTS* 90, 8a-9b, biography of Hua Wên-ch'i for *k'ai-tao*.

Ngo-hou, 遏後, I have interpreted as a special regiment for defence against attacks from the rear; *CWTS* 22, 4b-8a. And an important regiment for border defence was the *ching-pien* 靜邊; *CWTS* 59, 7b-10a.

Chu Wên's career and were not abandoned until after he had become emperor.[33]

Chu Wên used his immediate kin both in the army and in the administration. In addition to his eldest son, he gave commands in his army to several nephews and to his sister's son who was appointed a cavalry officer in the guards. Chu Wên was not given to the mass adoption of sons which was a widespread practice in the imperial armies,[34] but he did have several important adopted sons. One of them, Chu Yu-wên, whom he had adopted as a boy, became an able administrator of his finances. He was treated like Chu Wên's own sons and was even thought fit to inherit the Liang

[33] *Wu-tai Shih-pu* 1, 1a (quoted in *CWTS* 7, 7a and *HWTS* 2, 10a), describes Chu Wên's policy of 'executing whole sections' (*pa-tuei chan* 拔隊斬) of the army for returning without their section officers and the need to tattoo men to discourage desertion. *TFYK* 195, 13a-b, records Chu Wên's decision to abandon the tattooing system at the beginning of his reign, largely in order to induce tattooed deserters to give up banditry and return to their homes. Also in *HWTS* 2, 9a; and in *TCTC* 266, K'ai-p'ing 1 (907)/11/*jên-yin*

[34] Prominent examples were the 'sons' of the eunuch commander of the imperial armies, Yang Fu-kung; *TCTC* 258, Lung-chi 1(889)/11th month and Ta-shun 2(891)/9/*i-mao*. This came from an older practice developed by the eunuchs of adopting eunuch boys. Its extension to the army commanders might have been influenced by the practice of bestowing the imperial surname (*tz'ŭ-hsin* 賜姓) as a reward for military success. Later on, the emperor himself was also to use the method for gaining loyal adherents, for example, the adopted son of Yang Fu-kung, Yang Shou-li, was given the Li surname some time after 888 in order to win him away from his eunuch 'father'; *TCTC* 258, Lung-chi 1(889)/11th month.

It is interesting to note that two of Chu Wên's greatest enemies, Li K'o-yung (the Turk 'barbarian') and Li Mao-chên (originally named Sung Wên-t'ung) were both bestowed with the imperial surname and that both of them adopted all their best commanders as sons. Another man who adopted all his officers, Wang Chien, the founder of the state of Shu in Szechuan, was, like Li Mao-chên, also from the imperial army.

A number of studies by Japanese scholars on 'Stepsons' (*chia-tzŭ* 假子 as distinguished from *yang-tzŭ* 養子) in the T'ang and the Wu-tai have recently appeared. K. Shino's two articles in *Hiroshima Bunrika Taigaku Shigaku Kenkyu Kinen Ronso* and in *Shi Nihon Shigaku*, no. 6, however, have not been available to me. The authoritative survey of the status of adopted sons is still that by N. Niida; in his *Tō Sō Hōritsu Bunsho no Kenkyu*, pp. 512-542 and his *Shina Mibunhō shi*, pp. 772-802.

throne.[35] Others were adopted when they were adults, the most important being a merchant of Pien Chou who had contributed sums of money and also brought a large number of retainers with him to join Chu Wên. He was made a commander of one of the best infantry regiments and later became one of Chu Wên's regular field commanders.[36]

[35] Biography of Chu Yu-wên has not been preserved in *CWTS*, see *HWTS* 13, 13b-14b and *TCTC* 268, Ch'ien-hua 2(912)/6/*ting-ch'ou*.

Chu Wên's eldest son, Chu Yu-yü; *CWTS* 12, 4b-5b. The two most prominent of his nephews were Chu Yu-ning (biography in *CWTS* 12, 2a-3b) and Chu Yu-lun (biography in *CWTS* 12, 3b-4b). Two other sons of his who became emperors after him, Chu Yu-kuei (912-913) the son of a camp follower, and Chu Yu-chên (913-923), were still too young to be of any help to him. Three other nephews, the sons of his eldest brother, might have been old enough, but Chu Wên was not impressed by them, and after Chu Yu-yü, Chu Yu-ning and Chu Yu-lun had died, all three in 903-904, he complained about the other sons and nephews being 'merely pigs and dogs'; *TCTC* 266, K'ai-p'ing 2(908)/5/*hsin-wei*. He was probably fonder of his sister's son Yüan Hsiang-hsien; biography in *CWTS* 59, 7b-10a.

[36] There is considerable confusion about this man arising from the different names he seems to have had. His biography in *CWTS* 19, 2b-3a, calls him Chu Yu-kung, alias Li Yen-wei, who, when adopted by Chu Wên, was first named Chu (Yu-)jang. But elsewhere in *CWTS* 62, 5a and 133, 1a (the biographies of two of the man's retainers), Chu Yu-jang was the adopted name of Li Jang, alias Li Ch'i-lang. The two seem to have been the same person, as pointed out in *TCTC* 259, Ching-fu 2(893)/2nd month and *K'ao-i*; and apparently supported by the *TFYK* 187 references to a Chu K'o-jang (error for Yu-jang?) between 888 and 892 (quoted in *CWTS* 1, 11a and 13b) and a Chu Yu-kung after 895 (quoted in *CWTS* 1, 14a-b and 15b-16a). *HWTS* on the other hand, considers the names to refer to two men; see 43, 2b and 8b-9a; 51, 3a; and 69, 1a.

Because of the difficulties of identifying him, his origins and early career have been obscured. His biography in *CWTS* 19, 2b-3a, says that he had served Chu Wên since he was a boy (*kuan-chüeh* 丱角), while in his retainers' biographies (also in *CWTS*, see above), he is said to have been a merchant (*ku-jên* 賈人), or an adventurer (*hao-shih* 豪士). We know nothing of the circumstances in which the three biographies were compiled. Chu Yu-kung himself was executed for murdering emperor Chao-tsung in 904 and of the two retainers, one died a rebel in 932 and the other defied imperial control until his death in 928. (A third retainer, K'ung Hsün, and the only one who died in imperial favour, has no biography preserved in *CWTS*). The circumstances of the three men's death must have influenced their official biographies. The difficulties have caused the editors of *HTS* in the biography of Chu Yu-kung (223 B, 7b) to call him a man of wealth at Pien Chou while the editors of *TCTC* say he had been Chu Wên's retainer since he was a boy.

There was also a team of personal officials (*ch'in-li*) of obscure origins whom Chu Wên employed in various capacities. An example of one of them was Chang T'ing-fan, an actor who had served as a guards officer in charge of reception before he was raised by Chu Wên to be an envoy dealing with difficult negotiations. He was later also appointed one of Chu Wên's governors. Another man, Chiang Hsüan-hui, was used as an army supervisor but was also sent as Chu Wên's special representative wherever there was trouble. He was later made a palace official to Emperor Chao-tsung and asked to arrange the emperor's murder. A third man, Ch'êng Yen, was an official for submitting memorials (*chin-chou kuan*), that is, an official of the governor's residence at the capital (*ti-li*). He was Chu Wên's eyes and ears at Ch'ang-an and his part in the attempt in 11th/900 to depose the emperor shows the extent of his influence at the court.[37]

There is little information about Chu Wên's civil administration. The records about a few men in his service show him to have been like the other governors in his willingness to use bureaucrats of more or less distinguished origins. His chief administrator (*chieh-tu p'an-kuan*) was a protégé of a high bureaucrat who had been ex-commander of the imperial armies against Huang Ch'ao. This administrator had been a financial expert and a commissioner of supplies and proved an invaluable help to Chu Wên. He was

(*TCTC*, *op. cit.*, the later editors, possibly Ssŭ-ma Kuang himself, disagreed with one of the co-editors, Liu Shu, who in his *Shih-kuo Chi-nien* said that Chu Yu-kung was a merchant). I have followed the *HTS* and the *Shih-kuo Chi-nien* (quoted in *TCTC op. cit.*, *K'ao-i*) for the details about a man who came into Chu Wên's service by way of adoption—his name was probably Chu Yu-kung.

[37] Chang T'ing-fan, *HTS* 223 B, 7a; also *TCTC* 259, Ching-fu 2(893)/4/*chi-ch'ou* and Ch'ien-ning 1(894)/6/*chia-wu*.

Chiang Hsüan-hui probably started as Chu Wên's retainer; *HTS* 223B, 6a-b. *CWTS* 16, 4a-b, says he was an army supervisor in the Ts'ang Chou campaign in 900. Other references to his special duties are in *TCTC* 260, Ch'ien-ning 2(895)/end of year; 262, Kuang-hua 3(900)/12/*wu-ch'ên*. For his role in Chao-tsung's murder, *TCTC* 265, T'ien-yu 1(904)/8/*jên-yin*. The third, Ch'êng Yen, is called a *ti-li* (邸吏) in *CWTS* 2, 4b and 18, 9b, and a *chin-chou kuan* (進奏官) in *TCTC* 262, Kuang-hua 3 (900)/11/*kêng-yin*. The two terms seem to have been interchangeable.

so trusted that the administration of Pien Chou was left entirely in his hands. Another trusted man was the assistant governor who was probably from an aristocratic family. He had been General of the Imperial Guards before he became an administrator to Chu Wên. As assistant governor, he was an important liason between Chu Wên and the court.[38]

Another administrator was a nephew of the powerful governor of the lower Yangtse region and the son of an imperial inspector who had also been a protégé of one of the highest court officials. He first served as an acting prefect and then became Chu Wên's administrator after 896. Also descended from a military governor was another of Chu Wên's assistant governors. This man's father and grandfather had both been prefects. After he had failed the imperial examinations, he was given the rank of General of the Metropolitan Guards and sent out to be a prefect. Unfortunately, his prefecture was already lost to rebels and he had to return. On his way back, he passed Pien Chou and was invited by Chu Wên to serve him. In 898, he was sent as assistant governor to Yün, one of Chu Wên's provinces.[39]

Chu Wên's personal secretary was from a minor bureaucrat family and had also failed the imperial examinations. He attached himself to one of Chu Wên's officials, a man from the same village, but was not given any employment. He then began to write memorials of admonition for others and his style attracted attention in the army and then the notice of Chu Wên himself. Having held no previous office, he was only made 'the sub-inspector of post

[38] No biographies of P'ei Ti and Wei Chên have been preserved in the *CWTS*. P'ei Ti is mentioned in *CWTS* 4, 2b-3a; two other fragments about him are also preserved in *TFYK* 211, 14b-15a; 716, 43a-b; and 721, 16b-17a; and the biography in *HWTS* 43, 7a-8a, follows these closely. Wei Chên is mentioned in *CWTS* 63, 3a and in *CTS* 20A, 18a. The only information about his early career is in *TFYK* 729, 12a. The biography in *HWTS* 43, 3a-b, gives little new information and omits the note on his early career in *TFYK*.

[39] Kao Shao's biography is in *CWTS* 20, 5a-b; his representations on Chu Wên's behalf are also recorded in *CWTS* 58, 11b. (Chou Lien-k'uan, 'T'ang Kao P'ien Chên-Huai Shih-chi k'ao', *Lingnan Journal*, pp. 41-43, argues from a memorial in Ts'ui Chih-yüan's *Kuei-yüan Pi-kêng Chi*, 4, 5a-b, that Kao Shao was probably not the nephew who worked for Chu Wên.)

Li Chên's biography is in *CWTS* 18, 9b-12a.

stations in order that he may specially take charge of despatches and memorials'. But a few years later, he was made secretary, and thereafter became Chu Wên's closest adviser on civil and military affairs.[40]

Not much is known about the financial support for Chu Wên's long campaigns. An important factor were the raids and extortions of an army living off the countryside and the little towns. The resources of Pien province were probably supplemented by supplies from neighbouring provinces for the war against the Ts'ai rebels and from his auxiliary provinces like Hua, after 886, and Mêng, after 888. In the beginning, grain and arms were not always adequate, and Chu Wên had to buy some of these from a neighbouring province.[41] More dependable were the governors who had accepted his leadership in Ho-nan. The self-appointed governor of the Eastern Capital was one, and the three brothers who succeeded each other as governors of $Hsü_3$ province (South of Pien) made regular contributions.[42] There were also the resources of men and supplies of each captured prefecture and province (see Table VI, A and B), increasingly important as Chu Wên's territory expanded. However, this was still inadequate and irregular methods of getting financial support from the merchants and landowners were probably used. Two interesting examples of these methods at Pien Chou are recorded. The first was the adop-

[40] Ching Hsiang's biography is in *CWTS* 18, 5b-9a. *TCTC* 257, Kuang-ch'i 3(887)/11th month describes Chu Wên's trust in him. In the *K'ao-i* for that date, the *CWTS* account of his influence on Chu Wên was criticized, and an account in a biography of Ching Hsiang in the *Chuang-tsung Lieh-chuan* was preferred.

[41] In 888, Chu Wên sent a military administrator (*ya-ya* 押牙) with 10,000 taels of silver to buy grain from the Wei governor. This man was killed in a mutiny against the governor and presumably the money was confiscated or the purchased grain withheld by the mutineers. The incident led Chu Wên to send an army to Wei to extract compensation. *TCTC* 257, Wên-tê 1(888)/2nd month; 3rd month and 4/*kuei-ssŭ*.

[42] The governor of Lo-yang, Chang Ch'üan-i, biography in *CWTS* 63, 1a-7a; the three brothers, Chao Ch'iu, Chao Ch'ang and Chao Hsü, biographies in *CWTS* 14, 5b-11b and *HWTS* 42, 7a-b. In both cases, other ties were involved. Firstly, they were all grateful to Chu Wên for saving them from rebel attacks. Chang Ch'üan-i was also a Huang Ch'ao follower, probably an acquaintance of Chu Wên's and certainly of some of his generals. The Chao brothers were related by marriage to Chu Wên since 885.

tion of the merchant already mentioned above (p. 68). The other was the formation of a special cavalry regiment (*t'ing-tzŭ tu*) consisting of the sons of wealthy families who had military talent and who could probably always be relied upon to provide their own arms, armour, horses and retainers and, if necessary, their own food supplies. In this way, Chu Wên was provided with a regiment at very little cost, if not also with a means of inducing the wealthy fathers to give him their fullest support.[43]

Another feature of Chu Wên's finances was his interest in the salt and transport commission. It was one of the few institutions still controlled by the bureaucrats at court. The commission seems to have regained financial importance because Chu Wên asked to be given control of it in 11th/889. As the commissioner, he hoped to use its resources to back his many campaigns. The request was refused. In 12th/893, possibly because he feared that the commission might fall into the hands of another governor, Chu Wên asked for the post again 'in order to facilitate supplies to the army'. Again he was refused.[44] The two incidents suggest that he was still looking for a more stable source of revenue and that he expected the court to help him in his campaigns which were still conducted in the name of the empire.

After 904 however, he had the resources not only of his own

[43] *CWTS* 64, 3a, in the biography of Wang Yen-ch'iu. Elsewhere the *t'ing-tzŭ tu* is called the personal troops, or the 'most trusted troops' (*tsui-ch'in-chün* 最親軍); in *CWTS* 16, 9b, biography of Chang Kuei-hou and *CWTS* 19, 8a, biography of Têng Chi-yün. From the three references, the regiment was probably formed about 893, when Têng Chi-yün escaped back from the Sha-t'o Turks and when Wang Yen-ch'iu was twenty years old.

[44] *TCTC* 258, Lung-chi 1(889)/end of 11/*chi-yu* and 259, Ching-fu 2(893)/12th month. How effective the commission was it is not possible to tell. It had little to do with the areas east of T'ung-kuan till after the Ts'ai rebels were driven south in 888 and probably never regained control over the salt lakes of the P'u province over which the troubles of 885-886 had begun. What tenuous hold it still had over the salt mines of Szechuan and north-west of the Great Wall near the far bend of the Huang Ho probably lapsed after 890. Chu Wên's interest in the post was partly strategic. He could have used his powers as commissioner as an excuse to interfere with the neighbouring provinces.

Also see *Pei-mêng So-yen*, 14, 5a, for the Chief Minister K'ung Wei's views on Chu Wên's request.

provinces but also of those of the empire. Whatever tribute was still sent to the emperor at Lo-yang was available to him. But his expenses had also increased and he still depended on *ad hoc* provincial supplies. An example of this is the help he received from the independent Wei province in the Ho-pei region. Lo Shao-Wei, the governor of this wealthy province of six prefectures and forty-six counties, was grateful to Chu Wên for having saved the province from the Sha-t'o Turks in 896 and from his northern enemies in 899. He sent armies to support Chu Wên in his major campaigns in Ho-pei in 900 and in eastern Ho-nan in 903. The expenses for the armies he sent were probably paid by the province.[45] Early in 906, he called in Chu Wên to deal with the notorious Wei castle garrison which he could no longer control. For this help he supplied all the needs of Chu Wên's armies for a year while they crushed the rebels in his provincial army. Later he

> urgently transported grain from Yeh (Wei Chou) to Ch'ang-lu (near present Ts'ang-hsien in Ho-pei) for 500 *li* in double tracks (of supply lines) without a break on the way.[46]

And at his provincial capital, Wei Chou, where Chu Wên had his headquarters, the governor

> slaughtered almost 700,000 cattle, goats and pigs and provided corresponding amounts of property and grain; he also paid bribes to the value of 1,000,000 (cash?).[47]

Chu Wên and his armies on campaign lived on this for a year. It is interesting to note that Lo Shao-wei continued this help. He saw that the province of Ch'ing (in eastern Shantung)

> had been free from war for many years and its store of grain was mountain-high while at the capital the soldiers and people were numerous and the food was increasingly short.

[45] *TCTC* 260, Ch'ien-ning 3(896)/intercalary 1st month and 6th month; 261, Kuang-hua 2(899)/3/*kuei-mao* to *jên-wu*; 262, Kuang-hua 3(900)/5/*kêng-yin*, ff.; 264, T'ien-fu 3(903)/3/*wu-ch'ên*, ff.

[46] *CWTS* 14, 3b.

[47] *TCTC* 265, T'ien-yu 3(906)/7th month. Cf. *CWTS* 14, 3b, where Chu Wên is said to have set up the offices of the Generalissimo (*yüan-shuai fu* 元帥府) in Wei Chou and the Wei governor supplied every one of his 'several hundred thousand men' with meat and drink and all the necessary equipment for their camps.

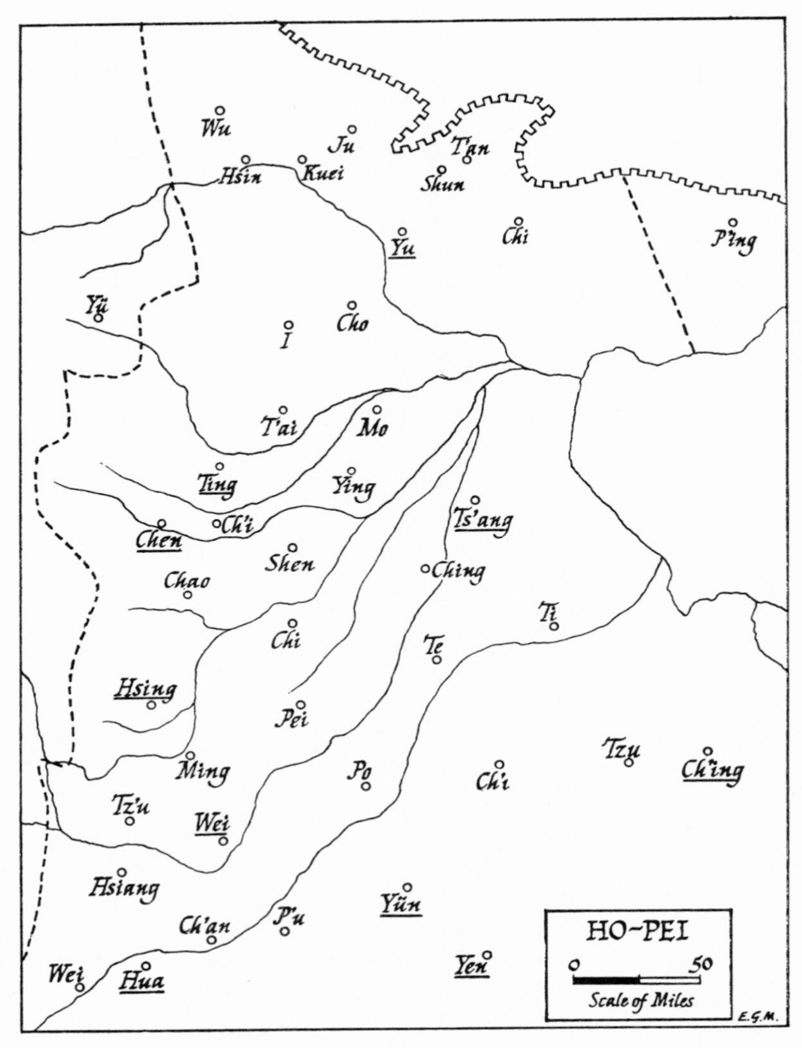

Map V

He offered to build 300 ships to transport grain up the Huang Ho to the mouth of the Lo (near Lo-yang); the annual supply to be expected was 1,000,000 piculs. It is no wonder then that

Chu Wên was genuinely sorry when Lo Shao-wei died in 909.[48]

Chu Wên had a personally chosen staff of military men and administrators to deal with the immediate problems of disciplining and expanding the armies. But as the number of provinces he controlled increased, there was the new problem of stabilizing the relationship between Chu Wên and those of his men he had recommended as governors or as prefects outside his province. Chu Wên's control of the provinces he had captured depended greatly on the loyalty of these men and on the measures he could introduce to check their power.

The problem of controlling more than one province had to be faced by Chu Wên in his third year as governor of Pien. He sent Hu Chên, his guards officer who had been a county administrator, to govern Hua province for him. The next year, in 887, the vacant governorship of Yang (Lower Yangtse) was given by the T'ang court to Chu Wên to be held in conjunction with that of Pien. He promptly sent his military deputy as deputy governor (*liu-hou*) at the head of an army. This was resisted both by the local garrison and by the governor of the intermediate province which lay between Pien and Yang, and Chu Wên had to accept a compromise by which he kept the title of governor but recommended the garrison officer in control to be his deputy.[49]

Although he failed to take over in Yang province, Chu Wên took advantage of the precedent of dual governorship. Three years later, he gave up his claim to Yang province in exchange for that of Hua. There is an interesting feature in this change. The governor, Hu Chên, had to be removed. Having been a governor, he could not return to Chu Wên's service, nor did Chu Wên wish to keep him in charge as acting governor. He was also not strong enough to resist Chu Wên. Finally, the court appointed him Grand General of the Metropolitan Guards and he had no more to do with Chu Wên. This move was Chu Wên's first success in controlling a

[48] *CWTS* 14, 4a-b. On Chu Wên's feelings for Lo Shao-wei, see *CWTS* 5, 7a-b and *TCTC* 267, K'ai-p'ing 3(909)/11/*wu-hsü* ff. and a long note in the *K'ao-i*.

[49] *CWTS* 1, 8b-9a (from *TFYK* 187); *TCTC* 257, Kuang-ch'i 3(887)/11/after *chi-hai* and after *wu-wu*; and Wên-tê (888)/1/*chia-tzŭ*.

subordinate governor. Chu Wên remained at Pien Chou and appointed Hsieh T'ung, an unsuccessful *chin-shih* candidate and an ex-secretary of his, to deputize for him as assistant governor of Hua. Hsieh T'ung had also been a prefect in Szechuan and a successful administrator. The appointment was justified, and in the next thirteen years, there was

in the province an increase in population of about fifty thousand households and in the army of several thousand men.[50]

This appointment was so successful that Chu Wên did the same when he forced the court to appoint him governor of a third province, that of Yün, in 898. He appointed two of the ablest bureaucrats in his service, one who had been his field command administrator to be the deputy governor and the other, who had been a court-chosen prefect and then his Pien prefectural assistant, to be the assistant governor.[51] When he was given his fourth province, that of P'u, however, Chu Wên took over himself. This was in 901 and when he campaigned in the west for the next three years, he used P'u Chou as his base. He appointed a cousin of the previous governor to be the chief administrator and transferred one of the Pien discipline officers (*tu yü-hou*) to take charge of the salt administration. Later on, when he returned to Pien Chou, he appointed an ex-defence commissioner who had been commanding his armies in Kuan-chung to be the chief commander of five prefectural armies based at P'u Chou.[52]

The other prefectures and provinces which came under him were more difficult to control. From 887 to 893, Chu Wên could barely keep the prefectures he captured. First, the garrison in

[50] Hu Chên, *CWTS* 16, 6b; Hsieh T'ung, *CWTS* 20, 1a-2a. The two men had both been Chu Wên's earliest assistants when he was still a supporter of Huang Ch'ao.

[51] The two men were Wei Chên and Li Chên, see notes 38 and 39 above.

[52] The chief administrator was Wang Tsan; *CWTS* 2, 5b and *TFYK* 211, 14b. His biography in *CWTS* 59, 5b-7a, says he was made a *pin-chu* (賓助) an 'honoured assistant' (?), which may have been an elegant description of an administrator.

The salt administration was left to Hu Kuei, an officer who had surrendered from the Yen provincial army in 897. He remained a chief discipline officer, now of P'u. Biography in *CWTS* 19, 9b-10a.

one of the prefectures in his own province turned against him and it took him two months to recapture the garrison town. Then, two prefectures which he had captured from Yün province had to be abandoned.[53] He then captured Su Chou in 888, but in 890, the garrison mutinied and went over to a rival governor. Chu Wên captured it again in 891 only after a year and a half of siege. This time, he made the first break from the previous practice of appointing a bureaucrat as prefect. Instead, he appointed one of his most senior officers as prefect and left him with large units of the army to defend it.[54] A policy of military administration of the prefectures was now adopted, and when another prefecture was captured later in 891, Chu Wên appointed another of his top commanders as acting prefect.[55] From then until the foundation of his dynasty, he used army officers as prefects in most prefectures and, as might be expected, always in the border prefectures. In this way, the prefectures had strong garrisons under soldier-administrators who built or repaired the walls of the towns and filled the granaries for defence against attack. The towns could thus hold out till the main army was sent to help them.[56]

The significant development here is Chu Wên's ability to employ earlier T'ang administrative practice for his own purpose. With Pien Chou as the new focus of power, he built up direct control

The chief commander of five prefectural armies was Hsü Huai-yü, one of Chu Wên's earliest followers (no. 10 in Table IV, see note 8 above). The five armies he commanded were P'u, Chin and Chiang (in P'u province), T'ung and Hua (nominally in Hua province).

[53] For Po Chou; *TCTC* 257, Kuang-ch'i 3(887)/6/*jên-hsü* and 8/*jên-yin*. For Ts'ao Chou and P'u Chou; *TCTC* 257, Kuang-ch'i 3(887)/10/*ting-wei*.

[54] *TCTC* 257, Wên-tê 1(888)/11th month, for the first capture of Su Chou; 258, Ta-shun 1(890)/4th month, for the mutiny; and Ta-shun, 2(891)/8th and 10/*jên-wu* for the recapture.

The senior officer appointed was Kuo Yen (no. 8 in Table IV), biography in *CWTS* 21, 6a-7a.

[55] *TCTC* 258, Ta-shun 2(891)/11th month, for Ts'ao Chou's surrender. The commander appointed was Huo Ts'un, one of the surrendered Huang Ch'ao officers (no. 5 in Table V); biography in *CWTS* 21, 2a-3b.

[56] Some examples are Wang T'an at Mi Chou not far from the Huai border, *CWTS* 22, 9b; and Têng Chi-yün at Têng Chou on the north Shantung coast, *CWTS* 19, 8b. An example of a prefecture which fell because the garrison was not reinforced in time was the same Mi Chou, the defences which Wang

of all the prefectures and deprived the new governors he appointed of the power to interfere with the prefects.

For the smaller area of Ho-nan, the control was successful. For example, the governor of $Hsü_3$ recommended by Chu Wên could govern his capital, but not the other prefecture whose prefect was at one period Chu Wên's eldest son and at another his adopted son.[57] Also, when $Hsü_2$ Chou was finally captured, the new governor appointed was Chang T'ing-fan who had been Chu Wên's personal official and then a prefect. The only other prefecture in the province was placed under one of Chu Wên's ablest field commanders at that time, Ko Ts'ung-chou. The governor was superior in rank and also closer to Chu Wên. He had a nominal right of inspection and his own prefecture was larger than that of Ko Ts'ung-chou. But though the latter was engaged in battles elsewhere throughout his period of office and therefore absent from his prefecture, it is doubtful if Chang T'ing-fan could take advantage of his absence.[58]

Ko Ts'ung-chou continued to be absent in the battlefield even when he was promoted to be deputy governor of the newly conquered Yen province (from 897). He was in the disastrous campaign against Huai-nan, and then fought in Ho-pei where he was also made acting governor of another province. While he was away, his family remained at Yen Chou and his relatives and retainers were left to supervise, on his behalf, the work of the various administrators and secretaries. The responsibility for defence, however, was in the hands of the garrison commander who was an officer of one of Chu Wên's regiments assigned to the province. The extent to which these deputies could interfere with the three prefects of Hai, I and Mi Chou in the province must have been negligible. The Hai Chou garrison commander had surrendered

T'an strengthened soon after its recapture; biography of Liu K'ang-ngai, the prefect who was killed, in *CWTS* 21, 8b-9a (no. 7 in Table IV).

[57] Chu Yu-yü was prefect after 892, biography in *CWTS* 12, 4b-5b; *TCTC* 261, Kuang-hua 2(899)/2nd month, still calls him prefect of $Hsü_3$ in 899. The adopted son, Chu Yu-kung, is called prefect of $Hsü_3$ in *CWTS* 1, 15b-16a (from *TFYK* 187) and *TCTC* 260, Ch'ien-ning 3(896)/end of 4th month.

[58] Chang T'ing-fan, see note 37 above. Ko Ts'ung-chou (from Huang Ch'ao's army, no. 4 in Table V), biography in *CWTS* 16, 1a-5a.

soon after, in 899, to one of Chu Wên's rivals, and the prefects of both I and Mi were top commanders of Chu Wên's army who led their own garrisons.[59] In fact, the army left at Yen Chou could not even defend the city itself, and in 903, it fell without a blow to the Ch'ing provincial army.[60]

At the end of 897, Chu Wên controlled eight provinces consisting of twenty-two prefectures. Of these, only Lo-yang and the capital of Hsü$_3$ province were not governed by men personally selected by him. In 898-901, he appointed an additional three governors and six prefects. Only in one of his newly captured provinces did he retain the governor, in this case a man who became his adopted son.[61]

After 901, Chu Wên succeeded in taking every province in Kuan-chung except two in the western part of the region. But the policy he followed in Kuan-chung was indecisive. After defeating the governor of Pin in 11th/901, he had merely taken as hostage the governor's wife and left him still in charge. The next year, in 11th-12th/902, his men captured Fu province and the governor surrendered. He first appointed an acting governor and, early in 904, a governor to that province. About this time, the governor of Pin turned against Chu Wên when his wife was returned to him. This seems to have taken Chu Wên completely by surprise. He had left so few of his troops at the neighbouring Fu province that

[59] Surrender of Hai Chou in 7th/899 in *TCTC* 261, Kuang-hua 2(899)/7th month. One prefect of I Chou was Hsü Huai-yü (no. 10 in Table IV, see note 8) and another of Mi Chou was Liu K'ang-ngai (no. 7 in Table IV).

[60] Ko Ts'ung-chou, in *CWTS* 16, 1a-5a; the invading commander of Ch'ing province, Liu Hsün, in *CWTS* 23, 1a-7a. On the fall of Yen Chou in 903, *TCTC* 263, T'ien-fu 3(903)/1/*ping-wu* and *K'ao-i*.

From the biography of Fang Chih-wên, *CWTS* 91, 1a-3a, it is clear that the governor recruited men for himself as retainers, and that some were left behind while he was commanding in the field. Further, when the governor was away, another of Chu Wên's commanders was left in charge of the garrison. This commander seems to have been away too when Yen Chou fell; *CWTS* 91, 1a, where Niu Ts'un-chieh is named as the officer (*pu-chiang* 部將) who garrisoned the town and was later in 903 sent by Chu Wên to save Yen Chou. From Niu Ts'un-chieh's biography (in *CWTS* 22, 6a), he seems to have been stationed at Hua Chou, to the north-west of Yen Chou, about 903.

[61] Chu Yu-ch'ien, governor of Shan, *CWTS* 63, 7a-b.

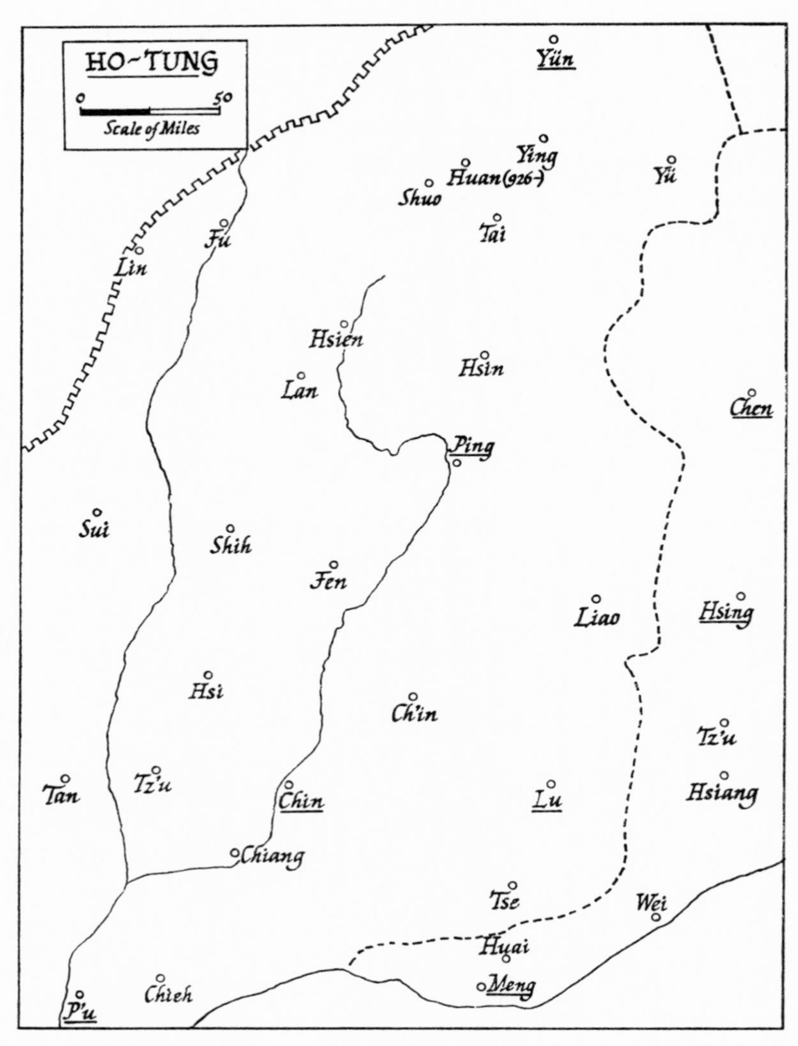

Map VI

in 6th/904 he had to abandon that province altogether. Within six months, he had lost two provinces. It was not until 11th/906 that Fu province was recaptured but again he could not hold it. The error of judgement over the Pin governor proved very costly to

Chu Wên. He was not to have a secure western border until his death.[62]

He was more successful on two other fronts. In 903, he sent an army against Ch'ing province in the east and in 905, another against Hsiang to the south-west. An interesting feature of the former campaign was the agreement in 9th/903 to accept the governor's surrender and to appoint prefects to all the prefectures in the province, leaving the governor as deputy governor at Ch'ing Chou, the capital. Although this was before the Pin governor turned against him, Chu Wên seems to have learnt that hostages were not enough to keep a surrendered governor under control. The compromise was accepted because it would have taken too long to capture the provincial capital.[63]

The other campaign against Hsiang in 905 was far more important. Chu Wên had to deal with a governor who had submitted to him in 898 but who was now against him. Chu Wên's swift victory, however, relieved his fears that other governors might do the same thing. He not only took all the prefectures of this large province, but also captured the neighbouring province farther to the south and reached, for the first time, a short stretch of the Yangtse.[64]

[62] The Pin governor was Yang Ch'ung-pên, *CWTS* 13, 12a-13b; and the Fu governor Li Mao-hsün, *CWTS* 133, 7a-b. The acting governor of Fu, Li Hui, was one of Chu Wên's earliest retainers (*CWTS* 19, 4b); *TCTC* 263, T'ien-fu 2(902)/11/*chia-yin*. The two Fu governors appointed by Chu Wên in 903-904 were Shih Shu-tsung (*CWTS* 19, 1a-2b) and Liu Hsün (*CWTS* 23, 1a-7a).

For the loss of Pin and the abandonment of Fu, *TCTC* 264, T'ien-yu 1(904)/1/after *wu-shên*, and 6th month. For the recapture of Fu, *TCTC* 265, T'ien-yu 3(906)/11th month. But the new governor, K'ang Huai-chên, was recalled to save Lu Chou; biography in *CWTS* 23, 9a-11b; also *TCTC* 266, K'ai-p'ing 1(907)/end of 1st month and 5/*jên-ch'ên*. *T'ang Fang-chên Nien-piao*, 1, p. 7302, says Li Yen-po was appointed Fu governor in 907 by Li Mao-chên of Ch'i.

[63] *CWTS* 2, 11b (from *TFYK* 187); *TCTC* 264, T'ien-fu 3(903)/9/*wu-wu*. Also *CWTS* 13, 6a-9a and *HWTS* 42, 2b-3a, biographies of Wang Shih-fan the Ch'ing governor.

[64] For the Hsiang campaign, *CWTS* 2, 14a-b (from *TFYK* 187); *TCTC* 265, T'ien-yu 2(905)/9/*hsin-yu*, ff.; *HTS* 186, 7a-b and *CWTS* 17, 5b-7a; biography of Chao K'uang-ning the Hsiang governor; and *CWTS* 22, 1a-4b, biography of Yang Shih-hou, the expeditionary commander and new Hsiang governor.

Chu Wên made comparatively little impression on the Ho-pei provinces. This meant that he had failed to solve the most persistent problem of T'ang provincial government since the An Lu-shan rebellion. After taking in 898 the smallest of the six provinces, Hsing, he had to be content with an alliance with two other governors, those of Chên and Ting. As for the strongest governor, that of Yu with his nine prefectures, Chu Wên could not stop him from expanding south. It was only in 906 that he made any progress. This was due to an internal struggle in the southernmost Wei province which led his ally, Lo Shao-wei, to call him in to crush the mutinous provincial army. But he gained nothing else in Ho-pei and it was from this area that his Turkish enemies were ultimately to destroy his small empire in 923.

Chu Wên's greatest failure was against his old rival Li K'o-yung. His men were at the gates of Ping Chou twice, once in 3rd-5th/901 after he had taken most of the southern prefectures in the province, and once in 2nd-3rd/902 when he had taken Ch'ang-an and was virtual master of North China.[65] He failed to drive Li K'o-yung from the strategic Ping Chou and because of this, the dynasty Chu Wên founded was never free from the danger of the tribesmen. In fact, when he lost Lu prefecture (Ho-tung region) to Li K'o-yung, it so distressed him that he was rushed to depose the last T'ang emperor before he had really completed his work of unification.

In 1st/903, Chu Wên was still too unsure of his power to force the emperor to move to Lo-yang. He had to be content to control the court in a way the Kuan-chung governors had previously done—by leaving parts of his army at Ch'ang-an under his nephews to form the Imperial Guards.[66] There was, however, one important

[65] The fortress of Ping Chou was impenetrable till almost eighty years later in 979 when the Sung emperor destroyed the last recalcitrant state in the empire. This strengthening of its defences was completed by Li K'o-yung in 900; *TCTC* 262, Kuang-hua 3(900)/end of 2nd month.

For the sieges of Ping Chou, see *CWTS* 2, 5a-b and 7b; *CWTS* 26, 11a-b and 12a-13a; *TCTC* 262, T'ien-fu 1(901)/3/*kuei-mao*, ff. and 263, T'ien-fu 2(902)/3/*wu-wu*, ff.

[66] The practice of leaving a part of a governor's army to supervise the emperor and the court was introduced in 1st/901 by the governor of Ch'i at

difference. Following the advice of the Chief Minister, Ts'ui Yin, he had all the eunuchs at the court killed and forced the emperor to order all governors to kill their eunuch Army Supervisors. This was Chu Wên's most important act. By this, he ended more than a century of eunuch domination in the court and opened up possibilities for a new kind of political structure.

Chu Wên left the court in the hands of Ts'ui Yin. The latter soon saw how weak he was without a fighting force to back him. Unwilling to be Chu Wên's stooge, he tried to rebuild the imperial army. For this, he was killed.[67] Chu Wên finally ordered the emperor to be moved to Lo-yang. In 1st/904, the emperor left Ch'ang-an for the fourth and last time, and his departure marked the end of Ch'ang-an as a political centre.

The last three years of the T'ang dynasty were really the uncertain beginnings of the Liang. Chu Wên groped for the prefect timing of the official transfer. But his fear of another restoration was great. On Chao-tsung's way to Lo-yang, Chu Wên killed every one of the emperor's men down to the last palace servant and replaced them by his own guardsmen. Chu Wên's most able followers filled the palace, including the nine palace commissions (the *nei chu ssŭ*). By 8th/904, the hostility of several governors drove him to murder the emperor and put a boy of twelve on the throne.[68] But the right moment still evaded him.

Chu Wên's cumulative power had met its first reversals twice in Kuan-chung in 904. His successes in 905-906 were marred by two more failures along the Huai river borders to his south. The inconclusiveness of his campaigns became a strain on his suppor-

the request of the Chief Minister Ts'ui Yin. This was called *su-wei* (宿衞). *TCTC* 262, T'ien-fu 1 (901)/1/after *ping-wu*.

Chu Wên left 10,000 men to take over the barracks of the imperial Shên-ts'ê Armies under his nephew Chu Yu-lun. He also appointed three of his men to be commissioners to police the palace grounds, the 'imperial city' and the Ch'ang-an metropolis. *TCTC* 264, T'ien-fu 3(903)/2/*i-wei*.

[67] *TCTC* 264, T'ien-fu 3(903)/end of year and T'ien-yu 1(904)/1st month and 1/*wu-shên*.

[68] *TCTC* 264, T'ien-yu 1(904)/intercalary 4th/*kuei-mao* and *wu-shên*, with a note by Hu San-shêng on the nine *nei-chu-ssŭ shih* (內諸司使); and 265, T'ien-yu 1(904)/8/*jên-yin*, ff., on the emperor's murder.

ters at the court. He had already killed the two marshals of the imperial army who had been responsible for the emperor's murder although they had been appointed by him. By the end of 905, he had executed not only some of the remaining chief bureaucrats, but also four of the men he had appointed as palace commissioners.[69] The rivalry among his men had grown acute because of his indecision. So had the disillusionment of the governor of Lu province, Ting Hui. In the last months of 906 when Chu Wên was preparing to take all of Ho-pei, the turning point came—not upwards as he had hoped, but downwards with the surrender of Lu province to Li K'o-yung. There could be no greater blow to his prestige, for Ting Hui had been the earliest of his supporters and the first head of his guards at Pien Chou more than twenty-three years ago.[70]

Chu Wên hurried back to Pien Chou when he heard the news. Ill and harassed and past fifty-four years in age, he felt that he could not delay the transfer any more. Inauspiciously, while his armies were being beaten back in Ho-pei and while Li K'o-yung's army was massing only a little more than a hundred and twenty miles north of Lo-yang, Chu Wên ascended the throne on 18/4th/907.[71]

[69] Chu Wên killed the two marshals two months after the emperor's murder in 10th/904; *TCTC* 265, T'ien-yu 1(904)/10/*chia-wu*. The execution of the bureaucrats took place in 6th/905; *TCTC* 265, T'ien-yu 2(905)/6/*wu-tzŭ*; and of the palace commissioners six months later, *op. cit.*, 12/*ting-yu* and *chia-yin*.

[70] *CWTS* 59, 1a-2a (Ting Hui, no. 2 in Table IV); also *CWTS* 26, 14a; and *TCTC* 265, T'ien-yu 3(906)/intercalary 12th month. (The imperfection of our present text of the first seven chüans of *CWTS* is clearly seen here. This incident is not preserved in the *TFYK* chüan 187 which has been used to fill most of the lost first chüan. The re-compilers of the present text have noted the important omission; *CWTS* 1, 17a, commentary).

[71] *TCTC* 266, K'ai-p'ing 1(907)/4/*chi-yu* and *chia-tzŭ*.

CHAPTER FOUR

The Liang Court and the T'ang Restoration 907-926

The T'ang aristocratic society had undergone great changes since the reign of Empress Wu (684-705). By the ninth century, the aristocrats had accepted the newly distinguished literati on their terms and many of the distinctions between the two groups had been removed. The broadened base of official society, however, was still not broad enough to satisfy the increasing number of families which had acquired wealth and education during the century. Men like Huang Ch'ao, Li Shan-fu and Li Chên who had failed the *chin-shih* examinations and resented their exclusion from the refined coteries at the T'ang court, each found his own way to shake the foundations of that society. Huang Ch'ao joined a major rebellion in 875 and later became its leader. Wherever his troops went, he did not spare the scions of the ruling families, and at Ch'ang-an he encouraged a veritable blood-bath. Li Shan-fu went into the service of the independent Ho-pei warlords and indulged his hatred of court bureaucrats there. As for Li Chên, he joined Chu Wên's provincial service, and was so bitter about the aristocrats that he advised the execution of many of them and even asked that their corpses be thrown into the Huang Ho as an act of defilement.[1]

There were others who were less educated but no less hostile. They were mainly the officers and men of the imperial and provin-

[1] Huang Ch'ao; see *HTS* 225C, translated by Howard S. Levy. Li Shan-fu urged the warlord's son to murder the distinguished bureaucrat Wang To in 884 (*Pei-mêng So-yen*, 13, 1a-b). Li Chên; see *CWTS* 18, 9b-12a; *TCTC* 265, T'ien-yu 2(905)/5/*i-ch'ou* and 6/*wu-tzŭ*.

cial armies who did not hesitate to take advantage of any weaknesses in the ruling groups to seize whatever power they could. They readily recruited the lawbreakers, the malcontents and the hungry poor to help them stake their claims by force. Eventually, the excluded majority in the vast T'ang empire joined together, however uneasily, to bring about 'the downfall of aristocratic politics'.[2]

In the preceding two chapters, the last thirty years of the T'ang have been briefly considered on two levels. On the one hand, there were the courtiers who had become ineffectual because they had been wholly isolated from the source of their power in the provinces. On the other hand, there were the army officers and adventurers who had parcelled out the empire and developed powerful provincial governments. In the example of Chu Wên, the stages of development have been traced to show the foundations of provincial power. This chapter takes up the problem of how the structure Chu Wên had built up was fitted into the T'ang court organization, and how that organization was changed in the process. This is followed by a consideration of the T'ang Restoration in 923 which was really a conscious but unsuccessful attempt to return to the conditions before the Liang. The reaction against the Liang was ineffective largely because the courts presided over by the last T'ang emperors had become obsolete and because Li Ts'un-hsü, the man who restored the dynasty, was himself a product of the T'ang provincial system. Ultimately, his own organization differed very little from that of Chu Wên.

The most important political changes were already being prepared during the last four years of the T'ang. The convention of a formal dynastic break at 907 has long clouded over the importance

[2] 'Kizoku-seiji no Botsuraku' in T. Hori, 'Tōmatsu Sho Hanran no Seikaku-Chūgoku ni okeru Kizoku-seiji no Botsuraku ni tsuite', *Tōyō Bunka*, no. 7, p. 52 ff., where some of the main social and political changes in ninth-century China are surveyed. For the economic background of these changes, see Y. Sudō, 'Tōmatsu Gōdai no Shoen-sei', *Chūgoku Tochi Seidoshi Kenkyu*, Tokyo, 1954, pp. 9-64; and for the changes in the provinces, see Y. Sudō, 'Gōdai Ketsudoshi no Shihai Taisei', *Shigaku Zasshi*, nos. 4 and 6. I owe much of the background for this and the later chapters on the Wu-tai period proper to Y. Sudō's articles (more specific references will be given as the points arise).

of the years 903-906 to the Wu-tai period. To all intents and purposes, the T'ang court then was under Chu Wên's control and the destruction of the eunuchs and the imperial regiments was as much part of the foundation of the Liang as the last stage in the fall of the T'ang. By emphasizing the mistake of the Chief Minister Ts'ui Yin in advising Chu Wên to murder the eunuchs, traditional historians have neglected the *effects* of this act on the rise of the new group of men who replaced them in the palace.[3]

There are reasons for this neglect. The replacement of the eunuchs by Chu Wên's personal followers was made not so much to staff the palaces and superimpose his provincial type of government upon the court structure, as to observe and finally to murder the emperor. The units which Chu Wên left behind at the capital under his nephew were there to prevent any revival of imperial power. These were merely temporary measures introduced to smooth the path of a dynastic change and not institutional changes in themselves. There was nothing equivalent to these measures in the Liang government after 4th/907. But though the purpose of the appointments of 903-904 was peculiar to a period of transition, the fact was that the traditionally eunuch-held posts were thrown open to minor provincial officials whose only distinction was that they had worked for the most successful governor, in this case Chu Wên, and to officers who had begun their careers in his private army. The precedent of employing them in the palaces was to turn the provincial retainer and army service into a springboard to the palace and military administration.

All the seven palace commissioners known by name had obscure

[3] The historian Ssŭ-ma Kuang allows himself a long comment on the eunuchs and their massacre, see *TCTC* 263, T'ien-fu 3(903)/1/*kêng-wu*, ff. Although he recognized the baneful influence of the eunuchs on civil government, he still criticized Ts'ui Yin's part in causing their death and thus removing one of the main bulwarks of the late T'ang dynasty. This attitude, that with the execution of the eunuchs the T'ang empire must inevitably come to an end, has been echoed by traditional Chinese historians until very recent times. It has, however, little foundation, for the empire was in no condition to recover by 903, whether the eunuchs were spared or not. The attitude merely reflects the moral disapproval for Ts'ui Yin because he supported Chu Wên against a group which had provided a stable element in the T'ang imperial survival.

origins. Chang T'ing-fan, the ex-actor and guards officer of Pien province, and Chiang Hsüan-hui, Chu Wên's retainer, have been considered before in Chapter Three. A third man, Wang Yin, had been adopted by a powerful family, but appears to have been of lowly origins. This is certainly true of the fourth, K'ung Hsün, who was an adopted son of a wet-nurse in Chu Wên's family; his origins were so obscure that one contemporary scribe noted that 'it is not known what his surname really was'. As for the fifth, Hu Kuei, he had started his career in a provincial army and had been an officer of one of Chu Wên's rival governors. There are no records of the origins of the remaining two, Ying Hsü and Chu Chien-wu.[4]

If all these men had been executed for their part in the dynastic transfer in 907, there would have been some justification for ignoring them when considering the Liang. But at least three of them survived: Wang Yin and K'ung Hsün, the two senior palace attendants, and Hu Kuei, the Commissioner of the Imperial Gardens and Manors. Wang Yin continued as a senior palace attendant till 6th/912 and had, by that time, so gained the confidence of the prince who was to murder Chu Wên that he was appointed military governor of a border province.[5] K'ung Hsün also continued as a senior palace official and was later made a defence commissioner of a prefecture. He lived on to the Later T'ang dynasty and even played a vital part in putting the usurper Li Ssŭ-yüan on the throne in 926 after the brief 'restoration' period had come to an end. He was then appointed one of the heads of the powerful Military Secretariat, and allied himself with the imperial family by marrying his daughter to Li Ssŭ-yüan's third son. By the time he died in 931, he had been viceroy of Lo-yang and governor

[4] Wang Yin, also known as Chiang Yin, was adopted into the great Wang family of P'u province; biography in *CWTS* 13, 13a-b. K'ung Hsün, also known as Chao Yin-hêng, had been a retainer of the Pien Chou merchant Li Jang before becoming one of Chu Wên's men; *HWTS* 43, 8b-9a. The contemporary scribe was the author of *Pei-mêng So-yen* (15, 5a-b).

Hu Kuei, *CWTS* 19, 9b-10a. Ying Hsü and Chu Chien-wu were the commissioners of the armoury and the imperial kitchens; in *TCTC* 265, T'ien-yu 2(905)/12/*chia-wu*.

[5] *CWTS* 13, 13b.

of two provinces. Two years later, his daughter became empress.[6] As for Hu Kuei, the third survivor, he returned to the imperial army and rose to become one of the highest commanders.

None of these men could be said to represent a new group of politically powerful men whose descendants continued to dominate later history. Wang Yin's family was destroyed after an abortive rebellion in 914, and K'ung Hsün's when his son-in-law was deposed in 3rd/934. Hu Kuei's family was disgraced after his execution in 911 for extortion.[7] But they were, as the products of the last T'ang court of 903-906, an important link between the power group that was to emerge and the eunuchs who had been murdered in 903.

Chu Wên seemed prepared to experiment with the basis of central government and began by giving more power to the palace officials.[8] In 905, against the wishes of the leading T'ang bureaucrats, Chang T'ing-fan, actor, guards officer, prefect, governor, palace commissioner and chief of metropolitan police, was made President of the Court of Imperial Sacrifices (*t'ai-ch'ang ch'ing*). Chu Wên's intention to experiment was clear, for this department was traditionally one of the sacred precincts of bureaucrat government. But the appointment was not successful and Chang T'ing-fan was disgraced later that year. Two years later, after the new dynasty was founded, the most important and successful change was introduced. This was when Chu Wên established the office of Commissioner of the Military Secretariat, a post which had been held by eunuchs until 903 and abolished in 905.[9] Chu Wên

[6] *HWTS* 43, 8b-9a and *CWTS* chüans 32-41, *passim*.

[7] For Wang Yin's rebellion, *CWTS* 13, 13b and *TCTC* 269, Chên-ming 1(915)/2nd month. For the death of empress K'ung in 4th/934, *WTHY* 1, p. 10 and *CWTS* 15, 10a. For Hu Kuei's execution, *CWTS* 19, 10a and *TFYK* 445, 21b-22a.

[8] *TCTC* 265, T'ien-yu 2(905)/3/*chia-shên*. For Chang T'ing-fan's disgrace, *op. cit.*, 12/*chia-wu* to *chia-yin*.

[9] The post of *nei shu-mi shih* (內樞密使) was created in the eighth century when the office of privy affairs was taken away from the chief ministers and placed under the eunuchs; Hsiang An-shih, *Chia Shuo*, quoted in *CWTS* 149, 6a. But an earlier reference, in the *Hsü Shih-shih* (續事始) of Fêng Chien (馮鑑, active in the state of Shu in Szechuan, before 963), has been

had by this time decided to abandon the attempt to make bureaucrats of his ex-retainers. Instead, he threw open a post long associated with the inner palace and appointed to it his ex-secretary, Ching Hsiang, who was from the ranks of the minor bureaucracy. In this way, Ching Hsiang was given access to the inner palace, a privilege usually given to eunuchs and occasionally conceded to imperial favourites but never officially bestowed to non-eunuchs during the T'ang.[10]

There is little detailed information on the work of the Commissioner of the Ch'ung-chêng Hall. His duties were

preserved in Yeh Mêng-tê, *Shih-lin Yen-yü*, 4, 8a-b. This names the first *nei shu-mi shih* as the eunuch Tung Shu, and dates his appointment in the reign-year Yung-t'ai (765) of Tai-tsung. The Commissioner was at this time relatively unimportant and nothing more is known of him and his immediate successors. Cf. *Wên-hsien T'ung-k'ao*, 58, 1a, which names Tung T'ing-hsiu instead of Tung Shu, and calls him *ts'an-chang shu-mi shih* (參掌樞密事).

CWTS 149, 5b, says the Commissioner's duty was to convey the emperor's will outside the inner palace. *Pei-mêng So-yen*, 6, 10b and 10, 9b-10a, show how, by the end of T'ang, the Commissioners were as powerful as chief ministers.

More details of the Liang Commissioner of the Ch'ung-chêng Hall and his relations with the chief ministers in *TCTC* 266, K'ai-p'ing 1(907)/4/*hsin-wei* and *HWTS* 24, 25b (see next page note 11). Also *Wên-hsien T'ung-k'ao*, 58, 1a-b.

The first non-eunuch Commissioners of the Military Secretariat were appointed by Huang Ch'ao in 880-883; Fei Ch'uan-ku (*HTS* 225C, 5b; Howard S. Levy, *Biography of Huang Ch'ao*, p. 30) and Li Tang (*CWTS* 19, 10a). Li Tang was so trusted partly because he had earlier contacts with the T'ang eunuchs and was familiar with the ways of the T'ang palace services.

[10] *CWTS* 18, 8b-9a. How far this was due to Chu Wên's fondness for Ching Hsiang's wife is not clear. Ching Hsiang's wife had been a concubine of Huang Ch'ao's second-in-command, Shang Jang, and the governor of Hsü$_2$, Shih P'u, before being captured by Chu Wên and given to Ching Hsiang when his first wife died. She continued to wander freely into Chu Wên's bedroom, and after 901, received the title of Lady of State (*kuo fu-jên* 國夫人). She showed

'arrogance and extravagance in her carriages and clothes. All (her) maids had pearls and kingfisher feathers as ear ornaments. (She) had a separate set of attendants to take charge of (her) correspondence and accounts, and sent (her) agents to establish relations with the various governors. The successes of women in recent times were not comparable to hers. The courtiers all attached themselves to her. The favour and trust accorded to her and her voice in public affairs were not below that of (Ching) Hsiang.' (*CWTS* 18, 9a). Also *HWTS* 21, 4a-b.

to provide advice, to participate in discussions on policy and, from within the (inner) palace, to receive the emperor's decisions and convey them in writing (by *hsüan* 宣) to be acted upon to the chief ministers. When the chief ministers wished to make requests (to the emperor) outside the hours of official audience, and when (they) had further requests to make after receiving the emperor's orders, all (the requests) were put in memoranda (*chi-shih* 記 事) through the Ch'ung-chêng Hall to be considered (by the emperor). On getting the (imperial) decisions (the Commissioner) then conveyed them again (by *hsüan*) to the chief ministers.[11]

Although the Commissioner had no executive powers, these duties meant, in fact, that he could supervise all affairs of policy and even influence decisions on grand strategy and on the highest civil and military appointments.

Under the Commissioner was an administrator (*p'an-kuan*) who was later made his assistant. At first he was probably one of Chu Wên's personal followers who was also given access to the inner palace, but the post was held by a bureaucrat later in the dynasty.[12] There was also a palace staff for the Commission, for example, a palace official was the transmitter of directives (*ch'êng-chih*) and

[11] *TCTC* 266, K'ai-p'ing 1(907)/4/*hsin-wei*. Also in *HWTS* 24, 25b, where a commentary by Hsü Wu-tang explains *chi-shih* as a kind of memorandum. For the nature of *hsüan*, see Sung Min-ch'iu, *Ch'un-ming T'ui-ch'ao Lu, hsia* (chüan 3), p. 37 and p. 40; and Shên Kua, *Mêng-ch'i Pi-t'an*, 1, pp. 62-63. Sung Min-ch'iu gave a brief account of the draft copies (*ti* 底) of Liang 'proclamations' (*hsüan*) made by the Ch'ung-chêng Hall Commissioner, Li Chên, in the years 917-918, and still preserved in the History Office in Sung times. Shên Kua says that the *hsüan* was first used in late T'ang as a preliminary 'proclamation' addressed to the Imperial Secretariat by the eunuch Commissioners of the Military Secretariat. He adds that in the Liang, the Ch'ung-chêng Hall Commissioner was concerned only with conveying imperial decisions to the chief ministers and did not interfere yet with the latters' executive powers. There is, on the other hand, little evidence in the contemporary sources of the Liang that the chief ministers exercised any power independently of the palace commissioners and the imperial favourites.

[12] *WTHY* 24, p. 289. The only assistant commissioner mentioned in our sources, however, was Chang Hsi-i, who seems to have been a fairly junior bureaucrat; *CWTS* 9, 8a. Nothing else is known of him, except that he was executed when the Liang was destroyed in 923; *CWTS* 30, 4a. As the bureaucrat-Scholars of the Ch'ung-chêng Hall were all spared, this suggests that he had drawn attention to himself because he had wielded considerable power.

probably one of the most important of the Commissioner's subordinates.[13] At the same time, younger T'ang bureaucrats were brought into the service as Scholars of the Ch'ung-chêng Hall. Two secretaries of the Ministries of Civil Office and War respectively were first appointed as Scholars in 11th/908. One of them is known to have come from an aristocratic family.[14] In this way, the Commission was not only the meeting-place between retainer and bureaucrat but also became a bridge between privy and public affairs and between the inner and outer groups of administrators. This shows how Chu Wên, although keen to try new ways of government, was also willing to compromise with the T'ang basis of government.

The most important feature of the Commission was that the two Commissioners of the Liang, Ching Hsiang (4th/907-9th/912) and Li Chên (9th/912-10th/923), were appointed for an indefinite period as were the T'ang eunuchs. The principle seems to have been service through a whole reign. The continuity thus provided by the two men, all through the ministerial and palace changes during the two major reigns (907-912 and 913-923), gave a valuable stability to political power at the Liang court.

Another commission which had been in the hands of the eunuchs became of great importance under the control of Chu Wên's personal followers. This was the *hsüan-hui yüan*, that is, the commission in charge of the emperor's palace staff. In the proclamation of 5th/907, the commission was given control over the new groups of imperial attendants who had taken over most of the outside duties of the eunuchs.[15] These men, mostly from

[13] *TCTC* 268, Ch'ien-hua 1(911)/6/before *i-mao*, and *K'ao-i*. Shih Yen-ch'ün is called a *shou-chih* (受旨). Hu San-shêng's commentary says this was changed from *ch'êng-chih* (承旨) because of a dynastic taboo.

[14] *WTHY* 24, p. 289. The aristocrat was Li T'ing; *CWTS* 24, 1a-3a. The practice of appointing young bureaucrats was continued till the end of Liang. Both the Scholars in 10th/923, Lu Ch'ung and Liu Kuang-su, were disgraced by the new regime; *CWTS* 30, 3a. Liu Kuang-su may have been related to the Liu Ch'ang-su who was a *chin-shih* graduate after 907 if not the same man whose name was wrongly recorded in one instance; *CWTS* 128, 7b.

[15] *WTHY* 24, p. 291. Three grades of attendants were involved. The *kung-fêng kuan* (供奉官) were not the same as those of the T'ang

the provincial offices, also took on special administrative, diplomatic and even military work which had in the past often been the responsibility of bureaucrats.

Two of the Commissioners of Palace Attendants (*hsüan-hui shih*), Wang Yin and K'ung Hsün, have already been shown to have

grouped around the Han-lin Academy or under the control of the Imperial Chancellery and Imperial Secretariat (see Yeh Mêng-tê, *Shih-lin Yen-yü*, 7, 2b-3a and Shên Kua, *Mêng-ch'i Pi-t'an*, 1, pp. 20-21) or those in the *HTS* Monograph on Officials whose place at the court can be seen from R. des Rotours' translation of the term as 'fonctionnaires à la disposition du tribunal des censeurs' or as 'fonctionnaires à la disposition de l'empereur' (*Traité des Fonctionnaires*, Index, p. 960 and pp. 982-983). At the end of T'ang and in the Wu-tai, the military grade of the *kung-fêng kuan* had become more prominent. These had been developed from the seventh-century *kung-fêng kuan* of the east and of the west (*tung-hsi t'ou kung-fêng kuan* 東西頭供奉官) or 'gardes à la disposition de l'empereur' (*kung-fêng shih-wei* 供奉侍衞, *Traité des Fonctionnaires*, p. 547); also see *Mêng-ch'i Pi-t'an*, 1, p. 19. In *Shih-lin Yen-yü*, 5, 10b, there is a note about the military grade of *kung-fêng* (*kuan*) who were mentioned with other palace bodyguards like the *tso-yu pan* (左右班) *shih-chin* (侍禁) and the *tien-chih* (殿直). Also note Huang Ch'ao's use of his retainer, Hua Wên-ch'i, as *kung-fêng tu-chih* (供奉都知); *CWTS* 90, 8a.

Another group of attendants mentioned in the *WTHY* 24, were the *tien-ch'ien shou-chih* and *kuan-hsüan* (?) (殿前受旨，官宣), probably officers of, or officials attached to, the palace guards assigned to convey messages from the emperor to the court offices. The third group were the left and right *nei-chih* (內直) who were junior officials attached to the palace (inner) service; cf. *tien-chih* of palace guards above.

The *hsüan-hui shih* (宣徽使) was an eunuch's office introduced in the T'ang to supervise the various palace services and the accounts and other records of the eunuch organization. Later in the T'ang, these commissioners became so powerful that they had ousted the bureaucrats in charge of the Imperial Courts (*shih* 寺) from the palaces and were classed with the Commissioners of the Military Secretariat as the 'four (chief) ministers' (two *hsüan-hui shih* and two *shu-mi shih* were appointed at a time); *Pei-mêng So-yen*, 6, 10b; also see *Shih-lin Yen-yü*, 3, 6a. *Pei-mêng So-yen* notes the exceptional case of the eunuch Yen Tsun-mei who considered the eunuchs as merely *kung-fêng kuan* and thought that the eunuch *shu-mi shih*, Yang Fu-kung, had usurped the authority of the chief ministers; 10, 9b-10a. Also see *Wên-hsien T'ung-k'ao*, 58, 4b-5a.

later graduated to important provincial appointments. Of the later Commissioners, Chang Yün was from a great merchant family, and Chao Hu, a cousin of one of Chu Wên's sons-in-law, was descended from generations of provincial army officers. They were both extremely wealthy and powerful men in the court of Chu Yu-chên (913-923). Chang Yün was later raised to govern two important provinces, and Chao Hu was considered one of the men behind the throne and so powerful that he was immediately condemned to death when the dynasty ended.[16]

The main group of attendants controlled by this Commission were the *kung-fêng kuan* who were recruited from the sons of officials and army officers as well as from the lower ranks of the provincial staff. The most prominent was Tuan Ning who, from being a county registrar and then Chu Wên's retainer, rose through the palace service to be a prefect, an Army Supervisor, a palace commissioner and, finally, the chief commander of the Liang armies. He was the first of the palace commissioners who were to dominate the imperial armies later in the Wu-tai period. Another man, Shih Yen-ch'ün, became an important member of the staff of the Ch'ung-chêng Hall.[17] In the provinces, the attendants were respectfully treated as if they were personal representatives of the emperor. In 910, two of them were given the command of troops

[16] Chang Yün, *CWTS* 90, 5a-6b. Chao Hu, the cousin of Chao Yen, Chu Wên's son-in-law; *CWTS* 14, 11b, and mentioned in *CWTS* 9, 7b.

It is possible that the Chao Ku reported as being one of the men behind the throne in 8th/923 (*CWTS* 29, 12a) and mentioned in the edict of 16/10th/923 ordering his arrest and execution (*CWTS* 30, 3a-4a; also *TCTC* 272, T'ung-kuang 1(923)/10/*pin-hsü*) was the same man as Chao Hu. Chao Ku and Chao Yen are called 'near relatives of the Chu (imperial) family' in the edict, and Chao Hu is said, in *CWTS* 14, 11b, to have been executed together with his cousin Chao Yen. The influential *hsüan-hui shih* could also be expected to be included in the list of the highest Liang officials to be executed, and only Chao Ku is mentioned in the list and *not* Chao Hu.

[17] Tuan Ning, *CWTS* 73, 3a-5a. Shih Yen-ch'ün, *TCTC* 268, Ch'ien-hua 1(911)/6/before *i-mao*; in the *K'ao-i*, it is shown that Shih Yen-ch'ün was called a *kung-fêng kuan* in one source and a transmitter of directives (*shou-chih*) in other sources. It is probable that the wider term *kung-fêng kuan* covered some of the lesser officials of the highest palace commissions.

A notable *kung-fêng kuan* was the son of a prominent governor; *HWTS* 69, 8a. This suggests that the palace staff was also linked to the hostage system employed to control the governors.

of an allied army which might have resented the use of actual imperial commanders. Others were sent as envoys to the Tangut governor of Hsia province and to the Khitans. One of their important functions was the carrying of secret instructions; for example, after his murder of Chu Wên in 6th/912, Chu Yu-kuei sent one of them from Lo-yang to his brother in K'ai-feng ordering the execution of the heir apparent.[18]

The attendant officials also supplied a reserve for the various palace commissions (*nei chu-ssŭ shih*). These had been cut down to nine after the extinction of the T'ang eunuchs in 903, but almost all were re-established during the Liang dynasty. The *Wu-tai Hui-yao* enumerates twenty-six commissions, but only the commissioners of the five concerned with reception and imperial audiences, and with palace gates and entry permits were politically significant.[19] The ranks of the commissioners, as well as those of their assistants and the rest of their staff, were determined by sinecure titles in the Imperial Guards. These titles gave them standing amongst the bureaucrats of more distinguished families. The status of the palace officials was thus equal to that of army

[18] The two sent at the head of the Wei army in 910 were Tu T'ing-yin and Ting Yen-hui; *CWTS* 27, 6a. Tu T'ing-yin was also sent with Chang Han-mei (a brother of Chu Wên's daughter-in-law) to the Tanguts in 910; *CWTS* 5, 9b; while Lang Kung-yüan was sent to the Khitans in 920; *CWTS* 10, 3b. The attendant sent by Chu Yu-kuei in 6th/912 was Ting Chao-p'u; *CWTS* 8, 1b and *TCTC* 268, Ch'ien-hua 2(912)/6/*wu-yin*.

Another attendant, sent to pacify mutineers in Wei province in 915, was Hu I; *TCTC* 269, Chên-ming 1(915)/4th month.

[19] *WTHY* 24, p. 296. Twenty-nine commissions are enumerated, but two have been considered and one, the Commission for State Finance (*tsu-yung yüan*), comes under a different category and will be considered later in this chapter.

The five commissioners concerned with reception and imperial audiences and with palace gates and entry permits were the *k'o-shêng shih* (客省使), the *ying-chin shih* (引進使), the two *ko-mên shih* (閤門使) and the *ta-nei huang-ch'êng shih* (大內皇城使).

It is important to note that not all the commissions were under the control of lowly provincials. One of the *ko-mên shih* was Li Yü, a member of the T'ang imperial family: *CWTS* 6, 7b.

commanders and even of prominent governors temporarily out of office.

One of Chu Wên's innovations was to bring financial administration under the control of a palace commission. He set up the commission in one of his old gubernatorial residences which he named the Chien-ch'ang Palace, and put his adopted son, Chu Yu-wên, in charge. This commission of the Chien-ch'ang Palace took over the previous provincial organization for dealing with all Chu Wên's 'military equipment and supplies, taxes and miscellaneous revenues', and turned that organization into an imperial office for the control of the accounts and registers of the empire.[20]

In 2nd/908 Chu Yu-wên was succeeded by Han Chien, an able governor, and the Commission remained out of the hands of the bureaucrats. But this seemed to have been unsatisfactory, and eight months later, a Vice-President of the Ministry of War who was an ex-T'ang bureaucrat was appointed Assistant Commissioner. This arrangement was then found to be unsuitable and in 9th/909, the leading Chief Minister, Hsüeh I-chü, was concurrently made Commissioner and the bureaucrats seem to have gained control over the finances for the time. This control continued for fifteen months but the policy was once again modified when Li Chên, the upstart bureaucrat who hated the bureaucracy and had risen to high office in Chu Wên's service, was made the assistant in 12th/910 and allowed to wield the real power.[21]

This ambiguity in financial control was a reflexion of Liang government as a whole. There was an uncertain attempt to fuse the administrators from the provinces and those, including aristocrats, with long connexions with the T'ang court. This was changed after Chu Wên's death when the Chien-ch'ang Palace

[20] *WTHY* 24, p. 289; *CWTS* 3, 7a and 149, 6b.

[21] *WTHY* 24, p. 290; *CWTS* 149, 7a. Han Chien had been Salt and Transport Commissioner; *CWTS* 15, 3b. Hsüeh I-chü had also been Salt and Transport Commissioner as well as head of the Department of Public Revenue, but his biographer says there was nothing outstanding in his career worth recording; *CWTS* 18, 3a.

Li Chên was of bureaucrat origins, but had rejected the prevailing standards of T'ang bureaucracy. At the time of his appointment, he was probably President of the Ministry of Finance; see *CWTS* 18, 9b-12a.

was abolished and the ex-Huang Ch'ao officer and governor of Lo-yang, Chang Ch'üan-i, was made Commissioner of National Economy (*kuo-chi shih*), taking over 'all the gold, grain and army equipment previously of the Chien-ch'ang Palace'.[22]

The control over finances was never again returned to the bureaucrats. Instead, the third Liang emperor set up a new palace commission and appointed his brother-in-law, Chao Yen, to take charge of it. Chao Yen had been prefect, commander of the palace armies, general of the Imperial Guards and palace commissioner and his rank, Vice-President of the Ministry of Finance, was merely a nominal link with the bureaucracy. Under him, the Commission of State Finance (*tsu-yung yüan*) extended the imperial control of provincial finances farther than at any time since the Huang Ch'ao rebellion. He was the leading figure in the Liang court and was sought out as a public enemy when K'ai-fêng fell to the later T'ang in 923.[23]

The position of the old T'ang bureaucrats has been variously suggested above. The Liang emperors found it necessary to re-employ all those who were willing to serve and depended on them to set up the formal structure of an imperial court. But the shadow of several executions of bureaucrats by Chu Wên hung over the survivors. The executions had shown their precarious position without any doubt. Ts'ui Yin had hoped to challenge

[22] *WTHY* 24, p. 290; *CWTS* 149, 7a.

[23] Chao Yen's biography in *CWTS* 14, 8a-b and *HWTS* 42, 3b-35a. The *tsu-yung shih* was created in the eighth century as a temporary appointment and revived during the Huang Ch'ao rebellion for the specific task of 'urging tax deliveries' (*ts'ui-chêng* 催征); *Wên-hsien T'ung-k'ao*, 61, 5a. Liang Mo-ti revived it again to replace the *Chien-ch'ang yüan shih* and the *Kuo-chi shih*. The significance of the *tsu-yung yüan* was that it had supreme powers in imperial finance. It could exact additional taxes and could give loans at high rates of interest. See *CWTS* 149, 7b-8a; more important is the memorial by Tou Chuan of 3rd/924 in *WTHY* 24, p. 290.

The Liang Chief Minister, Chao Kuang-fêng, is said in his biography in *CWTS* 58, 2a, (but not in *HWTS* 35, 13b-14a) to have been a *tsu-yung shih*, but this was probably an error because of the various financial officials he had been, like the Salt and Transport Commissioner, the official in charge of the Department of Public Revenue and the Commissioner of the Yen-tzŭ Treasury; *CWTS* 8, 7b and 14a.

Chu Wên in 903 and was killed in 1st/904 because of it. P'ei Shu and more than thirty others had had their corpses thrown in the Huang Ho in 6th/905 for lack of full-hearted co-operation and, at the end of 905, Liu Ts'an was publicly executed in spite of his co-operation.[24]

Furthermore, the upper ranks of the bureaucracy and their families had been greatly depleted in numbers since 880 when two major series of executions were carried out in 881-882 and in 886-887. Many of the families left the metropolitan areas for Szechuan and South China or returned to their estates to live away from politics. The younger members of some of the families moved to provinces hostile to Chu Wên and continued to serve the T'ang cause among his enemies.[25] The few senior bureaucrats who remained with the Liang thought it wise to remain passive and limit their own scope of activity. Thus, although the full quota of high bureaucratic offices was filled, including most of those of the Censorate and the other organs of criticism, none of the bureaucrats seem to have achieved any kind of distinction. Another factor in their inactivity was the importance of Chu Wên's provincial staff which overwhelmed them through the palace offices closer to the emperor. It is doubtful if Chu Wên, a governor for twenty-four years, ever trusted the hereditary ruling class; there is certainly little evidence that he fully utilized the T'ang machinery of government. But an important element in our lack of information about the Liang bureaucrats was probably the omissions of contemporary historiography. The Liang dynasty was never regarded as legitimate (*chêng-t'ung*) during the tenth century—the T'ang 'restoration' had condemmed Chu Wên's treachery and the historians obliterated the dynasty from official

[24] Ts'ui Yin's execution in *TCTC* 264, T'ien-fu 3(903)/end of year and T'ien-yu 1(904)/1/*i-ssŭ*. P'ei Shu's execution, with more than thirty others, in *TCTC* 265, T'ien-yu 2(905)/3/*chia-shên*; 5/*i-ch'ou*, ff. and 6/*wu-tzŭ*. Liu Ts'an's execution in *TCTC* 265, T'ien-yu 2(905)/12/*chia-wu*, ff. and *chia-yin*.

HWTS 21, 3a, says Chu Wên 'killed almost all the great ministers of T'ang'. This statement is strongly criticized in Wu Chên, *Wu-tai Shih Tsuan-wu*, p. 14.

[25] The best-known of these men were Li Hsi-chi (*CWTS* 60, 1a-4b), Lu Ju-pi (*CWTS* 60, 8a-b) and Lu Chih (*CWTS* 93, 1a-2b) who joined Li K'o-yung, and others like Lu Ch'êng (*CWTS* 67, 4b-6b) and Tou-lu Ko (*CWTS* 67, 1a-2b) who joined Wang Ch'u-chih, the governor of Ting province in Ho-pei.

records. Thus many of the bureaucrats who survived to the Later T'ang and after would have gladly forgotten their work in the 'false' dynasty for support of which several of them had been penalized in 10th/923. And most of those who died during the Liang had distinguished relatives and descendants who had no wish to immortalize their families' part in collaborating with the dynasty.[26]

There are glimpses of bureaucratic activities from time to time, for example, in their control of finances from 909-912 and in various reforms made in Liang law and court rites. But no estimate of their political power is possible from such glimpses. It is significant that Ching Hsiang who had held great power in the Military Secretariat from 907-912 was promoted to be Chief Minister after 912 in order that he might be relieved of his power. Also, when (after 920) two Chief Ministers struggled for the influence they still had in the administration, one of them was saved from disgrace only through the intervention of a palace commissioner.[27]

As for imperial examinations, the basis of the highest bureau-

[26] The list of those Liang bureaucrats penalized in 10th/923 is given in *CWTS* 30, 3a (reproduced in *TCTC* 272, T'ung-kuang 1(923)/10/*ping-hsü*). Of the eleven men mentioned, eight have biographies in the *CWTS*, but the biographies merely give lists of the offices they had held and say nothing of what the men did during the Liang. As the eight men all lived till after 930 and had a second career when they were re-admitted into the court, the biographies deal largely with the later years of their lives. See *CWTS* 58, 4a-b and 11b-12a; 68, 3a-b, 4b and 4b-5a; 92, 1a-2b, 9a-10a and 10b-11b. The three men without biographies are Jên Tsan and Liu Kuang-su (both Liang *chin-shih* graduates), and Lu Ch'ung.

One of the highest Liang bureaucrats who died during the dynasty, Yang Shih, had a distinguished son, Yang Ning-shih. Yang Ning-shih, of whom there is a detailed biography in the *CWTS*, does not seem to have recorded anything about his father's work as Chief Minister. There is no biography of Yang Shih in the *CWTS* and the *HWTS* (35, 6a-b) draws a pathetic picture in a few sentences. (There may have been a biography of Yang Shih in the original *CWTS*, but it probably said no more than what is now preserved in the *HWTS*).

[27] Ching Hsiang, in *CWTS* 18, 7a-b. The two Liang Chief Ministers after 920 were Li Ch'i and Hsiao Ch'ing; see *CWTS* 58, 8a-b. New sets of Liang statutes and regulations were drawn up and six senior bureaucrats were kept busy for more than a year on the work. The collection, submitted in 12th/910 was in 130 chüans; *CWTS* 147, 1a-b (still preserved in the 11th century; *Ch'ung-wên Tsung-mu*, 2, pp. 82-83).

cratic recruitment, these were held in thirteen of the sixteen years of the Liang. Totals of 179 *chin-shih* graduates and 34 other graduates are recorded, and several of these graduates were to play an important part in later history.[28] The examinations kept alive the T'ang bureaucratic traditions and gave opportunities to younger men to fill the depleted ranks of the bureaucracy. On the whole, the bureaucrats continued to provide a literate and respectable administration for the dynasty, but there was never any question of their regaining political eminence. They were not the ones who benefited immediately from the destruction of the eunuchs which one of their members, Ts'ui Yin, had advised in 903.[29]

[28] The totals for each year have been preserved in the *Wu-tai Têng-k'o Chi* which the *Wên-hsien T'ung-k'ao* has preserved in quotation; 30, 2b.

Two of the most prominent Liang graduates were Ho Ning (*CWTS* 127, 5a-7a; see detailed bibliography in *HWTS* 56, 1a-6a) and Ts'ui T'o (*CWTS* 93, 5b-6b), both distinguishing themselves as chief examiners of later bureaucrats. Ho Ning also became a Chief Minister in the Chin dynasty. Others who distinguished themselves in later dynasties were Hsiao Hsi-fu (*CWTS* 71, 3a-4a; the *TFYK* 729, 14b, says he was a Liang *chin-shih*), Lu Shun (*CWTS* 128, 7b-8b), Yen K'an (*Sung Shih*, 270, 1a-2a) and Wang I-chien (*Sung Shih*, 262, 8a-b). An important graduate without a biography in the *CWTS* was Jên Tsan (mentioned in *CWTS* 30, 3a; 36, 6a; 40, 5a and 7a; 42, 7a; 44, 4a-b, 8a and 9b; 78, 5a; also in *TFYK* 475, 18b).

[29] In his sociological study of Chinese gentry, *Conquerors and Rulers*, *passim*, W. Eberhard supports his theory of the political power of the gentry with the example of Chu Wên's dynasty. He notes that the failure of Liang was largely due to Chu Wên's summary treatment of the gentry class, but gives no evidence of how exactly the opposition of this class brought the dynasty down. I think he has over-emphasized the role of the bureaucracy and has not given enough consideration to the provincial armies from whose ranks came the military governors who finally destroyed the Liang. It cannot be maintained that these governors resisted the dynasty for the sake of the gentry nor can evidence be found that they were of gentry origins. Further, the gentry were not averse to the idea of serving the Liang or any other 'illegitimate' province-empire. A considerable number of men of the most distinguished T'ang families including men descended from the imperial Li family (for example, Li Yü and Li T'ao; *CWTS* 6, 7b and *Sung Shih* 262, 5b) were willing to work for Chu Wên. It is necessary to distinguish their political impotence, and even servility to the new régime, from their reluctance to exert their powers and from their passive opposition.

It must be noted, however, that Chu Wên did not reject the institution of bureaucracy itself. His friendliness to some T'ang bureaucrats has been noted in his relations with the poet Tu Hsün-ho (Chang Ch'i-hsien, *Lo-yang Chin-shên Chiu-wên Chi*, 1, 1a-4a). Also well known were his many efforts to recruit new

It has often been pointed out that the Wu-tai was a period of 'military men's politics'. A strong indication of this seems to have been present in the Liang palace service and many examples of army officers replacing the bureaucrats in financial and administrative offices have already been mentioned. But the duties these officers were allowed to perform and the power they wielded did not depend on their military power. Although they continued to hold military titles which connected them with the Sixteen Imperial Guards (*shih-liu wei*), these titles were only sinecures with little military or political influence. They were really Chu Wên's trusted men and exercised the power which that trust had given them. Their 'politics' was not that of 'military men' but merely that of 'inner officials' (*nei-ch'ên*). This kind of 'politics' has to be distinguished from what generals and commanders of the imperial armies were able to do.

When Chu Wên became emperor, he retained personal control over the main armies which remained with him at the capital. He divided other sections of the armies among the commanders whom he had sent out as military governors to defend the border provinces. His main armies, part of which had already been used in the T'ang palaces in 903-906 first as Guards and then as a substitute for the disbanded Shên-ts'ê Armies of the eunuchs, were re-named and largely fitted into the T'ang system of Six Armies. Each of the Six Armies had a Marshal (*t'ung-chün*) and various other subordinate commanders. Of the six, the Left and Right Lung-hu Armies ranked first and second and the Marshal of the Left Lung-hu Army was the first choice as an expeditionary commander as well as being the Commissioner of the Emperor's Camps and thus, Chu Wên's chief deputy. This Marshal was the nearest to a permanent chief commander Chu Wên ever permitted. Several other armies were created but no marshals were appointed for them, only commanders (*tu chih-hui shih*) or commandants (*chün-shih*).[30]

men into the imperial administration, for example his successive edicts in 907, 7th/908, in 909 and in 9th/910, collected in *TFYK* 213, 7b-9a.

[30] *WTHY* 12, p. 156. Two Sung historians commenting on the growth of the Emperor's Personal Army (*shih-wei ch'in-chün*) refer significantly to the

The earliest marshals appointed in 904 were the two men who later arranged the murder of T'ang Chao-tsung. The murder made them politically undesirable in Chu Wên's eyes and they were executed soon afterwards. The first Liang Marshals of the Left Lung-hu Army are not known for their political activity, although one of them, Liu Han, was appointed not for his fighting record but for his administrative and disciplinary work with the armies.[31] They were, however, potentially dangerous. Some of them resented the strict control exercised over them, and the *coup d'état* of 6th/912 was in fact accomplised with the backing of the Marshal of the Lung-hu Army, Han Ching. He was approached by Prince Chu Yu-kuei who was the commanding officer of the emperor's personal bodyguards, the K'ung-ho regiment, and agreed to use his troops to help the prince murder Chu Wên.[32]

Eight months later, another successful *coup d'état* overthrew Chu Yu-kuei and Marshal Han Ching and placed Chu Yu-chên on the throne. A major figure in this *coup* was another Marshal, that of the Left Lung-wu Army, Yüan Hsiang-hsien. He was an imperial cousin who was concurrently the commander of the armies at Lo-yang, the Western capital of Liang. Within eight months, two Marshals had successively been king-makers. But at this stage, the power which each of these Marshals wielded was, in fact, limited. The eventual failure of the first Marshal and the quick success of the second show this clearly. The two *coups* were determined largely by factors outside the capital, by the intervention of the

Liang 'cavalry and infantry at the capital' (*tsai-ching ma-pu chün* 在京馬步軍) before considering the Army in Li Ssŭ-yüan's reign; Ou-yang Hsiu, *HWTS* 27, 13b and Yeh Mêng-tê, *Shih-lin Yen-yü*, 6, 1b-2b.

This has been discussed by T. Hori, 'Gōdai Sōshu ni okeru Kingun no hatten' *Tōyō Bunka Kenkyujo Kiyō*, 4, pp. 89-96 and his survey has been expanded by H. Kikuchi, 'Gōdai Kingun ni okeru Jiei Shingun shi no seiritsu' *Shien* 70, pp. 58-66. The two studies show that although a formal Emperor's Army did not exist in the Liang, some of the bodyguard units at the capital were the precursors of such an Army later on. For a consideration of the Emperor's Army, see Chapter Six.

[31] *CWTS* 20, 2b-4a.

[32] The *CWTS* section on the murder of Chu Wên is now lost. The most detailed accounts of this event are in *HWTS* 13, 14b-15a and *TCTC* 268, Ch'ien-hua 2(912)/6/*wu-yin*.

most powerful governors of the empire, Yang Shih-hou of Wei (in Ho-pei) and Chu Yu-ch'ien of P'u (in Ho-tung). It was the hostility of these two governors to Chu Wên's murderer which ultimately brought about his downfall, and without the armed support of Yang Shih-hou, Chu Yu-chên and the second Marshal would probably not have ventured against Chu Yu-kuei.[33]

After 913, there is no record of the exercise of political power by the Marshals. The military men closest to the emperor were the imperial relatives, chiefly members of the Empress Chang's family. Chang Han-chieh, for example, was the commanding officer of the imperial bodyguards and influenced the appointments of military governors and expeditionary commanders. He and his brothers and cousins were some of the most powerful men in Chu Yu-chên's court. They, like the palace officials with whom they shared the highest political power, all had various military connexions and were mostly descendants of newly risen provincial army officers.[34] But the political activities of all these men were not dependent on their army careers. It would be more accurate to say that their control over sections of the central armies was dependent on their status in the palace and it was this status which gave them political power. An excellent example to show where the real source of power lay is in the career of Tuan Ning. Tuan Ning rose from retainer to palace commissioner and then to chief commander of the imperial expeditionary armies, all through his access to the inner palace.

What is clear is that 'military men's politics' in the Liang did not

[33] Yüan Hsiang-hsien's biography in *CWTS* 59, 8b, calls him Marshal of the Left Lung-*wu* and not Lung-*hu* Army, while in the *CWTS* Basic Annals (8, 4b) and the *TCTC* 268, Ch'ien-hua 3(913)/2/*jên-wu*, he is called Marshal of the Lung-*hu* Army. The *HWTS* also gives both titles, Lung-*wu* in his biography (45, 17b) and Lung-*hu* in the Basic Annals (3, 2a). As Yüan Hsiang-hsien was concurrently chief commander of the armies at the capital and the Lung-hu Marshal was the most senior of the imperial commanders, it is likely that the biographies are wrong.

[34] *CWTS* 16, 8b. The Empress Chang's family refers to the sons of Chang Kuei-pa, Chang Kuei-hou and Chang Kuei-pien (nos. 6,7 and 8 in Table V). Chang Han-chieh was also sent to supervise the commander-in-chief of the imperial armies; *CWTS* 10, 10b and 30, 1a. He and his brothers and cousins were all executed in 10th/923 (*CWTS* 30, 4a).

stem from the imperial army. The only men who wielded power as military men were, in fact, not at the capital, but in the provinces. Chu Wên had been prescient enough not to allow the power of the army to develop in the capital, but he was unable to curb the growing power of the military men he had sent to defend his frontiers. These border-governors formed the real threat to the court and continued to do so for several more decades. It was really the politics of these men which can be said to characterize the Wu-tai period, and the impact of their power will be examined in the following chapter.

It seems clear that there were new focal points in the Liang court while the traditional power groups of the T'ang were partly displaced. But there is a significant gap in our sources left by contemporary historians for the ten years' reign of the last Liang emperor.[35] This gap has made it very difficult to make an appraisal of the power factors in the later Liang court. Also, the reticence of the bureaucrats about their own activities and the willingness of later historians to place the blame for the fall of Liang on the imperial relatives have obscured the importance of the changes which had taken place under this first plebian ruling group since the Former Han dynasty. Furthermore, the Liang was succeeded by a T'ang 'restoration' (923-926) which set out to reject everything that the Liang emperors had done. This has certainly obscured the fact that for twenty years, 903-923, members of Chinese provincial families who had risen to power by wealth and military activities, and not by nobility or learning, had dominated the court. The following analysis of the Restoration attempts to show how the Liang developments were consciously neglected but did, in fact, survive.

When Li K'o-yung, leader of the Sha-t'o Turks, died in 1st/908,

[35] In my article on the Wu-tai Veritable Records and the *Chiu Wu-tai Shih*, *Asia Major*, VI/1, I have discussed the fact that the reign of Liang Mo-ti was without Veritable Records; see also *Ch'ung-wên Tsung-mu*, 2, p. 49 and *Sung Shih*, 263, 4a.

The *Chiu Wu-tai Shih* has been affected by the gap in the Records and has only three chüans of the Basic Annals for Liang Mo-ti's reign of ten years as compared with seven chüans for the five and a half years of Chu Wên's reign.

his son, Li Ts'un-hsü, inherited the tribal army as well as the provincial army of Ping province. Li Ts'un-hsü was then a young man of twenty-two who had had no opportunity to prove his qualities of leadership before his father's death. But after suppressing an attempt to depose him, he began to show that he was a natural leader. He disciplined the Turkish tribesmen and devised strict rules for the mixed armies of 'tribesmen and Chinese' (*fan-han*) in battle. He also began to reorganize the administration with an eye to winning over the Chinese population.[36]

The slogan which he used to rally other provincial armies against Chu Wên was the restoration of the T'ang. Li Ts'un-hsü, like his father before him, employed several aristocrats who had been driven from the court by the rival factions more willing to collaborate with Chu Wên. They were given secretarial and legal posts and their employment gave weight to the professed intention to restore the T'ang. But the far more important work of military supervision and financial administration was in other hands. The eunuchs and some of Li Ts'un-hsü's retainers took charge of the first, and the accounts officials and other retainers of the second.[37]

[36] *CWTS* 27, 3a-b, for the attempt to remove Li Ts'un-hsü. In the biography of Li Ts'un-chang, an old trusted retainer of Li K'o-yung, there is a description of how the tribal army was subdued and the administration reformed; *CWTS* 53, 8a. Also *TCTC* 266, K'ai-p'ing 2(908)/5/after *hsin-wei*.

Li Ts'un-hsü began to use the power of official appointment granted to his father by T'ang Chao-tsung and appoint regular officials for Ping province; *ibid*. In this way, he may have put a stop to some of his father's past extortionate practices. One of these which must have embittered the gentry was to put a son of a wealthy family in charge of the treasury each year and to make the family answerable for any 'inadequacy' by death and confiscation of their property. For the story of a man who survived the first year and was begged by relatives to do another term, see *Sung Shih*, 255, 7b.

Li Ts'un-hsü also made rules for the armies on march which improved discipline (*Wu-tai Shih-pu*, 2, 2a-b, but this leaf in the edition available to me is missing, and I have translated from the text quoted in *CWTS* 34, 12a-b):

'Before the enemy is sighted, the cavalry troops are not to be mounted. If the positions of the infantry and the cavalry have been fixed, they may not change their allotted place to avoid any danger. If the units advance separately agreeing to meet at an appointed time and place, they may not be late. Further, any man who dares speak of illness while marching shall be executed.'

The same source also describes how Li Ts'un-hsü wrote popular songs which his soldiers sang in battle.

[37] The distinguished eunuchs were Chang Ch'êng-yeh, originally the Army

Li Ts'un-hsü's victory over the Liang in 10th/923 was followed by an attempt to put the clock back to the last years of the T'ang. There was a demand for aristocrats to be chief ministers. There was a return to power of the eunuchs. The capitals were again Lo-yang and Ch'ang-an, and K'ai-fêng once more became a provincial city. There were acclamations that history was repeating itself and that the T'ang, like the Han, was due to have its Kuang Wu-ti. But there were differences. The court had changed in the sixteen and a half years under the Liang. Also, fifteen years as a military governor had accustomed Li Ts'un-hsü to the provincial system of government which the Liang had adapted to the needs of an imperial court.

Three groups of officials could be distinguished at the new court from the start. There were the emperor's powerful retainers and there were the eunuchs who once again flourished in the environment of the inner palace. Then there were the ministers, secretaries and censors, both the newly appointed and the survivors from the Liang, who tried either to please both the powerful parties or to align themselves with one of them.

Outside the court, there was the political pressure exerted by the central armies. These consisted of Li Ts'un-hsü's tribal and Chinese army as well as the surrendered troops of the Liang. Two large armies which had been bitter enemies for a quarter of a century had now to be reorganized and merged. They also had to be paid. This was a burden which induced Li Ts'un-hsü to revive the centralized financial machinery of the Liang and give the Commission of State Finance great power over the provincial governments. And outside of the capital, there were his military governors

Supervisor of Li Ts'un-hsü's father (*CWTS* 72, 1a-4b) and Li Shao-hung (*CWTS* 72, 6a-b). The senior retainer officers were Kuo Ch'ung-t'ao (*CWTS* 57, 1a-10b), Chang Hsien (*CWTS* 69, 1a-4a) and Mêng Chih-hsiang (*HWTS* 64 A, 1a-b). Provincial finances were in the hands of men of lowly origins like K'ung Ch'ien (*CWTS* 73, 5a-b) and Mêng Ku (*CWTS* 69, 7a-b and *TFYK* 483, 29a-b).

More important than the ex-courtiers and their families were the northern literati (chiefly of Ho-pei and Ho-tung) who entered Li Ts'un-hsü's service. The most distinguished of them was Fêng Tao, Li Ts'un-hsü's secretary during the successful years just before the end of the Liang (*CWTS* 126, 1a-2a).

and the Liang governors who had submitted to his rule. The Liang governors had been returned to their provinces where, with their wealth and private armies, they could also take sides in the struggle at the court.[38]

Thus, in spite of Li Ts'un-hsü's declared intention to restore T'ang, the *chieh-tu shih* form of provincial government which had influenced the Liang court also influenced the political structure of his court. He introduced the retainers of his province into the palace administration. He also saw the need for a new kind of chief minister to be the bridge between the inner and outer groups of officials. And he found it expedient to recognize the difference in specialized skill which divided the court bureaucrats who dealt largely with formal and ritual affairs from the officials of provincial origins who had financial and diplomatic ability.[39]

But this aspect of Li Ts'un-hsü's government has been largely obscured by the more spectacular role of the imperial favourites in his court. A great deal has been written about these favourites, especially their part in Li Ts'un-hsü's downfall. Those who drew most attention to themselves were the actors and musicians who entertained him in his favourite pastime. The emperor, who was said to have preferred sport and drama to affairs of government, has often been used as a warning to others. But the importance of these men has been exaggerated. There is no convincing evidence that they dominated state affairs. One of them, Ching Chin, had taken advantage of imperial favour to advise the emperor on military and civil affairs and unwisely persuaded him to execute one of the more powerful governors and his family. Another,

[38] Although the Liang governors offered no military resistance against Li Ts'un-hsü, they could not immediately be removed. For the way Li Ts'un-hsü dealt with them, see Chapter Five. For the support Li Ssŭ-yüan received in 926 from Liang governors and army officers, see Chapter Six; see biographies of Huo Yen-wei (*CWTS* 64, 1a-2b) and K'ung Hsün (*HWTS* 43, 8b-10a). Also see biography of the Liang commander-in-chief, Tuan Ning, for his use of his great wealth to influence court politics (*CWTS* 73, 3a-5a).

[39] Cf. the remarks made by Sung Min-ch'iu about the T'ang practice of using military and literary men interchangeably (*wên-wu ts'an-yung* 文武參用) and how the Sung continued this practice (*Ch'un-ming T'ui-ch'ao Lu*, 1, p. 11). This was certainly not true of the first half of the Wu-tai period.

Shih Yen-ch'iung, was noted for his part in angering the Wei provincial garrison and a third, Kuo Ts'ung-ch'ien, incited a regiment of imperial bodyguards to mutiny in 4th/926.[40] All three thus played their part in Li Ts'un-hsü's downfall, but they did not represent a coherent group which made a conscious bid for power. They catered for the tastes of a theatre-loving emperor who was foreign and cared little for Chinese social distinctions. They were in some ways a phenomenon similar to the eunuch favouritism which Li Ts'un-hsü revived in his court.

The return of the eunuchs to power after twenty years was much more significant and clearly the most pronounced feature of Li Ts'un-hsü's reign. The Liang palace commissioners were for the most part replaced by them. So were the various groups of palace attendants (chiefly the *kung-fêng kuan*). Most of them had gained office and wealth from lowly origins in the last quarter of a century and were now rendered unemployed. Many of them were probably re-absorbed into other administrative positions in the capital, but many others returned to their homes in the provinces as the heads of newly rich and influential families.[41]

[40] Ching Chin was the most powerful of the three, *CWTS* 31, 7b; 34, 2b-3a. In *HWTS* chüan 37, *passim*, Ou-yang Hsiu devoted a chapter to actors and showed Li Ts'un-hsü's fondness for drama and sport.

For Shih Yen-ch'iung, see *CWTS* 34, 3a-b; *TFYK* 698, 5a-b and 11b-12a. For Kuo Ts'ung-ch'ien, see *CWTS* 34, 11b and *TCTC* 274, T'ien-ch'êng 1(926)/3/*chia-ch'ên* and 275, T'ien-ch'êng 1(926)/4/*ting-hai*.

[41] The eunuchs did not take over all the palace commissions. A Liang palace commissioner like Liu Sui-ch'ing was retained in his office; *CWTS* 96, 5b. Other men from Chuang-tsung's provincial government were employed in the palace commissions like the reception official Yang Yen-hsün (*CWTS* 90, 10b-11b) and the guards officer Liu Ch'u-jang (*CWTS* 94, 8b-10b). There were also men of literati origins like Hsüeh Jên-ch'ien (*CWTS* 128, 6b-7a) and a man who had been a prefect, Li Yen (*CWTS* 70, 5a-6b).

The important use of eunuchs as *kung-fêng kuan* can be seen in the developments following the Shu campaign at the end of 925; *CWTS* 33, 5a, notes the key eunuch appointments, while *CWTS* 57, 7b-9b, describes the complex intrigues initiated by the eunuchs. Also see *TCTC* 274, T'ung-kuang 3(925)/12th month, ff.; intercalary 12/*hsin-hai*; and T'ien-ch'êng 1(926)/1/*kêng-shên*, ff.

An important example of an ex-Liang palace commissioner who was employed in responsible posts by Li Ts'un-hsü and later emperors was Lou Chi-ying; *CWTS* 9, 1b; 37, 3b; 39, 4b and 42, 7b; also *TFYK* 497, 18a. His biography in *HWTS* 51, 15a-b, describes his part in the attempted *coup d'état* in 937 against the founder of the Chin dynasty. His origins were obscure, and he

This was not the only significant result of the eunuchs' return. The eunuchs were so confident that they were really back in power again that many of them provoked the envy and hatred of their rivals, that group of Li Ts'un-hsü's retainers and others of lowly provincial origins who were also hoping for preferment in the new court. The antagonism which they aroused among the officials who felt that the Liang court had worked perfectly well without these interfering eunuchs became so acute that only the emperor could save them. And this Li Ts'un-hsü could not do for long. When his armies mutinied and killed him in 926, it also marked the end of the eunuchs. After 926, they were permanently excluded from imperial government. Thus their two and a half years of borrowed time reflected the fundamental changes that had taken place since 901 when their predecessors had last tried to be king-makers.

This failure of the eunuchs to retain power was largely due to their inability to regain control of military affairs. Li Ts'un-hsü had built his power, as Chu Wên had done, on the provincial form of government in which the governor had his own military adviser and the eunuch was a representative of the central government. He therefore revived the Military Secretariat (*shu-mi yüan*) in place of the Liang Ch'ung-chêng Hall, but did not let the eunuchs dominate it. Instead he appointed his most trusted ex-retainer, Kuo Ch'ung-t'ao, who shared the control of the Secretariat with the leading eunuch. The eunuchs then strenuously opposed Kuo Ch'ung-t'ao in an effort to challenge the influence of the emperor's ex-retainers. And it was largely this opposition which provoked the violent reactions against the emperor, their sole patron, in 1st-3rd/926.[42] The ex-retainers successfully prevented the eunuchs from controlling the armies. Their two leaders were Kuo Ch'ung-t'ao who dominated the military administration, and Chu Shou-yin who commanded the army at the capital. These two men represent-

made a marriage alliance with the son of a disreputable Liang governor of bandit origins. The families of these two men seem to have flourished, and were influential enough to attempt a rising against the new Chin régime.

[42] For the *shu-mi yüan*, see note 9 above; also *WTHY* 24, p. 289 and *CWTS* 149, 6a. The struggle between Kuo Ch'ung-t'ao and the eunuchs is briefly summarized in *CWTS* 57, 4a-10b.

ed the new political group, the former extending his authority to civil government as a new chief minister, and the latter checking the ambitions of professional soldiers who were highly-placed army commanders.

How far Kuo Ch'ung-t'ao and his immediate following usurped the traditional influence of the bureaucrats which was supposedly restored at this time has been difficult to estimate. The historians who started to write in 928 of Li Ts'un-hsü's reign were influenced by the political conditions of their own time. The emperor under whom they served had overthrown Li Ts'un-hsü, and yet had for sentimental reasons not changed the name of the dynasty. As bureaucrats, these chroniclers would be expected to take the side of Kuo Ch'ung-t'ao as a man more sympathetic to the bureaucrats than the eunuchs and the various favourites. A further complication was the disgrace and execution, only a year before in 927, of the two chief ministers who had served with Kuo Ch'ung-t'ao through the whole of Li Ts'un-hsü's reign.[43] With this background, it is not improbable that Kuo Ch'ung-t'ao's part in civil government had been given more weight than was due, and that the two chief ministers who were no credit to bureaucratic traditions were proportionately belittled. It is significant that the historians also tried to show that Kuo Ch'ung-t'ao's dictatorial powers were partly responsible for Li Ts'un-hsü's downfall.[44] To do this, they might easily have over-stated his part in all matters.

Li Ts'un-hsü had from the beginning sought men from the most distinguished families to be his chief ministers. The emphasis

[43] Tou-lu Ko (*CWTS* 67, 1a-2b) and Wei Yüeh (*CWTS* 67, 2b-4a) were the two chief ministers disgraced in 7th/926 and finally executed in 7th/927. For the details of their disgrace, see *CWTS* 36, 8b-10b and 38, 9b; and *TCTC* 275, T'ien-ch'êng 1(926)/7/*chi-mao*.

[44] *CWTS* 57, 1a-10b, *passim*. Two Sung essays on Kuo Ch'ung-t'ao differ slightly from each other about this effect of his power. Su Ch'ê emphasizes the error of attacking Shu which Kuo Ch'ung-t'ao had encouraged for his own gain while Ho Ch'ü-fei stresses Li Ts'un-hsü's mistake in sending him to Shu. But they both agree that Kuo Ch'ung-t'ao's great power and the threat to that power by the eunuchs had driven him to lead the ill-fated Shu campaign, and that this made it easier for Li Ssŭ-yüan to destroy Li Ts'un-hsü. I have not been able to consult the two essays, having read them only in quotation in the commentaries to the *HWTS* (24, 15b-16b).

being on social origins and not on ability and experience, there was obviously no intention to lean on them greatly for efficient government. For example, although Tou-lu Ko was a member of a distinguished family and was put in charge of state finances in 11th/923, this was only a temporary measure and the administration was soon afterwards, and for the rest of the reign, in the hands of K'ung Ch'ien, an accounts official of lowly origins from the provinces who had proved himself earlier.[45]

Also, two of the chief ministers during Li Ts'un-hsü's reign were bureaucrats who had collaborated with the Liang and had been promoted to their present positions by Tou-lu Ko and Kuo Ch'ung-t'ao respectively for their knowledge of the preceeding court. Their career with the illegal Liang dynasty, however, must have discouraged them from doing anything which might prejudice their providential advancement in the new court. In fact, the relations between these two ministers and their sponsors reflect the whole court with its three divisions of the emperor's retainers and provincial staff, of restored T'ang bureaucrats and of Liang collaborators. The more distinguished of the two ex-collaborators, Chao Kuang-yin, gave way to his sponsor Kuo Ch'ung-t'ao on all affairs of government and only made one ineffectual attempt to curb the power of the eunuchs. On the other hand, when it came to 'the successive changes in the rites, music and (other) institutions', no one could challenge his 'empty talk and arrogant arguments', and even the senior minister, Tou-lu Ko, 'could only agree respectfully'.[46] The other collaborator, Wei Yüeh, accepted the views of Kuo Ch'ung-t'ao as well as those of his own sponsor, Tou-lu Ko, in all matters. He did, however, resent Kuo Ch'ung-t'ao's power. When Kuo Ch'ung-t'ao was murdered, Wei Yüeh sent two of his protégés to defame the dead man's name for an unpopular decision made long before his death.[47]

The restored T'ang bureaucrats were in a different position.

[45] See note 49 below.

[46] *CWTS* 58, 3a, in Chao Kuang-yin's biography.

[47] *CWTS* 67, 3a-b and 148, 5b-6b. Kuo Ch'ung-t'ao's part in causing many bureaucrat families to lose the certificates of office they had acquired by illegal methods is dealt with later.

They had either escaped north to join Li Ts'un-hsü and his allies in the last days of the T'ang dynasty or had started as secretaries or administrators in the northern provinces. Those who had served at court had forgotten what it had been like twenty or more years before. They were often indistinguishable from the administrators who had newly risen from the lower ranks of the provincial staff through special ability, long service as retainers, or through marriage relations with their governors' families. They were therefore more willing to accept the leadership of someone from this group like Kuo Ch'ung-t'ao.

The sources point to Kuo Ch'ung-t'ao as the prototype of a new type of bureaucrat. The power he wielded in both civil and military matters may be compared with that of the bureaucrats of aristocratic origins before the Huang Ch'ao rebellion. He had, in fact, been encouraged by the other ministers to identify himself with the aristocrats, and he soon saw himself as a descendant of the famous general Kuo Tzŭ-i of the eighth century. These pretentions coloured his attitude to government officials for he began to inquire into the family background of new candidates and to favour pedigree blood to loyal service.[48] But nothing could change the fact that he was an upstart who had himself risen to power without benefit of either blue blood or a literati education.

The extent of his authority can be seen in the way he frequently interfered with bureaucratic government. One example concerned the controversy over the post of Commissioner of State Finance (*tsu-yung shih*). The post was first held by a man of similar origins as himself with a professional accountant as assistant. Through his recommendations the post passed to a Chief Minister in 11th/923; but when it was found that the Minister had taken loans of a few hundred thousand cash from the public coffers, Kuo Ch'ung-t'ao forced him to resign. He continued to dictate the choice of the

[48] *CWTS* 57, 10a. The *HWTS* records that when he cried on the grave of Kuo Tzŭ-i, those who heard of it laughed; *HWTS* 24, 14b. Kuo Ch'ung-t'ao's importance was always acknowledged by the bureaucrats. His great ability has been fully dealt with in a whole chüan in the *CWTS* and in half a chüan of the concise *HWTS* and in the *TCTC* 272-274, *passim*. He has also inspired several essays by Sung scholars, notably by Su Ch'ê and Ho Ch'ü-fei, already mentioned in note 44 above.

candidate to be appointed, and called upon Wang Chêng-yen, another bureaucrat, to take over in 1st/924. He might well have been responsible for the decree of the same month ordering the three economic organs, the Board of Finance, the Department of Public Revenue and the Salt and Transport Commission, till then in the hands of the older bureaucrats, to be placed under the control of the Commission of State Finance. In 8th/924, however, he did not object to the promotion of the professional accountant mentioned above to replace the ineffectual Wang Chêng-yen.[49] In 11th/923, he also created the Commission for Internal Affairs (*nei-kou*) merely to please the eunuchs, although this meant duplicating the work of checking 'the cash, grain and registers of the empire'. He did this in the face of strong bureaucratic criticism that it was a policy of 'nine shepherds for ten sheep'.[50]

Another example of this power concerns some of the malpractices among the T'ang bureaucrat families. When Kuo Ch'ung-t'ao heard that T'ang officials had been selling their certificates of office (*kao-ch'ih*) to their younger relatives and that the Ministry of Civil Office had been appointing these men indiscriminately, he reported the matter. The Chief Ministers, who did not dare to oppose him, ordered an investigation which resulted in the removal of about 1,200 officials out of a total of only 1,250. These officials had their certificates destroyed, and a memorial complaining about this two years later said that there were 'some who died in their inns and others who cried on the roads'.[51] This was a blow to the traditional ruling class. Rightly or wrongly, a large proportion of men from distinguished families had their names removed from the service registers and fresh opportunities were created for the sons of lesser families. Although for two years men were afraid

[49] *CWTS* 73, 5a-b (from *TFYK* 924) gives a full account of the complex struggle for control of the Commission of State Finance. Also *TCTC* 272, T'ung-kuang 1(923)/11/*wu-wu*; 273, T'ung-kuang 2(924)/1/*chia-ch'ên*, *chia-yin* and *wu-wu*; 2/*chi-ssŭ*; 4/after *kêng-ch'ên*; 7/*jên-yin*; and 8/*kuei-yu*.

[50] *CWTS* 72, 6b. Also *CWTS* 31, 9b; 149, 7a-b; 57, 5b. Also *TCTC* 273, T'ung-kuang 2(924)/2/after *hsin-ssŭ*.

[51] *CWTS* 148, 5b-6a; *TFYK* 632, 11a; also *TCTC* 273, T'ung-kuang 2(924)/3/after *kêng-hsü*. According to *TFYK* 632, 11a, the number of officials removed would have been about 1,300, while *CWTS* 32, 7a, and *TFYK* 632, 10a, say that 'seven or eight out of every ten' were removed.

to go to the court for examination, and for the 2,000 vacancies in 925 only sixty men were appointed,[52] the effect of this measure

[52] *CWTS* 148, 6a, and *TFYK* 632, 11b, the memorial submitted by the protégés of one of the Chief Ministers (Wei Yüeh). These men were taking advantage of Kuo Ch'ung-t'ao's execution to accuse him of having wrongly caused the dismissal of so many potential officials, and the figures may have been exaggerated.

Kuo Ch'ung-t'ao's original memorial is partially preserved in *CWTS* 32, 6b, and fully preserved in *TFYK* 632, 9a-10b (also in *Ch'üan T'ang Wên*, 844, 4a-5b). It complains of forgery and nepotism bringing about the neglect of genuine talent among those who were poor and uncorrupt, and calls for an investigation. It asks for informants to come forward and recommends various forms of reward and punishment. It draws attention to the protection given to false candidates by influential officials (*hsing-shih* 形勢). It also notes the delay in selecting candidates by the various Establishment Offices and the heavy debts the candidates incurred at the capital which would probably encourage them to be corrupt when given office. Both the *CWTS* and *TFYK* note the great resentment against Kuo Ch'ung-t'ao for the investigation which followed.

The importance of the certificates of office (*kao-ch'ih* 告赤 or *kao-shên* 告身) at this time is difficult to estimate. During the last years of T'ang and the sixteen years of Liang, many of the poorer and lesser officials had not been able to afford the cost of getting these certificates (*TCTC* 275, T'ien-ch'êng 1(926)/11/*chia-hsü*). Three months after the Restoration, in 1st/924, it was decided to limit the issue of certificates to the highest officials and officers (*WTHY* 14, p. 179). Four months later, in 5th/924, candidates for office who had not *lately* been court officials or were not examination graduates, were asked to produce their past certificates (*WTHY* 13, p. 166). This was about the time of Kuo Ch'ung-t'ao's reform, according to the dating in *TCTC* 273, (T'ung-kuang 2(924)/3/after *kêng-hsü*), but the *CWTS* 32, 6b, and *TFYK* 632, 9a, date Kuo Ch'ung-t'ao's memorial in 9th/924.

The extent of Kuo Ch'ung-t'ao's reform must have been considerable, and many innocent officials may have been affected. In Li Ssŭ-yüan's first proclamation of amnesty in 28/4th/926, a fresh investigation was ordered for those men whose certificates had been destroyed in 924, and the examination departments were asked 'to remove only the false (candidates)'. (*TCTC* 275, T'ien-ch'êng 1(926)/4/*chia-yin*; this constitutes the last part of the amnesty proclamation. It is missing from the proclamation preserved in *CWTS* 36, 1b, and stands separately in *TFYK* 632, 12b.)

By the end of 926, however, the certificates seem to have gained a different kind of significance. It was first decided to award them to the officials at no cost, and then decided to award them to all classes of officials. As a result, tens of thousands were issued annually in the years after 930. *TCTC* 275, T'ien-ch'êng 1(926)/11/*chia-hsü*.

On the nature and function of *kao-shên* in T'ang and Sung times, see N. Niida, *Tō Sō Hōritsu Bunsho no Kenkyu*, pp. 793-806. Niida calls it 'a writ of

on later standards of recruiting for office must be considered.

Our sources for the years 923-926 have concentrated on the supreme power of Kuo Ch'ung-t'ao and his struggle with the imperial favourites and the eunuchs. It was a struggle which is shown to have brought the disaffection in the army to a climax early in 926. Apart from a few references to military personalities close to or disliked by the emperor, there is little to tell us how the provincial armies of mixed tribesmen and Chinese were reorganized into imperial armies or how they were integrated with the old Liang armies. The biographical material shows that the officers of the new Six Armies included commanders from Li Ts'un-hsü's crack troops as well as from the Liang armies, but there is no information about how the rank and file were distributed among them. Marshals were appointed to the Six Armies, but they were placed under the Controller of the Six Armies and Various Guards (*p'an liu-chün chu-wei shih*).[53] This office was finally given to Prince Chi-chi, but as he was already influential at the court as the heir apparent, there is no clue to the political power attached to the office. It was probably a titular one, like the Prince's other titles.

Li Ts'un-hsü did not immediately delegate any of his military powers at the capital. His top-ranking officers had each been

official appointment'. He reproduces part of the *kao-shên*, dated 755, found at Tun-huang by Aurel Stein (British Museum, S. 2575) in Plates XIII and XIV; and also quotes (on pp. 804-805) a Sung *kao-shên* of 996 found by P. Pelliot at Tun-huang (Pelliot 3290 in Paris).

[53] For the position of the *p'an liu-chün* with regards to the emperor who retained his personal troops around him, see T. Hori, 'Gōdai Sōshu ni okeru Kingun no hatten' *Tōyō Bunka Kenkyujo Kiyō*, 4, pp. 89-100, and H. Kikuchi, 'Gōdai Kingun ni okeru Jiei Shingun Shi no seiritsu' *Shien*, 70, pp. 66-70.

The biographical sources are the following (in the *CWTS* unless otherwise mentioned):

Li Ts'ün-hsü's officers	*Liang officers*
Chang Yen-ch'ao (129, 10a)	P'an Huan (94, 2b)
Chang T'ing-wên (94, 5b-6a)	Shên Pin (95, 8a)
Kuo Yen-lu (94, 7a)	Lu Ssŭ-to (90, 13a)
Hsiang-li Chin (90, 17a)	Yo Yüan-fu (*Sung Shih*, 254, 9a)
Li Chien-ch'ung (129, 5a-b)	An Ch'ung-yüan (*CWTS* Basic Annals, 30, 10a and 34, 3b-9a).
Hsia Lu-ch'i (*CWTS* Basic Annals, 31, 6a)	

rewarded with a province and others with a prefecture. All of them had been given troops with which to defend their territories and some of these had been drawn from the central army. In the event of a large-scale campaign, some of the provincial forces were recalled to augment the expeditionary army sent from the capital. There was a chief commander, Li Ssŭ-yüan, but he was also a governor and not permanently stationed at the capital.[54]

Of the army officers, there were two who dominated the court. They did so not through their position in the armies, but because they were imperial favourites. Chu Shou-yin had been Li Ts'un-hsü's domestic retainer since they were boys, while Yüan Hsing-ch'in, one of the imperial 'sons', had once saved his life. Because they were favourites, they were given higher commands than they merited. Chu Shou-yin was made the Chief Discipline Officer (*tu yü-hou*) against the advice of Li Ssŭ-yüan. In 2nd/924, the emperor revived the Liang practice of having a commander of the troops at the capital and appointed Chu Shou-yin commander, that is, as the deputy to the emperor himself. In this position, Chu Shou-yin was able to deny help to save the emperor from the mutiny of the imperial bodyguards two years later.[55] As for Yüan Hsing-ch'in, so favoured that he could marry a favourite concubine of the emperor, he was given an expeditionary command at a critical time and his failure led indirectly to the revolt of Li Ssŭ-yüan.[56]

The decisive factor, however, in the influence of army officers was the relationship they could establish with other groups close to the emperor. Both Chu Shou-yin and Yüan Hsing-ch'in were close to the imperial household, the eunuchs and the actor-favourites. Li Ssŭ-yüan was saved from suspicion of his loyalty by the friendship of a leading eunuch during the precarious first months of 926. And Kuo Ts'ung-ch'ien, the actor who became an officer in the imperial bodyguards in the four Ts'ung-ma Chih cavalry regiments, sought to strengthen his position by 'adopting' Kuo

[54] *CWTS* 35, *passim*, for Li Ssŭ-yüan's career before he became emperor; see Chapter Six.

[55] *CWTS* 74, 4b-5b; *TCTC* 275, T'ien-ch'êng 1(926)/4/*ting-hai*.

[56] *CWTS* 70, 1b-3a; *TCTC* 274, T'ien-ch'êng 1(926)/2/ *jên-yin*, *ting-wei*, ff. and 3/*ting-mao*, after *hsin-wei*, *chia-hsü* and *wu-yin*.

Ch'ung-t'ao as his uncle. He also became an adopted son of Prince Li Ts'un-ngai who was Kuo Ch'ung-t'ao's son-in-law. Our sources suggest that had the 'uncle' and 'father' not been executed, Kuo Ts'ung-ch'ien would not have led the mutiny which caused the death of the emperor on 1/4th/926.[57]

Chu Wên and Li Ts'un-hsü had set out to fight for the throne and found their dynasties. They represented the initial struggle to replace a distinguished but weak dynasty. In the process of doing so, they had both found it necessary, for different reasons, to retain the framework of T'ang government.

Within that framework, Chu Wên had introduced a new factor of imperial power. This was his provincial staff, consisting of men of lowly origins who replaced the eunuchs and ousted some of the bureaucrats from the palaces altogether. Chu Wên was not, however, hostile to bureaucratic institutions. The T'ang bureaucrats were deprived of active political power, but the administrative functions of the bureaucracy remained. In this way, the bureaucrats prepared for the time when their traditional power could be restored to them.

The T'ang Restoration reacted against the Liang developments in two ways, both somewhat superficially. The eunuchs were brought back and aristocratic government was made respectable again. But Li Ts'un-hsü's long years as a governor made him unable to restore all T'ang practices. His provincial and retainer staff were brought into the palace service alongside the eunuchs. The abler members of his staff were raised to the highest court offices, and the revived 'aristocratic government' was largely controlled by one of these men. Liang precedents could not be kept out of his government altogether. Eventually, the various compromises to accomodate the old and the new were to be the foundations on which his successor, Li Ssŭ-yüan, began to build up a new kind of court.

The Liang and the T'ang Restoration can further be compared

[59] *CWTS* 34, 11b-12a; *TCTC* 274, T'ien-ch'êng 1(926)/2/*chia-ch'ên* and 275, T'ien-ch'êng 1(926)/4/*ting-hai*.

through their policies towards the provinces. The instability of both the dynasties was chiefly the product of strong political and military pressure from the provinces. In the next chapter, the way the four emperors of 907-926 attempted to control the provinces and the extent to which they succeeded or failed are examined to complete the picture of the structure of power during this crucial transitional period.

CHAPTER FIVE

The Control of the Provinces 907-926

In Chapter Three, it was shown that when Chu Wên united all of Ho-nan under his control in 897, that control did not depend on his being appointed the governor of Ho-nan. All he had to do was to appoint his army officers and senior retainers to be governors of the existing provinces in the region. Once his power was consolidated, he could confidently extend it to the provinces in the adjoining regions of Ho-pei, Ho-tung, Kuan-chung and Shan-nan East. And as he conquered each province, he continued with the policy of appointing army officers and retainers as governors. In this way, it may be said that Chu Wên's new empire was largely modelled on that of the T'ang.

During the early stages of empire-building, there was no real control of the provinces short of conquest and Chu Wên had to fight long and hard for every province. But after 900, he accepted a system of alliances by which the governors of Wei, Chên and Ting in Ho-pei bowed to his claims to leadership. The bond with the governors of Wei and Chên was strengthened by the marriage of his daughters to their sons. But these provinces remained independent of Chu Wên's administrative machinery. Only Wei province submitted to some control in 906-907, but even there, he had to wait for the death of the governor in 910, three years after he was proclaimed emperor, before he could directly take over its government.[1] After this, Chu Wên was encouraged to try to take the neighbouring Chên province by force. The frailty of the alliances was soon apparent. When the Chên governor was driven to call in Chu Wên's great enemy Li Ts'un-hsü and his tribesmen to help him, the other Ho-pei 'ally', the governor of Ting province, refused to support Chu Wên. Within a month, most of Ho-pei

[1] *CWTS* 5, 9a; 149, 18a-b.

had become totally independent of the Liang empire.[2] From these campaigns in 910-911, it is clear that there still could not be any control over a province without a military victory. Imperial authority still had to be won in the field and the alliances were made only as a respite before a further struggle.

In the provinces Chu Wên had conquered, his relations with the governors of his own choice were more stable as might be expected. On the borders, he had sent his ablest generals as governors, several of them being concurrently commanders of expeditionary armies. By being expeditionary commanders, the governors were allowed to have with them large sections of the imperial armies. Although these troops were replaced and transferred from time to time, it is not known how frequently this was done and how successfully the transfers prevented the growth of strong personal loyalties between the governors and their men. The border provinces were not regarded as sources of public revenue. This often encouraged the governors to take advantage of their own military importance and neglect their administrative responsibilities to the centre.

Within Ho-nan itself, governors were not appointed for their military talents. Greater efforts were made to administer these provinces efficiently because of the revenue they yielded. Chang Ch'üan-i and Han Chien, for example, were employed as governors not because of any past service with Chu Wên but only because of their proven administrative genius.[3]

When Chu Wên became emperor, there were six leading governors in the empire, five on the borders and the sixth, Chang Ch'üan-i, in Ho-nan. Of the five men governing border provinces, three were officers who had been under some of Chu Wên's rivals and then had surrendered to him — Yang Shih-hou in 888, Liu Chih-chün in 891 and Chu Chien (adopted as a son) in 899.[4] The

[2] *CWTS* 27, 6a-9b; 54, 3b; and *TCTC* 267, K'ai-p'ing 4(910)/11/after *hsin-hai*, ff. and 12/*hsin-ssŭ*, ff., and Ch'ien-hua 1(911)/1/*ting-hai* and 2/*chi-wei*, ff.

[3] Chang Ch'üan-i, *CWTS* 63, 1a-7a. Han Chien, *CWTS* 15, 1a-4a; his activities as an independent governor who contributed to the downfall of the T'ang dynasty have been briefly considered in Chapter Two.

[4] Yang Shih-hou, *CWTS* 22, 1a; Liu Chih-chün, *CWTS* 13, 9a; and Chu Chien (re-named Chu Yu-ch'ien), *CWTS* 63, 7a-b.

other two, Wang Ch'ung-shih and Kao Chi-hsing, were officers who had been with Chu Wên almost from the beginning. One of them had been specially recruited in Chu Wên's first years as governor and the other had been a retainer of an adopted son and was later taken into Chu Wên's own service.[5]

The sixth man, Chang Ch'üan-i, was, like Chu Wên, an old member of Huang Ch'ao's army. He was trusted with the control of the city of Lo-yang and also asked to direct from there the administration of Mêng (907-908), Shan (908-909) and Hua (910-911), all provinces in Ho-nan. He was entrusted with these posts chiefly because of his great experience in administration and his remarkable success in re-building Lo-yang from the ruins of several conflagrations.[6]

Of these six men, only Chang Ch'üan-i gave long service to the dynasty. Three of them were serious threats to Chu Wên's successors while Wang Ch'ung-shih and Liu Chih-chün gave him trouble in his lifetime. Of the latter two, the first was executed in 5th/909 for suspected treachery and the execution led to the rebellion of the second. This rebellion in turn gave the opportunity for another rising. The two rebellions proved to be very dangerous: the first almost cost Chu Wên his territories in Kuan-chung, and the other was crushed only after a difficult three months' siege by a large force.

The following features of the first revolt show some of Chu Wên's problems in the border provinces. Liu Chih-chün, the governor who led the rebellion, was called to Lo-yang in 5th/909 after the execution of his colleague and neighbour. His brother, who was kept as an officer and a hostage in Chu Wên's personal army, suspected that Chu Wên meant to kill Liu Chih-chün and, by a bluff, escaped to join him. When he decided to revolt, Chu Wên sent back

[5] Wang Ch'ung-shih, *CWTS* 19, 3a-b; Kao Chi-hsing, *CWTS* 133, 1a (as the founder of the small state based on Ching Chou on the Yangtse, his biography appears in several works, but there is no new information on his early life). The man whom Kao Chi-hsing served was Li Jang. On the origins of the latter and his adoption by Chu Wên, see Chapter Three, note 36.

[6] *CWTS* 63, 1a-7a and a detailed account of his service to Lo-yang in Chang Ch'i-hsien, *Lo-yang Chin-shên Chiu-wên Chi*, 2, 1a-6b (the importance of Chang Ch'i-hsien's account is noted in *Jung-chai Sui-pi*, 14, 3b-4b).

his nephew, another hostage, with a promise of full pardon. But the gesture was ignored. A great part of the imperial units stationed at the governor's capital supported the rebel and the Army Supervisor, the administrators and the officers who refused to join in the revolt were unable to stop them.[7] Then the garrison at Ch'ang-an which resented the recent execution of their governor also supported the rebellion and imprisoned their new governor. The rebels appealed to the neighbouring governor of Ch'i, one of Chu Wên's enemies, and received immediate help from him. The strategic T'ung-kuan Pass between Kuan-chung and Ho-nan was captured. It was only through the swift action of the commander of the Imperial Guards that the Pass was recovered and the Kuan-chung provinces saved.[8] The rebellion was crushed within one month, but it had been very dangerous and the results could not have been foreseen. The extremely high reward offered for the rebel governor alive—ten thousand strings of cash, the governorship of a province, a manor and a mansion at the capital[9]—suggests that there was some lack of confidence in the imperial officers. The section leader (*shih-chiang*), the camp official (*ya-kuan*) and twenty others who caught the governor's brothers were rewarded by a special edict which divided among the men a large cash reward and the monthly salary of a prefect.[10]

The second revolt followed quickly in 7th/909. This took place in Hsiang province (south-west of the Ho-nan region) and was the result of the recall of its governor to deal with the first rising. There seems to have been a struggle among three main groups at the provincial capital. When the governor left, the administration came into the hands of the hereditary garrison force (*ya-ping*). The new deputy governor (*liu-hou*) brought his own retainers with him and tried to take over again on behalf of the imperial government. The third group was stationed outside the governor's residence. This group consisted of units of the imperial armies assigned to the

[7] *CWTS* 4, 13b and *TFYK* 210, 17a-b and *TCTC* 267, K'ai-p'ing 3 (909)/6/*i-wei*.

[8] *CWTS* 13, 9b-10a; 22, 2a-b; 23, 3b; *TFYK* 218, 15a-b; and *TCTC* 267, K'ai-p'ing 3(909)/6/*i-wei* and 6/*i-mao*.

[9] *CWTS* 4, 10b-11a; *TFYK* 216, 19a-b.

[10] *CWTS* 4, 11a-b; *TFYK* 210, 21b-22b.

province and was led by the provincial commander and a number of other officers. When the mutiny led by the first group, the *ya-ping*, broke out, it was aimed at ousting the deputy governor and his retainer force. The commander and officers of the imperial troops outside were invited to join the revolt. This led to a bitter division in the army. The commander and his closest officers refused to support the rebellion and had to escape when other officers agreed to take over its leadership. The struggle was extended to the prefectures where the prefect of Fang supported the rebels and the prefect of Chün opposed them, each with his own unit of the imperial armies.[11] This gives a picture of how Chu Wên had depended on the natural antagonism of various groups to keep a form of balance in the provinces.

Two factors led to the defeat of the Hsiang rebels in 9th/909. One was the disunity of the garrisons which Chu Wên had counted on and quickly exploited. The other was the result of a long-term policy which deserves closer examination here. Two months before the revolt and after the governor had been recalled, the province was divided into two and its resources reduced by a third. Its two northern prefectures, forming the new province, were placed in loyal hands and these also provided an unobstructed route for imperial forces sent to crush the revolt. This division of large provinces into smaller ones was a T'ang policy which Chu Wên had already used in creating the province of Hsing (in Ho-pei) in 6th/908 and in cutting Fu province (in Kuan-chung) into two after its recapture in 4th/909. In 5th/909, two new provinces were created out of the metropolitan area of K'ai-fêng and the large Hsiang province. After the rebellion in T'ung province, its only other prefecture, Hua Chou, was raised to the status of a province; this is a remarkable example of how the concept of province was being radically changed, the two new provinces each consisting of no more than *one* prefecture. In 910, the next year, P'u province in Ho-tung was also divided in two. Thus in three years, from 4th/907 to 4th/910, seven new provinces were created, without any increase in territory in the Liang empire.

[11] *CWTS* 4, 13a-b; 64, 8a; and *TCTC* 267, K'ai-p'ing 3(909)/7/*wu-yin*; 8/*hsin-yu* and 9/*ting-yu*.

With one exception, Sung province created out of the old Pien province, the new provinces were created on the borders.[12] Although these divisions of the provinces did not altogether deter governors from rebellion, the long-term effect of having permanently reduced the resources available to at least six governors was an important contribution to the later attempts to control the provinces.

It has been shown how the five leading border governors were potential and actual threats to the Liang dynasty. There were, however, at least twelve others, not members of the imperial family, who were loyal during the rest of Chu Wên's reign. Of these, three were old friends from Huang Ch'ao's army, two were officers of the Pien army who had served Chu Wên since 883, two had been recruited from neighbouring garrisons, and three had been officers under Chu Wên's rivals and had surrendered in 886, 897 and 903 respectively. Of the remaining two, one was a surrendered governor who was valued for his administrative ability, and the other was a border Chinese who had helped to take Fu province (in Kuan-chung) in 909 and was in return given a small border

[12] Hsing province was first created out of the three Ho-pei prefectures of Lu province in 10th/883 (*TCTC* 255, Chung-ho 3(883)/10th month). Chu Wên captured Hsing province in 898 and broke it up again into three prefectures (*CWTS* 16, 3b; 16, 8a; and 22, 6a; and *T'ang Fang-chên Nien-piao*, 8, p. 7497). He created Hsing province again in 6th/908; *WTHY* 24, p. 292.

Fu province was cut up and Yen province created with a local army officer, Kao Wan-hsing, as governor (*CWTS* 132, 8a), but Fu province remained in Liang control only until 912 (*CWTS* 21, 5b) after which Kao Wan-hsing seized it for his brother, Kao Wan-chin. After the latter's death in 918, Fu and Yen provinces became one again under Kao Wan-hsing himself (*CWTS* 132, 8a-b).

Sung province was created out of the metropolitan area of K'ai-feng and Têng province out of Hsiang province; *WTHY* 24, pp. 292-293.

Hua province was created in T'ang times and Han Chien governed it for fifteen years (887-901), but Hua Chou was attached to T'ung province in 905 (*T'ang Fang-chên Nien-piao*, 8, p. 7493). It is not clear when it was made a province again. K'ou Yen-ch'ing is called Hua governor after Chu Wên came to the throne (in 907?; *CWTS* 20, 9a) and in 11th/909 (*CWTS* 5, 4a), but as Hua Chou was still under a prefect in 6th/909 (*TCTC* 267, K'ai-p'ing 3(909)/6/*i-wei*), it is probable that the province was not re-established until after Liu Chih-chün's rebellion in 6th/909.

Chin province was created out of P'u province in 4th/910; *WHTY* 24, p. 293.

province to govern.[13] No pattern of appointment can be seen, though it may be pointed out that the first ten men had all been Chu Wên's officers and had been rewarded for success in battle and that they had all been prefects and militia or defence commissioners before their provincial appointments.

The attempts by Chu Wên to strengthen his hold on the border provinces were largely undone when he was murdered by his illegitimate son, Chu Yu-kuei, who was in turn murdered by the supporters of another son, Chu Yu-chên. In the eight months of the struggle between the half-brothers, four governors indicated their independence, the two in the Shan-nan East region (modern Hupei province), the adopted brother at P'u (in Ho-tung) and the commander of the Ho-pei expeditionary army. In addition to this, the governor of Fu was murdered and his province fell into the hands of the governor of the neighbouring Yen province. There was also a mutiny in $Hsü_3$ province and the murder of its able and loyal governor.[14]

Chu Yu-chên ascended the throne in 2nd/913. He managed to do this with the support of Yang Shih-hou, an expeditionary commander and also governor of Wei province. As a result of this

[13] The following twelve men were Chu Wên's governors in 909-912; references are from the *CWTS*:

1) The three from Huang Ch'ao's army: Chang Kuei-pa (16, 8b); Hua Wên-ch'i (90, 8b); Chang Kuei-hou (16, 10b).

2) The two from the Pien provincial army: K'ou Yen-ch'ing (20, 9a); Liu Han (20, 3b-4a).

3) The two recruited from garrisons neighbouring Pien Chou: K'ung Ching (64, 7b; also see *TCTC* 268, Ch'ien-hua 2(912)/end of year); Ho Tê-lun (21, 13a).

4) The three officers of Chu Wên's rivals: Niu Ts'un-chieh, 886 (22, 7b); K'ang Huai-ying, 897 (23, 11a-b); Liu Hsün, 903 (23, 3a-b).

5) The remaining two were Han Chien, the surrendered governor (15, 3b), and Kao Wan-hsing, the border Chinese (132, 8a).

[14] For the eight months, 6th/912-2nd/913, the most detailed material is found in *TCTC* 268, Ch'ien-hua 2(912)/6/*wu-yin* to Ch'ien-hua 3(913)/2/*kêng-yin*.

The four governors who became independent were Kao Chi-hsing of Ching (*CWTS* 133, 1b), K'ung Ching of Hsiang (*TCTC* 268, Ch'ien-hua 2(912)/end of year), Chu Yu-ch'ien of P'u (*CWTS* 63, 7b-8a) and Yang Shih-hou who declared himself governor of Wei (*CWTS* 22, 3a-b). The murdered governor of Fu was Hsü Huai-yü (*CWTS* 21, 5b-6a) and that of $Hsü_3$ was Han Chien (*CWTS* 15, 3b-4a; *TCTC* 268, Ch'ien-hua 2(912)/6/*ping-shên*).

support, he could do little to try to recover his father's control over the extensive and wealthy Wei province until Yang Shih-hou died two years later in 3rd/915. The court was so relieved to hear of Yang Shih-hou's death that the formalities of official mourning could barely be kept up, and the ministers lost no time in cutting Wei province into two.[15]

The division of Wei province in the 3rd to 7th months of 915 was a crucial event in Liang history. The Wei provincial army refused to be broken into two together with the province, and being larger than the retainer force of the new governor, defeated this force and arrested the new governor. The events show the uncertain relationship between that provincial army and the imperial armies. 60,000 men of the imperial forces were stationed about twenty miles south of Wei Chou but only 500 men were sent into the city as the court was afraid to force the issue with the army. When the revolt came, the small imperial force was helpless against the Wei army and its commanding officer barely escaped with his life.[16] This led to the eventual loss of the province and all territories in Ho-pei to Li Ts'un-hsü, leader of the T'ang loyalists.

Although the Liang emperors failed to subdue the border provinces, considerable progress was made in dealing with the provinces in Ho-nan. This was clearly a minimum achievement for an 'empire'. Much, in fact, had already been done by Chu Wên during the last years of T'ang. Nevertheless, the progress in Ho-nan was his chief contribution as emperor to the task of centralization under the later dynasties. By integrating the provinces there, he established a firm base for ventures into other regions. The fact that no rebellion in Ho-nan was ever successful throughout the Wu-tai period testifies to his success.[17]

[15] *CWTS* 22, 3b-4b; 8, 7b; *TCTC* 268, Ch'ien-hua 3(913)/2/after *jêng-wu* and *kêng-hsü*; 269, Chên-ming 1(915)/3/after *ting-mao*.

[16] *CWTS* 8, 8a-10b; 23, 4a-6a; 21, 9b-10a; *TCTC* 269, Chên-ming 1(915)/3/ *chi-ch'ou* to 7th month, *passim*.

[17] During the reigns of Chu Wên's sons (912-923), three rebellious governors in Ho-nan were removed. The governor of $Hsü_2$ on the south-eastern border was defeated in 914-915 in spite of some help from the armies of Huai-nan; *CWTS* 8, 6b-7a and *TCTC* 269, Ch'ien-hua 4(914)/9th month and Chên-ming 1(915)/2nd month.

In 918-919, the surrendered officer from Yu Chou, Chang Wan-chin, who

The background to the Liang integration of Ho-nan can be filled in by a survey of the imperial links with the provincial governments. Army Supervisors (*chien-chün shih*) were appointed for those governors who commanded the imperial armies to battle, but there is no record of their activities in the provinces themselves. Nor is there record of the Military Deputies (*hsing-chün ssŭ-ma*) who were important figures during the T'ang.[18] Their place in the provincial armies seems to have been taken by the commanding officers of the imperial units stationed in the provinces, the Provincial Commanders (*ma-pu tu chih-hui shih*). These Commanders and their officers were probably known to the governors and nominated by them to their provinces. But this was not always so, as in the example of the Commanders in Hsiang province in 909, Liu Ch'i and Ch'ên Hui, who had been appointed independently of the new governors. Liu Ch'i had been Chu Wên's own retainer officer, and so had Chang Lang, another man who had a long career in prefectural and provincial armies. The Commanders had independent careers and some were promoted to be prefects

had been appointed governor of Yen province, rebelled and tried to get help from Li Ts'un-hsü. Although he was able to hold out against a siege for fourteen months, he was eventually defeated; *CWTS* 13, 14b and 9, 10a (and commentary); *TCTC* 270, Chên-ming 4(918)/8/*chi-yu* and 271, Chên-ming 5(919)/10th month.

In 921, one of the emperor's cousins rebelled at Ch'ên Chou and there was a chance of his brother, then governor of Shan province, coming to his help. Again, the imperial armies were quick to remove both the princes; *CWTS* 10, 4a-b, 6b, 8a-b; 12, 1b; *TCTC* 271 Lung-tê 1(921)/4th month and 7th month.

After the Liang, there were the risings of Chu Shou-yin at K'ai-fêng in 927 (*CWTS* 74, 5b), of Chang Ts'ung-pin at Lo-yang in 937 (*CWTS* 97, 5a), of Yang Kuang-yüan at Ch'ing Chou in 943-944 (*CWTS* 97, 8b-9a) and finally that of Mo-jung Yen-ch'ao in 952 (*CWTS* 112, 3a-5b, *passim*). But none of the risings succeeded. Only that of Chang Ts'ung-pin at Lo-yang was a serious threat to the reigning emperor and this was because of the mutiny of a large part of the imperial armies while on their way to a campaign against a rebel governor in Ho-pei; *TCTC* 281, T'ien-fu 2(937)/6/after *ting-wei*.

[18] It is possible that during the Liang, Military Deputies were not appointed and that Provincial Commanders were the highest military men under the governors; cf. the events of the Hsiang rebellion in 909 (*TCTC* 267, K'ai-p'ing 3(909)/7/*wu-yin*).

Examples of Army Supervisors later in the Liang are Tuan Ning, the ex-palace officer (*CWTS* 73, 3b-4a) and Chang Han-chieh, the Empress Chang's brother (*CWTS* 10, 10b and 30, 1a).

in prefectures not under the control of their previous governors.[19]

The assistant governor (*fu-shih*), usually a bureaucrat, also had a greater importance than in the T'ang. When the governor was away in the battlefield, the responsibility for defence and government was left to his assistant and the Provincial Commander. For example, when the governor of Yün was murdered by mutineers in 9th/916, it was the assistant governor, P'ei Yen, who led the provincial troops against the mutineers. A few months later, P'ei Yen became a prefect.[20]

[19] Liu Ch'i, *CWTS* 64, 8a; Ch'ên Hui; *CWTS* 5, 1b and *TFYK* 435, 2a-b (also see *TCTC* 267, K'ai-p'ing 3(909)/7/*wu-yin*), and Chang Lang, *CWTS* 90, 14b-15b.

Liu Ch'i rose from being Chu Wên's retainer officer to be an officer in Hua and then Hsü$_2$ province before going to Hsiang; and neither of the Hsiang governors, Yang Shih-hou (905-909) and Wang Pan (909) had ever been at Hua and Hsü$_2$ provinces. Chang Lang was an officer in two prefectural armies and one provincial army before becoming Provincial Commander at Yün province under Tai Ssŭ-yüan (*CWTS* 64, 5a-b). But in the battles north of the Huang Ho he fought under Tuan Ning, the Army Supervisor (see *CWTS* 10, 9a), and was promoted prefect. After his promotion, however, the new Provincial Commander, Yen Yung, was left to defend the provincial capital, Yün Chou (*CWTS* 10, 9b), while Tai Ssŭ-yüan commanded the imperial armies in battle.

Other examples of a Provincial Commander's independent career were Chu Ching and Huang Kuei. Chu Ching had been Commander at Yün province before being appointed prefect in 917 to another province under a different governor (*CWTS* 9, 1a). Huang Kuei had been Commander for several years under Huo Yen-wei of Pin province and then was made a prefect in Hsü province and then in Chin province while Huo Yen-wei was transferred to Hua and then to Yün province (*CWTS* 8, 11a; 9, 4b and 7a-b; 9, 1a; and 64, 1b).

On the other hand, Chiang K'o-fu was his governor's *ya-ya* (and thus was probably in his governor's retainer service) as well as Provincial Commander. His promotion to prefect may have been due to the court's desire to separate him from his governor; *CWTS* 9, 5a.

Y. Sudō, in his article 'Gōdai Ketsudoshi no Shihai Taisei', *Shigaku Zasshi*, pp. 304-309, lists all the Commanders in the Wu-tai without distinguishing between the governor's retainer commanders (*ya-nei tu chih-hui shih*), often the governor's sons, and the emperor's own officers or officers in the imperial armies sent to command units in the provinces. Although the two kinds of Commanders were not always distinguishable, I think there is enough evidence for us to think that the Provincial Commanders in the Liang were appointed by the court and were not part of the governor's own organization.

[20] *CWTS* 22, 10a; *TCTC* 269, Chên-ming 2(916)/9/*chi-mao*; and *CWTS* 9, 1b.

There was the appointment of bureaucrats, as in the T'ang, to serve as administrators, secretaries and legal administrators, but most of them seem to have been nominated by their governors. In Ch'ing province, for example, Wang Chêng-yen the administrator was the governor's nominee and he followed his governor when he was transferred to the Ho-pei province of Wei. When the governor surrendered to Li Ts'un-hsü soon afterwards, Wang Chêng-yen was obliged to continue under Li Ts'un-hsü and work against the Liang.[21] The career of Wang I-chien, however, was different. He was a protégé of the governor of Shan (in Ho-nan), Prince Chu Yu-hui. After graduating as a *chin-shih*, he held successive secretarial posts under the governors of Pin and Hua (both in Kuan-chung). When the Hua governor was recalled, he continued under the new governor Yin Hao. He retired after Yin Hao's death, but later served another governor, this time at Têng province (in Ho-nan).[22] His career reflects an independence of both the court and the governors and emphasizes his purely

The function of the assistant governor is not very clear. In the Ho-pei province of Wei, the governor, Yang Shih-hou (6th/912-3rd/915) had Li Ssŭ-yeh as his assistant. When the governor died in 915, the garrison force built up by him, the *Yin-ch'iang Hsiao-chieh* regiment, mutinied and killed Li Ssŭ-yeh (*CWTS* 69, 5b). This suggests that Li Ssŭ-yeh may have been a loyal bureaucrat appointed by the court who was hostile to Yang Shih-hou's private army. Yet he does not seem to have had control over any imperial force in the province.

[21] *CWTS* 69, 4a; *TCTC* 269, Chên-ming 1(915)/6/*kêng-yin*.

It must be noted that while most of the original provincial staff of Wei province remained there throughout the period of Liang domination (906-915), many members were drawn into the Liang court. Examples were Sun Chih (*CWTS* 24, 3b-4a), K'ung Mieh (*TFYK* 729, 14b; and 513, 11a; see *CWTS* 68, 6a) and Liu Tsan (*CWTS* 68, 7a-b).

There is indirect evidence that the provincial officials were appointed by the court some time before the fall of the Liang. See *WTHY* 25, p. 301, in the memorial of 8th/924 (also in *CWTS* 149, 13b).

[22] *Sung Shih* 262, 8a. After being the protégé of Prince Chu Yu-hui, he served Han Kung, the governor of Pin (after 916) and Li Pao-hêng, the governor of Hua (until 918). Yin Hao died some time after 920. Wang I-chien retired and then served two short terms of office at the Liang court before going to Têng province. If this last appointment was in 923, it is probable that he served Tai Ssŭ-yüan who had just been disgraced for being defeated in battle (*CWTS* 64, 5b; *TCTC* 272, T'ung-kuang 1(923)/Intercalary 4th/*kuei-mao*).

administrative functions. But the non-committal attitude to imperial politics of both Wang Chêng-yen and Wang I-chien was characteristic of many Liang bureaucrats. The attitude was largely brought about by the fact that the bureaucrats were never in a position to check their governors in any way.

The most important imperial policies towards the provinces were those aimed at limiting the governor's power as far as possible to his own prefecture. The average province had two or three prefectures apart from that controlled by the governor. It has been noted that Chu Wên restored the status and privileges of the other prefects by appointing some of them from distinguished officers of the imperial army. These officers had fuller control of their own garrisons than had been previously possible and were in a better position to resist any attempts by the governor to encroach upon their rights. For example, in the revolt in Hsiang province in 909, it has already been shown how the prefects were free to choose which side they wanted to support. The independence of the prefects was also safeguarded by appointments which prevented a governor from having his subordinate officers as prefects in his own province and from sending such officers to usurp the prefects' powers.[23]

Another means of protecting the status of the prefects was to raise several important prefectures to be special defence or militia

[23] In 9th/910, for example, Chu Wên was actually able to extend his Ho-nan practice to Ho-pei as the following edict illustrates:

'The prefects of the province of Wei-po have, of late, left the administration to inspecting officers (*tu-yu* 督郵, officers sent by the Inspectors, *kuan-ch'a shih*, i.e. the governors) thus allowing the departmental officials (*ts'ao-kuan* 曹官) to usurp authority and rendering the prefects superfluous. In order to accord with established practice and to stop irregularities, all the prefects are allowed to assume sole control (*chuan-ta* 專達) according to the regulations of the various prefectures in Ho-nan.' (*CWTS* 149, 18a; *TFYK* 191, 8b-9a, which is quoted in *CWTS* 5, 9a-b).

This reform of local government was modelled on the recommendations made to T'ang Hsien-tsung almost a century earlier (see Chapter Two, note 2). That the Liang re-employed this method of control so long afterwards and found it effective reflects the persistence of the problem, if not also the lack of a more original solution to it.

areas in which the prefects were made concurrently defence or militia commisioners. Three defence and three militia prefectures (*fang-yü* and *t'uan-lien chou*) had been created by the end of the Liang, further reducing the resources of the governors of at least four provinces, those of Yün and Hua and those of Sung and Hsü$_2$, the provinces to the north-east and to the south-east of K'ai-fêng. The commissioner was allowed the independent control of more troops than was the prefect and could also communicate directly with the court on military matters.[24] It seems likely that these commissioner-prefects, as well as the ordinary prefects, were allowed to nominate their own staff of administrators and secretaries or to have them appointed by the court, and that a governor could not influence the appointments in the subordinate prefectures of his provinces.[25]

In this way, the governor's control over his subordinate prefects

[24] During the latter half of the T'ang, the court dealt with the prefectures of each province through the governor and did not communicate directly with each prefect. But by the end of Liang, even prefects who were not defence or militia commissioners dealt directly with the Commission of State Finance; *TCTC* 273, T'ung-kuang 2(924)/10/*hsin-wei*.

The three defence prefectures were Chêng Chou (of Hua province), Ch'i Chou (of Yün) and Ju Chou (probably of Hsü$_3$), *CWTS* 21, 10a, and 9, 2a-b; and the three militia prefectures were Po Chou and Ying Chou (of Sung province) and Su Chou (of Hsü$_2$), *CWTS* 20, 9a, and 16, 10b (the *T'ai-p'ing Huan-yü Chi*, 12, 11b, says that Po Chou was made a defence prefecture in 908).

[25] Wang Chêng-yen, for example, was nominated by his prefect, Ho Tê-lun, at Mi Chou, and continued in his service through two provincial appointments (*CWTS* 69, 4a). It is doubtful if the governor of Yen province (of which Mi Chou was a prefecture) had anything to do with Ho Tê-lun's choice. There is also the example of Chang Hsi, the administrator of Ti Chou, who was in the service of his prefect, Liu Chün-to, and was actually able to arrest one of the retainer officers sent by the governor; *Sung Shih* 262, 10a.

Some of the prefects seem to have controlled the *chên* garrison towns in their prefectures. The Su Chou militia commissioner and prefect, Yüan Hsiang-hsien, for example, was himself commander of Yung-ch'iao *chên* (*CWTS* 59, 8a); and it is possible that T'ung-hsü *chên* in Su Chou was under the prefect and not under the governor of the province of Hsü$_2$ (*TFYK*, 425, 23a). Also, Yeh-hsien *chên* was probably under the control of the prefect of Ju Chou (*TFYK* 435, 2b).

I have not dealt with the prefectural administrators and various secretaries because the Liang made no significant changes from the T'ang except to reduce the number of departmental secretaries from six to one in 10th/908 (*CWTS* 149, 11b).

was pruned down to personnel and financial supervision. These powers were officially placed in the hands of the Inspectorate administrator and secretary (the *kuan-ch'a p'an-kuan* and *chih-shih*). However, the governor's personal staff could, under cover of this office, exert pressure on the prefects concerning tax deliveries and possibly commercial enterprises, but this did not give the governor much scope for expanding his own military power. In fact, during the reign of Chu Yu-chên (913-923), the Commissioner for State Finance, Chao Yen, was able to ignore the governors and deal directly with the prefects, allowing them to petition and report to the court without reference to the governors at all.[26]

The independence of the prefect curtailed the power of the governor in another way. A major factor in provincial affairs during the T'ang had been the primarily unofficial influence of the local families, the 'Bureaucrat Families' (the *kuan-hu*), the 'Powerful Families' connected either with officialdom or the various armies within the empire (the *hsing-shih hu*) and other families with wealth and strong local ties (the *yu-li hu*, *hao-min*, *fu-hu*, etc.).[27] These families had risen as a consequence of the widespread development of manors and estates, and their position was usually both stable and permanent. Part of the function of each governor and prefect was, in fact, to be the link between the court and these families, to get their support for the régime as well as to act as a check on their great influence. In the course of doing so, both the governor and the prefect could hope to get strong local support for themselves.

During the Liang, the governors in Ho-nan had been prevented from having too strong a local support by being transferred frequently and at intervals of two to three years. But the use of independent prefects in their provinces was probably a more important factor. The prefects could limit the governor's share of local support to his own prefecture and, in this way, limit the

[26] *TCTC* 273, T'ung-kuang 2(924)/10/*hsin-wei*.

[27] Y. Sudō, 'Tōmatsu Gōdai no Shoen sei', *Chūgoku Tochi Seidoshi Kenkyu*, pp. 12-34.

number of families which could help him achieve independence from central control.[28]

The potential military power of a governor in Ho-nan was also successfully limited by the Liang emperors. This had been achieved by firm control of the provincial armies, by the revival of authority amongst the prefects and by the reduction in size of many of the provinces. Although a governor retained many social and economic privileges, there was an extension of central power. The problem was how this power could be extended farther to other regions.

It is true that the subjugation of Ho-nan was the result of twenty-nine years of constant fighting by Chu Wên, the longest period of empire-building granted to an emperor at this period. But he was the first man who did create some order in North China out of the empire broken up during the Huang Ch'ao rebellion. The inability to extend that order himself and to ensure that his successors could preserve it should not be allowed to hide the important though limited advances he made.

In contrast, the military victories of Li Ts'un-hsü, the leader of a

[28] I have drawn this hypothesis from observing the nature of revolts against the throne by governors in Ho-nan before and during the Liang and by comparing them with revolts by governors elsewhere during the early half of the Wu-tai.

The revolts in Ho-nan during the Liang were marked by the quick isolation of the governors in their provincial capitals and comparatively short sieges (see note 17 above). But during the T'ang up to 903, for example, it was necessary to take Ch'ing province prefecture by prefecture; *TCTC* 264, T'ien-fu 3(903)/3/*wu-wu* to 9/*wu-wu*, *passim*.

As for revolts elsewhere during the first twenty years of the Wu-tai, Liang Mo-ti was not only unable to remove any of Chu Yu-ch'ien's prefects from P'u province (in Ho-tung) but eventually lost a whole province (that of T'ung in Kuan-chung) to Chu Yu-ch'ien's son; *TCTC* 271, Chen-ming 6(920)/4/*chi-yu* to 9th month. Also, the fact that the governors of Chên, Ting and P'u had their own prefects and therefore the full resources of their respective provinces made Li Ts'un-hsü respect their rights and be content to have them as allies. In 921, Chên province fell prefecture by prefecture (*TCTC* 271, Lung-tê 1(921)/8/*chia-tzŭ*, ff.) and in 926, when the governor of P'u was executed, all the seven men he had appointed as prefects were also executed (*CWTS* 34, 2a-b; 63, 9a; *TCTC* 274, T'ien-ch'êng 1(926)/1/*kêng-ch'ên*). And as late as 928, the Ting governor dared to rebel because he had all the resources of his province of three prefectures; *TCTC* 276, T'ien-ch'êng 3(928)/4/*kuei-ssŭ* and 5th month.

confederation of tribal and Chinese armies and a professed T'ang loyalist, tend to obscure the failure of his administrative policies in his provinces. Li Ts'un-hsü was a great soldier who in 908 inherited three provinces from his father. Two years later, two governors in Ho-pei requested his help against Chu Wên, and after his victory early in 911, he became their acknowledged leader. By 914, he had captured the greatly coveted province of Yu and appointed a governor to it. Only three provinces in Ho-pei remained in Liang hands and these fell to him in 915-916 when the mutineers of Wei invited him to take over the control of that province. Within nine years he had gained territories almost as extensive as those the Liang had ever controlled. Of these provinces, apart from Ping and Wei which he governed personally, six were in the hands of men chosen by him or his father, while the two independent provinces of Chên and Ting lay enclosed by territories (Yu, Hsing and Ts'ang provinces) governed by his nominees.[29]

The first appointment as provincial governor had been made by Li Ts'un-hsü's father who sent the chief commander of his army, Li Ssŭ-chao, to Lu province in 12th/906. The latter remained there till his death in 922. There was no question of transferring or recalling him. Only a frail link, a eunuch Army Supervisor who played a passive role, bound him to Li Ts'un-hsü. In the sixteen years he was governor, Li Ssŭ-chao accumulated great wealth and left an immense fortune which his sons were able to use to turn against Li Ts'un-hsü and support the Liang as they did at a critical time in 3rd/923.[30]

As for the governors Li Ts'un-hsü appointed himself, the striking fact was that few of them actually governed their provinces.

[29] *CWTS* 27, 6b, ff.; 28, 1a-7b; *TCTC* 267, K'ai-p'ing 4(910)/12/*hsin-ssŭ* to 269, Chên-ming 1(915)/6/*kêng-yin*, *passim*.

At the end of 916, the six provinces governed by his or his father's nominees were Lu, Yün and Chên-wu in or north of Ho-tung and Yu, Hsing and Ts'ang in Ho-pei.

[30] Biography of Li Ssŭ-chao, *CWTS* 52, 1a-6a, which ends with a comment on his wife's ability to amass a large fortune for the family; and the biographies of his seven sons, *CWTS* 52, 6b-8b. Also *TCTC* 271, Lung-tê 2(922)/4/*chia-hsü* and 272, T'ung-kuang 1(923)/3rd month.

They retained their commands in Li Ts'un-hsü's central armies and several of them fought alongside him. Because he had also inherited his father's organization, Li Ts'un-hsü's choice of governors for each province was limited. Of the seven governors appointed before 923, all had started their careers as his father's retainer or army officers and stood in some order of seniority. Their appointments seem to have followed this order with the exception of Li Ts'un-chang, who was the oldest surviving member of his father's earliest supporters and a man experienced in administration and army training. More important, of the other six, five were his adopted brothers and cousins, all of them about twenty to thirty years older than he. They were indeed loyal officers, but their place in the family and their ranks in the army had predetermined their choice as governors.[31]

Li Ts'un-hsü had had considerable trouble with his allies in Ho-pei and it was not till late in 922 that he cleared Ho-pei of his potential enemies. But in Ho-nan he had no comparable difficulty. Once the Liang armies surrendered at the gates of K'ai-fêng, all resistance ended. Even the border governors who could have been dangerous decided not to oppose him. Their joint submission created a different kind of problem. Leaving their armies behind in their provinces when they came to pay court to Li Ts'un-hsü

[31] The seven governors appointed before 923 were (references are from *CWTS*):

Li Ssŭ-chao (52, 1a-6a)
Chou Tê-wei (56, 1a-6a)
Li Ssŭ-pên (52, 9a-10a)
Li Ts'un-shên (also known as Fu Ts'un-shên, 56, 6b-10b)
Li Ts'un-chin (53, 5b-7a)
Li Ssŭ-yüan (35, *passim*—later T'ang Ming-tsung, see Chapter Six)
Li Ts'un-chang (53, 7b-8b).

Chou Tê-wei succeeded Li Ssŭ-chao as commander-in-chief, and while he was alive (he died in 12th/918), Li Ssŭ-pên, Li Ts'un-shên and Li Ts'un-chin had all, at one time or another, been his deputies. Li Ssŭ-pên was captured by the Khitans in 8th/916, so Li Ts'un-shên succeeded Chou Tê-wei. Li Ts'un-chin died in 9th/922, and Li Ssŭ-yüan became deputy to Li Ts'un-shên. After the latter's death in 5th/924, Li Ssŭ-yüan succeeded him.

With the exception of Chou Tê-wei and Li Ts'un-chang, the governors were 'false' sons of Li K'o-yung and his brothers. On their comparative ages, see M. Kurihara, 'Tōmatsu Gōdai no Kafushi Teki Ketsugo ni okeru seimei to Nenrei', *Tōyō Gakuho*, pp. 444-445.

was a form of blackmail. If they were arrested or even detained, eighteen provincial armies under new leaders drawn from their families or their provincial commanders could cause great trouble to the new imperial armies which had barely gained a foothold south of the Huang Ho. Since the governors had come to acknowledge his claims, Li Ts'un-hsü was forced to accept them on their own terms.

His immediate decision was to re-instate all of them and he even adopted several into the imperial family.[32] But he intended ultimately to replace them with men of his own choice, and this was done by transfers and recalls and by executions. By 3rd/926, the eighteen governors were reduced to six, excluding one who was actually re-employed after having been recalled to the capital. Table VII shows the rate at which this was done. The extension into the reign of Li Ssŭ-yüan has been included to show when the last of the Liang governors disappeared from the scene. The whole process took little more than five years, and the relative ease with which this was done was chiefly due to the Liang emperors' success in rendering most of their governors militarily weak.

[32] *CWTS* 30, 5b-10b; *TCTC* 272, T'ung-kuang 1(923)/10/*chi-ch'ou*.
The Liang governors who came to Li Ts'un-hsü's court were (references are from the *CWTS*):

Yüan Hsiang-hsien* (59, 7b-10a)
Tuan Ning* (73, 3a-5a)
Huo Yen-wei* (64, 1a-2b)
Wên T'ao* (73, 2b-3a)
Tai Ssŭ-yüan (64, 5a-b)
K'ung Ching (64, 7b)
Kao Chi-hsing (133, 1a-2b)
Chu Han-pin (64, 5b-7b)
Han Kung (no biography, 30, 10a-b)
Chang Chi-yeh (no biography, 30, 10a)
Chu Yu-ch'ien* (63, 7a-10b)
Chu Ling-tê* (son of Chu Yu-ch'ien, 63, 8a-9a)
Kao Yün-chên (no biography, 30, 10a)
Hua Wên-ch'i (90, 8a-9b)
Chang Yün (90, 5a-6b)
Wang Tsan (59, 5b-7a)
Liu Ch'i (64, 8a-b)
Kao Wan-hsing (132, 7b-8b)

(* refers to governors who were adopted by Li Ts'un-hsü as 'false sons' (*chia-tzŭ*))

I have included Wang Tsan of K'ai-fêng and not Chang Ch'üan-i of Lo-yang because Li Ts'un-hsü had moved the capital to Lo-yang.

Li Ts'un-hsü executed one governor who was arrested at the capital. He was Chu Kuei, governor of Ch'ing (*CWTS* 30, 3b).

TABLE VII[33]

Re-employment of Liang governors, 923-928

	923	924	925	3rd 926	12th/ 926	927	928
Nos. re-employed at beginning of period	18	17	11	10	7	4	3
Died (d) or killed (kd)	1(d)	1(d)	1(d)	2(kd)	—	—	2(d)
Recalled	—	5	1	1	4	1	1
Retained in same province	15	6	3	2	1	1	—
Transferred	2	5	5	4	2	1	—
Re-employed after recall	—	—	1	1	1	1	—
Total still employed at end of period	17	11	10	7	4	3	—

Li Ts'un-hsü dealt successfully with two other governors in North China who had remained independent of the Liang. The provinces of Ch'i and Ching on the western borders of Kuan-chung were governed by a father and son who also bore the T'ang

[33] Biographical references of the eighteen governors have been given in note 32 above. More details on their later appointments and their replacement by Li Ts'un-hsü's own men (or later, by Li Ssŭ-yüan's) are found in the *CWTS* Basic Annals (chüans 30 to 39).

In the table, Wang Tsan died in 923, Yüan Hsiang-hsien in 924, and Kao Wan-hsing in 925. The two killed in 926 were Chu Yu-ch'ien and his son, Chu Ling-tê, and the two who died in 928 were Kao Chi-hsing and Huo Yen-wei. The deaths of Kao Wan-hsing and Kao Chi-hsing were not followed by the appointment of new governors from the court. In both cases, their sons succeeded them. Both the provinces were on the border and successfully resisted direct control from the court.

The governors recalled in 924 were Han Kung, Kao Yün-chên, Wên T'ao, Hua Wên-ch'i and Chu Han-pin. Tai Ssŭ-yüan was recalled in 925 and Chang Chi-yeh in 2nd/926. Those recalled after 4th/926 were Tuan Ning, K'ung Ching, Liu Ch'i and Hua Wên-ch'i who had been re-employed in 925. Chang Yün was recalled in 927 and Tai Ssŭ-yüan, who was re-employed in 5th/926, was recalled in 928. (Only one man was re-employed after 928. He was Chu Han-pin in 5th/929, who had made an alliance with the powerful Commissioner of the Military Secretarist, An Ch'ung-hui. He was finally recalled when An Ch'ung-hui was executed in 931).

imperial surname Li. Li Mao-chên, whose part in destroying the T'ang between 895 and 903 has already been considered (in Chapter Two), did not himself come to pay court but sent his son instead. The relations with the new T'ang court were simplified by his death in 4th/924. His son was allowed to succeed him at Ch'i and another son kept a hold on Ching. There was no resistance to the new dynasty, and the two sons were adopted as 'false' sons of Li Ts'un-hsü. In 925, they were completely awed by the army sent through Ch'i territory to conquer Shu.[34] In North China, only the two provinces in the Ordos north-west of Kuan-chung evaded Li Ts'un-hsü's control.[35]

The ruler of Shu in modern Szechuan and south Shensi was openly defiant, and less than two years after the capture of K'ai-fêng, the imperial armies were despatched against him. Within two months, from 9th-11th/925, nine provinces yielded with the collapse of Shu.[36] Li Ts'un-hsü had fulfilled a chief condition of empire-building—the swift extension of his empire. He did not, however, live to test his control of these new provinces. Four months later, his armies in Ho-nan and Ho-pei mutinied and the glorious T'ang Restoration was ended.

In the previous chapter, the swift collapse of Li Ts'un-hsü's armies in 3rd/926 was shown to have been largely owing to the distribution of the imperial armies at the time and the precarious balance of political power in the inner and outer palaces. But because the provincial governments were so closely involved with the military organization, the measures introduced to streng-

[34] *CWTS* 132, 1a-7a, biographies of Li Mao-chên and his two sons; *TCTC* 273, T'ung-kuang 2(924)/1/*kêng-hsü* and *kuei-ch'ou*; 4/after *i-hai* and 5/*jên-hsü*. In the Shu campaign, the governor of Ch'i was appointed commissioner in charge of military supplies and transport and was probably made to bear the burden of a considerable part of the initial outlay; *TCTC* 273, T'ung-kuang 3(925)/9/*ting-yu*.

[35] The two provinces in the Ordos were Hsia (under Li Jên-fu, *CWTS* 132, 10a-b) and Ling (under Han Shu, *CWTS* 132, 9a-b).

[36] For the start of the quarrel with Shu, *TCTC* 273, T'ung-kuang 2(924)/4 *chi-hsü* and 5/*wu-shên*. The swift victory against Shu in *TCTC* 273, T'ung-kuang 3(925)/9/*ting-yu*, ff.

The nine provinces were those of I (Ch'êng-tu), Tzŭ, Li, Sui and K'uei in Szechuan, Liang and Yang in south Shensi, Ch'in in Kansu and Ch'ien in northern Kueichow.

then the control over the provinces contributed a great deal to the disaffection of the commanders and officers.

The chief conflict of the court with the governors arose out of the appointments of eunuch Army Supervisors who had great influence at the palace. This was not new, there having been such Supervisors in all the provinces under Li Ts'un-hsü since 908. But they were unlike those in the later part of the T'ang dynasty who were powerless because imperial authority had been extremely weak then. By the time Li Ts'un-hsü became emperor, these Supervisors were men who could call on the support of a strong central army.[37]

At the same time, legislation was passed continuing the financial centralization of the last years of the Liang. The Commission for State Finance was given far-reaching control over all sources of revenue urgently needed to reward the imperial armies and maintain the new splendour and large staffs of an over-staffed court. The powers of the Commission were found irksome by the various governors as early as in 10th/924. There was a complaint lodged by the governors of Yün and Ch'ing against the Commissioner, K'ung Ch'ien, who had been appointed only two months previously. The governors accused him of directly controlling the prefectures without reference to the provincial government. He defended this as conforming to recent procedure. Although it was agreed that this Liang practice should be rejected and that the prefects should in future be approached through the governors, the Commissioner was able to ignore the edict and continue his direct control. This must have received the emperor's approval as he would not have dared to pursue his policy in the face of numerous powerful governors, including the eldest of the emperor's younger brothers, without at least his unofficial sanction.[38]

This complaint can also be considered as an expression of the

[37] In *TCTC* 274, T'ien-ch'êng 1(926)/3/after *ting-mao*, there are several instances of the Army Supervisor's power. In two cases, the governors were away, and the eunuchs sent their men against the retainers of the governors. In a third, the Supervisor tried to murder the governor. This suggests that the Supervisor had his own troops.

[38] *TCTC* 273, T'ung-kuang 2(924)/10/*hsin-wei*. Also in *HWTS* 26, 6a-b. The edict which was ignored appears briefly in *CWTS* 32, 7b.

governors' resentment against the scaling down of their privileges as compared with those of the prefects. For example, in 2nd/924, a memorial from the chief ministers had asked for a limit to be put on the number of friends or subordinates a governor could recommend to higher office. Three men per year were allowed to those whose provinces consisted of more than three prefectures, and two to those whose provinces consisted of three or less. This was a serious limitation for, by comparison, one man per year was allowed to the defence commissioners (*fang-yü shih*) who were no more than superior prefects.[39]

In the decree of 8th/924, the governors were allowed a wider choice of officials, the court appointing only the assistant governors and the two senior administrators. But more significant was the fact that the prefects were also allowed to nominate their staff.[40] This further confirmed the independence of the prefects.

The measures introduced by the new imperial government were incompatible with the accustomed autonomy of the late T'ang governors which was what some of the older ex-commanders probably expected from the Restoration. Many of them had been allowed to keep their large private armies. For example, the private army of the governor of Yu province was so large that when he died in 924, his son who was a mere prefect could not

[39] *WTHY* 24, p. 297; *CWTS* 149, 13a-b.

[40] *WTHY* 25, p. 301; and more briefly in *CWTS* 149, 13b.

This may also have been due to the policy of saving expenditure on salaries, see *CWTS* 73, 6a, which describes the recommendations of the Commissioner of State Finance, including one reducing the salaries of even court officials by half (also see *HWTS* 26, 6b). Another example is found in 4th/924 when there was a substantial cut in the number of provincial offices, designed to avoid redundancy and reduce expenses (*WTHY* 20, pp. 252-253).

A third example is the revised set of regulations concerning the salaries and allowances of the staff drawn up by the Commission for State Finance in 2nd/925. After requesting for a proclamation that the provincial governments should pay their staff according to the revised scales of salaries, there was included the following proviso:

'Apart from the assistant governor, the senior administrators, the secretary and the law administrator appointed (by the court), if the provincial office still appoints officials without authority, it is insisted that the governor of that province should himself meet the (salary) demands and may not draw upon the cash and goods pertaining to the government.' (*WTHY* 27, p. 336 and *TFYK* 508, 12a-b).

afford to maintain it and presented 8,700 of his men to the emperor.[41] As for Chên province, the governor's army of retainers was large enough to be distributed in three places at once in early 926—one group with the governor himself at the capital, another with his family in his provincial capital, Chên Chou, and a third with his eldest adopted son on patrol in Ho-pei.[42]

Apart from the accustomed autonomy of some of the governors, another factor contributing to the unstable relations between the court and the provinces was the varied origins of the governors. The tribal and border Chinese governors had had a special position in the court hierarchy, but there was a predominance of Chinese governors among those newly appointed after 923.[43] There were

[41] *CWTS* 32, 4a.

[42] In the accounts of Li Ssŭ-yüan's (the governor of Chên) revolt against Li Ts'un-hsü, the number of retainer officers by the governor's side can be seen; *CWTS* 34, 8a-b and 35, 7b-9b; *TCTC* 274, T'ien-ch'êng 1(926)/2/*chin-yin*, ff. In the biography of Wang Chien-li, the governor's retainers at Chên Chou are said to have saved his family from the Army Supervisor; *CWTS* 91, 4a and *TCTC* 274, T'ien-ch'êng 1(926)/3/before *kuei-yu*.

Li Ssŭ-yüan's eldest adopted son, Li Ts'ung-k'o, was sent on patrol, but on hearing of his father's revolt, he brought his troops together with the retainer army at Chên Chou to help him. He was most probably supported by a group of retainers in order to be able to persuade the imperial troops he was leading on patrol to join the revolt. *CWTS* 46, 2b and *TCTC*, *op. cit.*

[43] Of the seven governors appointed in the early years of Li Ts'un-hsü's leadership, 908-923 (see list of names in note 31 above), Li Ssŭ-yüan was a tribesman and Li Ts'un-shên was a Chinese from Ho-nan. The other five were from Ho-tung and the border regions north of Ho-tung and may have descended from sinicized tribesmen. By this time, however, they were 'border Chinese'.

After 923, twenty-eight new governors were appointed. Five of them were the emperor's brothers and only nominal governors for they do not seem to have left the imperial capital; see *HWTS* 14, 18b-21a. Of the other twenty-three, only seven were clearly tribesmen or border Chinese while sixteen were Chinese from various parts of North China (references are in *CWTS* unless otherwise mentioned):

Tribesmen

An Yüan-hsin (61, 2a-3b)
Chang T'ing-yü (65, 5a)
K'ang Yen-hsiao (74, 1a-4b)

Border Chinese

Kuo Ch'ung-t'ao (57, 1a-10b)
Chang Ching-hsün (61, 6b-7a)
Shih Ching-jung (55, 10a-b)
Chu Shou-yin (74, 4b-5b).

Chinese

Mêng Chih-hsiang (*HWTS* 64A, 1a-4b)
Chang Hsien (69, 1a-4a)
Lu Chih (93, 1a-2b)
Wang Chêng-yen (69, 4a-5b)

many who had served the Liang and, together with those Liang governors who had been re-employed, they found themselves new patrons either among the courtiers and the eunuchs of the inner palace or among the more senior governors. In this way, a new group whose loyalties were unpredictable were at work among the older adherents to the dynasty.[44]

The attempts at a greater degree of centralization were clumsy and inconsistent. Measures which had been introduced in Ho-nan after long years of preparation by the Liang emperors were too hurriedly adopted for other regions where local military power was still significant. They had been enforced by the intimidating presence of the eunuchs backed by the imperial armies. Thus, when the bulk of these armies was drawn off to the Shu campaign

Li Ts'un-hsien (53, 8b-10a)
Chao Tê-chün (98, 8b-10b)
Yüan Hsing-ch'in (70, 1a-3a)
Chu Ling-hsi (son of Chu Yu-ch'ien, 63, 9a-10a)
Mao Chang (73, 1a-2a)
Hsia Lu-ch'i (70, 3a-4a)
Tung Chang (62, 5a-8a)
K'ung Hsün (*HWTS* 43, 8b-10a)
Liu Hsün (61, 6a-b)
Chang Ts'ung-ch'u (alias Li Shao-wên, 59, 10b-11a)
An Ch'ung-yüan (90, 9b-10b)
Ch'ang Ts'ung-chien (94, 1a-2b).

Two other new governors were appointed, Li Ts'un-ching (*CWTS* 33, 8b) and Liu Ch'êng-hsün (appointed a deputy governor, possibly made a governor later on, *CWTS* 32, 15a), but no biographical information is available about the two.

Even if all the governors appointed in 908-926 are considered (including the five imperial brothers who were tribesmen), the number of Chinese is surprisingly high—seventeen out of thirty-five or almost half. And if the border Chinese were grouped with the Chinese instead of with the tribesmen, an even higher percentage would be reached, twenty-six out of thirty-five or about 74 %.

[44] Of the new governors (see list in note 43 above), K'ang Yen-hsiao, Tung Chang, Chu Ling-hsi, K'ung Hsün and An Ch'ung-yüan had served the Liang. Of these, Tung Chang had gained the good favours of Kuo Ch'ung-t'ao and K'ung Hsün those of K'ung Ch'ien, the Commissioner of State Finance. Chu Ling-hsi's father had initially bought the favours of several powerful eunuchs. In 926, K'ang Yen-hsiao, who resented Kuo Ch'ung-t'ao's liking for Tung Chang, started the critical Szechuan revolt, and late in 3rd/926, K'ung Hsün opened the gates of K'ai-fêng to the rebel Li Ssŭ-yüan.

Among the surviving Liang governors, Tuan Ning and Wên T'ao were prominent in winning favours with their great wealth at the new court among the eunuchs and the actor-favourites (*CWTS* 73, 4a-b and 3a). Huo Yen-wei became a follower of Li Ssŭ-yüan and supported his rebellion (*CWTS* 64, 1b-2b) and Chang Yün, also in possession of great wealth, turned against the prince Li Chi-chi in favour of Li Ssŭ-yüan at a critical time (*CWTS* 90, 5b-6a).

and various units mutinied both at home and in Szechuan, the governors who were able to do so quickly rid themselves of their intolerable burdens. In at least four provinces in Ho-nan and Ho-pei, the eunuch Supervisors were murdered.[45]

The murder of the Supervisors symbolized the end of a militant stage of provincial control. It is significant that one of the earliest and most important compromises made by Li Ssŭ-yüan six days after he took the throne on 14/4th/926, was to order the execution of the eunuch Supervisors and to discontinue their use altogether.[46]

This, among other compromises, was made to win the support of the provinces. It did not represent a breakdown of imperial control, but merely a retreat from the aggressive measures adopted by Li Ts'un-hsü. There was the need for more gradual methods of consolidation for the provinces in Ho-pei which had been independent for more than a century and a half, and for those in Ho-tung and Kuang-chung which had known no direct imperial interference for half a century. Only after two more decades of administrative reform and after the development of a new instrument of power, the Emperor's Personal Army, was it possible to extend the limited achievements of the Liang emperors in Ho-nan to the rest of North China.

I have so far emphasized the comparative success the Liang emperors had in depriving the Ho-nan governors of any considerable military power. But there were no notable changes during the whole period of 907-926 in the structure of local government which was built on the T'ang *chieh-tu shih* system. As long as this structure survived, the imperial government was never able to gain full control of the provinces.

This form of local government was based not on the bureaucrats and gentry sons appointed to provincial offices, but on the men who may be loosely grouped as 'retainers' (*yüan-sui*, *sui-shên* or

[45] *CWTS* 37, 2b-3b; 64, 7b; 91, 4a; *TFYK* 724, 20a; *TCTC* 274, T'ien-ch'êng 1(926)/3/after *ting-mao*.

[46] *CWTS* 35, 12a-b; *TCTC* 275, T'ien-ch'êng 1(926)/4/*kêng-tzŭ*. The compromises Li Ssŭ-yüan made to win the support of the governors are considered in Chapter Seven.

pu-ch'ü) and on the governor's personal staff (*ch'in-li*, *ya-li*). These men included relatives and household servants, armed bodyguards, and stewards in charge of the governor's landed property. They followed the governor from appointment to appointment. From time to time there were fresh recruits from all levels of society, frequently including bandits and soldiers of the imperial armies.[47]

The part played by these men in Chu Wên's rise to power has already been examined in Chapter Three. The important development after 907 was that the number of the governor's military retainers was at first subject to greater control. Only a few governors were permitted to have large private armies of personal troops as their *ya-chün*. After Chu Wên's death in 6th/912, however, this control was relaxed and Yang Shih-hou, for instance, built up the notorious Yin-ch'iang Hsiao-chieh regiment of several thousand men after he had seized Wei province. This regiment was so much larger than the retainer-group brought in by the new governor appointed in 3rd/915 that the governor's retainers were soon defeated in the mutiny which followed.[48] About this time, there is evidence that governors in Ho-nan were also allowed to have personal troops (*ch'in-ping*). The governor of Yün in 916 had gathered bandits into his service and was, in 9th/916, actually murdered by some of them.[49]

The *ya-chün* was essential to a governor's position. A governor who lost his *ya-chün* forfeited his right to govern, for he was no longer assured of his authority. But even if he had the support of a

[47] For the varied origins of the retainers and various levels of a governor's personal staff, cf. the researches of Y. Sudō, 'Gōdai Ketsudoshi no Yagun ni Kansuru ichi Kosatsu', *Tōyō Bunka Kenkyujo Kiyō*, *passim* (see brief references above, Chapter Three, note 6 and note 8).

See *CWTS* 22, 10b, which describes a Ho-nan governor during the Liang recruiting retainers from among bandits. Also *CWTS* 71, 6b, *TFYK* 716, 43b-44a, and *TFYK* 725, 13b-14a, which describe the career of an examination graduate, Shun-yü Yen, who joined the personal staff of Huo Yen-wei when the latter was only an army officer and remained with him until he became a governor. Shun-yü Yen was described as follows, 'although (he) was a private secretary (*mo-pin* 幕賓), (he) was like a family steward (*chia-tsai* 家宰)'.

[48] *CWTS* 8, 8b-9a; 21, 13a-b; 22, 3b-4b; *TCTC* 269, Chên-ming 1 (915)/3/ after *ting-mao*.

[49] *CWTS* 22, 10b; *TCTC* 269, Chên-ming 2(916)/9/*chi-mao*.

ya-chün, he still needed the acquiescence of the provincial army to his rule. Since there was a limit to the size of his retainer force beyond which it would arouse suspicion, the governor was more concerned with getting his retainer officers to command the local garrisons and the imperial troops sent to reinforce them. But this was not always possible, and he probably had to resort to influencing the appointments of the provincial commander and other officers of the local units of the imperial army. When the governor could do this, his armed retainers were kept to perform their original function of acting as his bodyguards or more intensively used in police and administrative duties.[50]

A relative, usually a son, led the armed retainers as the commander of the garrison at the governor's office and residence (the *ya-nei tu chih-hui shih*). Other retainers were headed by the *tu ya-ya* who were in fact the governor's deputies in most matters and especially in military and revenue administration. Under the *tu ya-ya* were four main groups of retainer-officials.[51]

Three of the groups worked mainly at the provincial capital. The most important were those *ya-li* called the *k'ung-mu kuan* (examining officials, chiefly of accounts) who were intermediaries between the imperial revenue departments and the county and village tax-collectors. They were responsible for problems of

[50] See pp. 121-128 and note 19 above. There is evidence that during Chu Wên's reign, the loyalty of retainer officers could not always be taken for granted. When Liu Chih-chün rebelled at T'ung Chou in 909, at least six of his *ya-ya* refused to rebel with him and had to be killed. Although Chu Wên's high posthumous rewards to these men point to their being a gratifying exception to the rule, the revolt in the governor's own ranks is significant. *TFYK* 210, 17a-b (quoted in *CWTS* 4, 13a-b).

[51] Y. Sudō, 'Gōdai Ketsudoshi no Shihai Taisei', *Shigaku Zasshi*, pp. 295-300, 311-313; 319-325; and 525 ff.

I have suggested a different way of grouping the governor's military retainers and personal staff from Professor Sudō's. Apart from the *tu ya-ya* (an equivalent to the *chung-mên shih* 中門使 in the areas controlled by Li Ts'un-hsü), there are roughly two groups of retainer officers (*ya-ya* 押牙), the *tu yü-hou* 都虞候 and the *chên-chiang* 鎮将, and two groups of executive staff (*ya-li* 牙吏), the *k'ung-mu kuan* 孔目官 and the *k'o-chiang* 客将 (also *t'ung-ying kuan* 通引官). In this way, the two sets of functions can be separated.

income and expenditure as well as for the organization of military supplies. Under them were special officers for tax supervision (*chien-chêng chün chiang*) sent to observe the work of the county magistrates and other officers given trading responsibilities (*hui-t'u chün-chiang*). The second group consisted of the men in charge of the governor's office, the adjutants and domestic retainers who arranged receptions for imperial envoys and representatives of other governors and prefects and also arranged interviews or hearings for others. These *k'o-chiang* or *t'ung-ying kuan* were not only protocol experts but were also advisers on 'external' affairs. The third group, the *tu yü-hou*, were probably members of the retainer garrison. They were officers in charge of military discipline, the military police and the prisons. They were also the governor's means of checking the provincial army and possibly its commanders as well when they were not men of the governor's own choice.[52]

The fourth group worked in the counties of the governor's prefecture. One of the chief ways a governor made full use of his resources was through these officers, the *chên-chiang* (also known as *chên-shih* or *chên-ngo shih*). They were sent to police the counties and supervise the magistrates (*hsien-ling*) from garrison towns called *chên*. The *chên* were developed at the expense of the *hsien* during the ninth century. The governors sent their senior retainers, each with a small force of retainers and with a team of clerks and accountants, to take over the control of the counties. Separate administrative offices were established at these *chên* which often became important towns and overshadowed the county capitals. Consequently, the magistrate's position fell to a lowly place and this was still so early in the Liang. Chu Wên found, on a visit to a *hsien* in T'ung Chou (in Kuan-chung), that the *chên* officer actually had a higher rank than the magistrate. He promptly reversed this in an attempt to revive the old authority of the magistrate.[53] But there was little improvement in the magistrate's position and the governors continued to send their own men to administer the counties.[54]

[52] Y. Sudō, *op. cit.*, pp. 311-313; and 319-325.

[53] *CWTS* 149, 18a and *WTHY* 19, p. 244; also *CWTS* 5, 6b, which quotes from *TFYK* 191, 8b.

[54] The development of the *chên* and the use of *chên-chiang*, etc. by the governors in the ninth and early half of the tenth centuries has been studied in great

I have not attempted to consider the details of the governor's organization which has been so exhaustively examined for the whole of the Wu-tai period by Professor Y. Sudō. The main features of the first two decades have been noted above in order to show the extent to which the provincial offices were duplicated. Almost every function, previously the sole responsibility of a court-approved bureaucrat, was now shared, if not actually usurped, by a governor's retainer or personal official. The formal structure of provincial government under the T'ang was reproduced in the governor's own organization which was built around his office and residence and developed according to his needs.

The great influence of this organization on local government had been felt in the T'ang. The organization had been affected by the social and economic developments of the ninth century and was to have an important effect on developments throughout the tenth. Particularly relevant to this study, however, was the growth of a new group of officials who began to dominate the imperial government soon after the fall of T'ang. A process of reproducing the provincial structure at the court was tentatively begun during the Liang and temporarily set aside by Li Ts'un-hsü. The full impact of the changes did not come to be felt until the middle period of the Wu-tai, 926-946, during which the political and military power of the palace staff was more clearly defined. This palace staff was

detail in K. Hinō, 'Tōdai Hanchin no Bakko to Chinso' (parts 2, 3 and 4), *Toyo Gakuho*, 27. His researches, especially the observations in the last four sections (part 3, pp. 196-212 and part 4, *passim*), have provided a valuable background to my understanding of the power of the governors.

The emphasis in this study being on imperial policy towards the provinces, however, I have been content to draw on his conclusions and keep within the scope of my work. I think I have said enough to show that, during and after the Liang in North China, imperial policy had begun to restrict the resources of the governors effectively in provinces close to the capital. This restriction was to be successfully extended into more distant areas stage by stage. The details of the *chên* organization should really be part of a study of local government, which I am not yet in a position to attempt.

Professor Hinō's studies mentioned above supplement an earlier article on the Wu-tai, 'Gōdai Chinso Kō', *Tōyō Gakuho*, 25. A less diffuse study of the *chên* under the *Wu-tai* governors has been of more value to me. This is the second part of Y. Sudō's 'Gōdai Ketsudoshi no Shihai Taisei', *Shigaku Zasshi*, 61/6, pp. 521-534.

drawn largely from the members of the organization the emperors had had when they had been governors. The successful transfer of the provincial staff to the imperial palace and their subsequent dominance in imperial government are some of the chief reasons the provincial organization has been called 'the fundamental political structure' of the Wu-tai period.[55]

[55] Y. Sudō, *op. cit.*, pp. 537-538. On pp. 536-537, Professor Sudō summarizes the features of the provincial organization which appear in imperial government. In Chapter Six, the summary is expanded into an examination of the courts of 926-946 and an attempt is made to estimate the significance of the group of men who had risen from provincial service.

CHAPTER SIX

Political Power at the Court 926-946

When Li Ts'un-hsü died in 926, Li Ssŭ-yüan ascended the throne if not unwillingly, certainly without ever expecting to do so. The more dramatic efforts to build a new empire by Chu Wên and the two generations of Sha-t'o Turk leaders had ended and were followed by a number of smaller struggles among officers who had risen from the tribal or the provincial armies. These officers had little or no claim to the throne and had to build up their authority by more cautious methods of compromise with their fellow officers, the most senior of whom were the military governors.

Li Ssŭ-yüan in his reign of seven and a half years (926-933) laid the foundations for the uphill task of consolidating imperial authority. He encouraged the recovery of bureaucratic influence which became important by the reign of his adopted son Li Ts'ung-k'o (934-936). He also established the institution of the Emperor's Army which was so developed by the emperors of the Chin dynasty (936-946) that it transformed the structure of power for the last decade of the Wu-tai period. A factor of immediate significance early in his reign was the growth in power of the group of men serving in the imperial palace. They had risen from personal service with the governors, and their rise to power was bound up with the way Li Ssŭ-yüan had come to the throne. Their importance to this study is in the way their place at the court reflects the political developments which the provincial organization of the T'ang eventually brought about.

Li Ssŭ-yüan was already fifty-nine years old when he succeeded Li Ts'un-hsü as emperor. He was the only surviving general of the men who had started their careers under the first of the great

Sha-t'o Turks, Li Ts'un-hsü's grandfather. He had not been a brilliant officer, but had contributed greatly to Li Ts'un-hsü's success against the Liang in 923. In 6th/924, when all his abler contemporaries were dead, he was made commander-in-chief of the 'Tribal and Chinese infantry and cavalry'. Although he was also an adopted member of the Sha-t'o Turk imperial family, he could not have expected the support which put him on the throne.[1]

The events that brought about the *coup d'état* which resulted in Li Ssŭ-yüan's ascension to the throne began with the execution of Kuo Ch'ung-t'ao, the Commissioner of the Military Secretariat, in 1st/926. A number of other executions followed and as a result there was considerable confusion at the court and in the provinces. On 6/2nd/926, a Ho-pei border garrison returning to their homes in Wei Chou mutinied and seized the city. Four days later, a large section of the imperial army returning from the Szechuan campaign rebelled, and three days after that the infantry garrison at Hsing Chou (in Ho-pei) seized the city. When an imperial favourite failed to defeat the mutineers at Wei Chou, several other garrisons in Ho-pei also mutinied. Loyal units of the imperial armies were recalled from the provinces and, together with a part of the emperor's own troops, were entrusted to Li Ssŭ-yüan to lead against the rebels.[2]

It cannot be known what happened at Wei Chou on the night of 8/3rd/926 when mutineers in Li Ssŭ-yüan's army handed him over to the rebels.[3] Li Ssŭ-yüan probably made a bargain with the

[1] *CWTS* 35, 1a-7b.

[2] *CWTS* 34, 1b-7b; 35, 7b-8a; also 57, 9b; 63, 9b-10a; 90, 1a-b; 74, 2b-4b; 70, 2a-b. Also *TCTC* 274, T'ien-ch'eng 1(926)/1/*chia-tzŭ*, ff.

[3] There is no reliable account of what happened to Li Ssŭ-yüan at Wei Chou. Our chief source, the *Chiu Wu-tai Shih*, was based on the two Veritable Records containing the official versions current in Li Ssŭ-yüan's lifetime that he was a victim of circumstances. The *Chuang-tsung Veritable Records* concerning the reign of Li Ts'un-hsü had had his approval, having been compiled in 929. The *Ming-tsung Veritable Records* for Li Ssŭ-yüan's own reign were compiled in 935-936, under the watchful eyes of his adopted son Li Ts'ung-k'o, by historians who contrasted his rule favourably with Li Ts'un-hsü's. See Wang Gungwu, 'The *Chiu Wu-tai Shih* and history-writing in the Five Dynasties', *Asia Major*.

Two later Sung historians disagreed about this official version that Li Ssŭ-yüan had been driven to turn against Li Ts'un-hsü. Ou-yang Hsiu took

rebel leaders for when he was released he made no attempt to attack them again. Instead, he gathered the remnants of his army, attacked the imperial grazing ground from which he took several thousand horses, captured a convoy of silk-laden boats on the Huang Ho and marched west to 'explain' his actions personally to the emperor.

The important features of his success were the willing support he received from the armies stationed in Ho-pei and the collapse of the emperor's remaining forces. In the race to enter the strategic K'ai-fêng, the emperor was defeated chiefly by several defections which reduced his army by about half. But the two decisions which put Li Ssŭ-yüan's power to rule beyond dispute were not made by army officers. The first was made by K'ung Hsün, the finance expert who had started on Chu Wên's personal staff and had become acting governor of K'ai-fêng. He decided to offer the resources of K'ai-fêng to the army which reached the city first. The other decision was made by Jên Huan, a man of bureaucrat origins who was also a cousin-in-law of Li Ts'un-hsü. He was an administrator of great experience and had become the executive officer of the armies led by prince Li Chi-chi in the Szechuan campaign. After the death of Li Ts'un-hsü and the suicide of prince Li Chi-chi, he decided to join Li Ssŭ-yüan with the 26,000 men of the Szechuan expeditionary army which had come under his control. K'ung Hsün and Jên Huan can be seen as representatives of the two branches of imperial administration which had been evolved in the first quarter of the tenth century. K'ung Hsün, the ex-retainer, was then appointed a palace commissioner while Jên Huan, the new bureaucrat, became Li Ssŭ-yüan's Chief Minister.[4]

the view that Li Ssŭ-yüan had joined forces with the rebels at Wei Chou while Ssŭ-ma Kuang (and his collaborators) merely modified the official account by showing that he was not entirely guiltless. See *HWTS* 5B, 27b-28a; 6A, 7b-9a, and *TCTC* 274, T'ien-ch'êng 1(926)/3/*chia-tzŭ* and *ting-mao*; before *kuei-yu*; *wu-yin*; *hsin-ssŭ* and *jên-wu*; *chia-shên*.

[4] K'ung Hsün has been considered before (*HWTS* 43, 8b-9a). For Jên Huan, *CWTS* 67, 11b-13b (*TCTC* 272, T'ung-kuang 1(923)/7/after *chia-tzŭ*, disagrees with *CWTS* and says that Jên Huan's brother, Jên T'uan was Li Ts'un-hsü's brother-in-law). See *TCTC* 274, T'ien-ch'êng 1(926)/3/*hsin-ssŭ* and 275, 4/*kêng-tzŭ*, *jên-yin* and after *kêng-hsü*; also 5/*ping-ch'ên*.

Li Ssŭ-yüan's unexpected success in the revolt not initially of his own making, and the broad basis of the support for him were important factors in the early decisions he made for his government. He had had no experience of imperial government, neither had his most trusted followers. Almost over night, a group of provincial officials was appointed to the highest palace commissions and began to wield great power. It was therefore necessary to give more responsibilities to the bureaucrats in order to provide continuity in imperial administration and to avoid having just a glorified provincial government at the court.[5] In this way, a measure of co-operation between the palace staff and the bureaucrats was necessary and their relationship affected the nature of imperial government as well as both the groups of men.

Political power remained largely in the hands of the emperor's men. Although several of Li Ts'un-hsü's palace commissioners were retained in office,[6] the main commissions were eventually filled by Li Ssŭ-yüan's provincial staff as can be seen in Table VIII.

Li Ssŭ-yüan modelled the higher ranks of his palace service on his provincial and retainer organization more as Chu Wên had done than had his immediate predecessor. In the early years of his reign, the few eunuchs who remained had negligible influence.[7]

[5] Other important decisions made by Li Ssŭ-yüan concern compromises to win over the provincial governors; see Chapter Seven where the compromises are considered in greater detail.

[6] The following are known to have been retained in Li Ssŭ-yüan's palace service (references are from *CWTS*):
Liu Ch'u-jang (94, 8b-10b) Yang Yen-hsün (90, 10b-11b) Liu Sui-ch'ing (96, 5b-6b) Hsüeh Jên-ch'ien (128, 6b-7a).

There was also Ch'ên Ssŭ-jang who was a bodyguard officer at the palace; *Sung Shih*, 261, 4b.

[7] The leading eunuchs had been executed or retired by Li Ssŭ-yüan. Those remaining at the palace were placed under Mêng Han-ch'iung who was brought to the palace from the provinces. Mêng Han-ch'iung enjoyed a short period of considerable power in 931-934, but was the last eunuch to do so in the Wu-tai; *CWTS* 72, 6b-7b.

Other important figures from Li Ssŭ-yüan's province were his Provincial Commander (also his son-in-law) who took over the imperial armies and the military police officer (*yü-hou chiang*) who saved his family and was given his own province to govern (Wang Chien-li, *CWTS* 91, 3b-4a; *TCTC* 274, T'ien-Ch'êng 1(926)/3/before *kuei-yu*). There were also several sons and adopted sons who filled various positions at the capital. They were later employed

TABLE VIII[8]

Provincial Office	*Name of Palace Commission*
Chief retainer officer (*chung-mên shih*)	Military Secretariat (*shu-mi*), 926-31.
Finance official (*yüan-ts'ung k'ung-mu kuan*)	Military Secretariat (asst.), 926; Palace Attendants (*hsüan-hui nan*), 927-28; 'state finance' (*san-ssŭ*), 930-31.
Reception officer (*k'o-chiang*)	Palace Attendants, 926-28; Military Secretariat, 928 and 930-33.
Reception officer	Palace Reception (*k'o-shêng*) (date?)
Reception official (*tien-k'o*)	Inner Palace Reception (*nei k'o-shêng*), 927; Palace Attendants, 928-30 and 931-32; Military Secretariat, 933-34.
Official in charge of Memorial Presentation (*chin-chou kuan*)	Inner Palace Reception, 926; Palace Attendants, 929-30 and 932-33; Military Secretariat, 933-34.
Garrison officer	Palace Reception, after 930.
Garrison officer	Palace Ushers (*ying-chin*) (date?).
Garrison officer	Palace Works (*tso-fang*) (asst.); Imperial Audience (*ko-mên*) (dates?)
Family servant	Imperial city (*huang-ch'eng*), after 926.
Eunuch domestic	Inner Palace Attendants (*nei-shih shêng*, also *hsüan-hui pei*) (dates?)

to govern provinces; *CWTS* 51, 3b-5b and 45, 1a ff. for the sons and *CWTS* 46, 1a-3b; 88, 12a-13a and 13b-15a; 123, 8a-9b for the adopted sons.

Two bureaucrat administrators also became prominent. They were Liang Wên-chü who rose quickly to be head of the Censorate and almost became a Chief Minister (92, 4a-b) and Shih Kuei who became a Secretary of the Military Secretariat (92, 4b-6a).

[8] In the table, the following were the provincial staff mentioned (references are from *CWTS* unless otherwise stated):
Chief retainer officer, An Ch'ung-hui (66, 1a, quoting from *TFYK* 309, 22a)
Finance official, Chang Yen-lang (69, 8a-b)
Two reception officers, Fan Yen-kuang (97, 1a-2a) and Li Jên-chü (70, 6b)
Reception official, Chu Hung-chao (66, 4a-b)
Official in charge of Memorial Presentation, Fêng Pin (*HWTS*, 27, 2b)
Three garrison officers, Chang Yen-po (97, 5b), Wang Ching-ch'ung (*HWTS* 53, 1a) and Wang Jên-hao (*Sung Shih*, 261, 4a)
Family servant, Ti Kuang-yeh (129, 2a)
Eunuch domestic, Mêng Han-ch'iung (72, 6b-7a).

As with the Liang palace, the work of guarding and administering the palace was largely in the hands of the Commission of Palace Attendants. Under the Commissioners were men previously in the palace service. These included men recruited from the imperial armies as palace guards and others, mostly the sons and relatives of governors and senior army officers who were partly hostages and partly serving an apprenticeship in imperial affairs. These men were given ranks in the Imperial Guards or in the Courts (*shih*) and Directions (*chien*), their ranks depending on the type of skills they had. Also as in the Liang, these men had duties outside the palace and often had administrative and diplomatic duties previously performed either by bureaucrats or by eunuchs.[9]

The significance of these men is not apparent because they were not themselves politically influential. But as men close to the emperor with important connections in the court, they continued the development in the Liang of a new power group derived from men of comparatively obscure origins. What was more immediately important, they were the men who helped the work of the palace commissioners and many of them were to play a part during the later dynasties.

For references to palace commissioners in this study, see *infra*, p. 89, note 9 and p. 109 ff. for the *shu-mi yüan* (also later in this chapter). For the *hsüan-hui yüan*, see *infra*, p. 92 ff. and note 15; and for the *san-ssu yüan*, the Three Offices of state finance, see later in this chapter. For a brief mention of some of the other commissioners, see p. 95 and note 19.

[9] A common term for them was 'the attending and following officials' (*shih-ts'ung chih ch'ên* 侍從之臣, *CWTS* 149, 16b) and they included men grouped as 'officials at the disposal of the emperor' (*kung-fêng kuan*) and officers attached to the palaces (*tien-chih*) (see Chapter Four, note 15).

Of the examples of these officials in Li Ssŭ-yüan's reign, five were sent as envoys—one to the Khitans (*TCTC* 275, T'ien-ch'êng 1(926)/7/after *jên-shên*), a second to the state of Wu (*CWTS* 38, 4b), two to the provinces in Szechuan (*CWTS* 41, 11a-b and 43, 6b, 8a-b) and one to the tributary state of Wu-yüeh (*CWTS* 40, 7b and *HWTS* 6B, 24b).

One of the two who were sent to Szechuan, Li Ts'un-huai, was a cousin of Li Ts'un-hsü's. He was sent by Li Ssŭ-yüan to negotiate with his uncle Mêng Chih-hsiang the powerful governor of Ch'êng-tu; *CWTS* 43, 6b, 8a-b; *TCTC* 277, Ch'ang-hsing 3(932)/6/*wu-wu*. The three sent to the other states were Wang Jên-hao and Ch'ên Ssŭ-jang, sons of prefects (*Sung Shih*, 261, 4a and 4b), and a son of a Liang governor and commander-in-chief, Ho Kuang-t'u (*CWTS* 23, 9a).

The most powerful of the palace commissioners during Li Ssŭ-yüan's reign was the Commissioner of the Military Secretariat (alternatively called the Military Secretary in this study). The first Commissioner, An Ch'ung-hui, was given overriding powers similar to those of Kuo Ch'ung-t'ao under Li Ts'un-hsü. An Ch'ung-hui, however, was barely literate and, as early as in 5th/926, two senior Hanlin Academicians were appointed as Scholars of the Tuan-ming Hall to help in the Military Secretariat. Although this was an important step in the recovery of bureaucrat influence, none of the Scholars appointed in Li Ssŭ-yüan's reign exercised any power independently of the Military Secretaries.[10]

For almost five years, An Ch'ung-hui and his supporters dominated the court. His ability and power aroused the envy of his fellow commissioners who had also been Li Ssŭ-yüan's retainers and this envy finally brought about his downfall. In Intercalary 5th/931, he was executed. Among the men who caused his death were Chu Hung-chao, an ex-reception official, Ti Kuang-yeh, domestic retainer and Mêng Han-ch'iung, a eunuch, all three having been with Li Ssŭ-yüan in his days as a governor.[11]

An Ch'ung-hui's death had important consequences. It left the central government weak and inactive. His two immediate successors, including one of the emperor's sons-in-law, were so frightened of the influence of the various palace commissioners that they did not dare exercise the power accruing to the Secretariat and resigned as soon as they could.[12] The two who succeeded

[10] *CWTS* 66, 1a-4a (where An Ch'ung-hui's biography is partially preserved) and *HWTS* 24, 16b-17a.

On the creation of the post of Scholar of the Tuan-ming Hall, *WTHY* 13, p. 173; *CWTS* 149, 8b-9a and 38, 1b; *HWTS* 28, 13b-14a; *Shih-lin Yen-yü*, 2, 12a.

Of the three men appointed Scholars in Li Ssŭ-yüan's reign, the most prominent was Chao Fêng; *CWTS* 67, 6b-8a; *HWTS* 28, 12b-18b. The other two Scholars were Fêng Tao (926-927) and Liu Hsü (931-932); *CWTS* 126, 1a ff. and 38, 2a; *CWTS* 89, 11a-13a; 42, 8a and 44, 1a.

[11] *CWTS* 66, 1a-4a. The three men have been mentioned in note 8 above. Also *TCTC* 277, Ch'ang-hsing 1(930)/9/*chia-hsü*; 12/*kuei-ch'ou*; Ch'ang-hsing 2(931)/1/after *ping-hsü* and Intercalary 5/*chia-wu*.

[12] The two successors were Fan Yen-kuang the ex-reception officer (*CWTS* 97, 1b-2a) and Chao Yen-shou the emperor's son-in-law (*CWTS* 98, 11a). Fan Yen-kuang had been appointed Military Secretary before (in 3rd/928) but

them, however, were less timid. One of them was Chu Hung-chao who had been one of the men responsible for An Ch'ung-hui's death and he had the support of the eunuch Mêng Han-ch'iung. Together, they were able to crush the attempted *coup d'état* of prince Li Ts'ung-jung in 11th/933. And after Li Ssŭ-yüan's death six days later they became the two most powerful men in the court of his son and successor, Li Ts'ung-hou.[13]

The fluctuations in the central government owing to the unstable conditions in the palace and the undefined power of the palace commissioner called for radical reforms. This was attempted by the emperor Li Ts'ung-k'o, the adopted brother of Li Ts'ung-hou, who usurped the throne in 4th/934. The first change he made was to appoint Han Chao-yin as Commissioner of the Military Secretariat. This was significant because Han Chao-yin had been his provincial administrator, a man of literati origins and not a retainer officer. The appointment was a break with the Later T'ang tradition and a new measure to increase the responsibilities of the bureaucrats. Li Ts'ung-k'o continued to connect the bureaucrats with the Military Secretariat and Han Chao-yin continued to be Military Secretary even after he was promoted Chief Minister a year later.[14]

he was sent out as acting governor of a province almost immediately (*CWTS* 39, 4a-b). He was then appointed Military Secretary again in 9th/930, four months before An Ch'ung-hui's dismissal, but does not seem to have exercised his powers until An Ch'ung-hui left the capital for the Shu campaign in 12th/930 (*CWTS* 41, 10a and 13a).

Also see *TCTC* 277, Ch'ang-hsing 2(931)/5/*chi-mao*.

[13] This was mainly because the young prince Li Ts'ung-hou left the province he governed to become emperor without bringing all his men and officers with him. One of his provincial officials advised him to take his provincial infantry and cavalry with him and predicted that he would fail to assert his authority when he did not do so. See Liu K'ai, *Ho-tung Hsien-shêng Chi*, 14, 4b.

Chu Hung-chao, *CWTS* 66, 4a-b; Mêng Han-ch'iung, *CWTS* 72, 6b-7a. The other Military Secretary was Fêng Pin; *HWTS* 27, 2b (see also note 8 above).

[14] *CWTS* 46, 8b and 10a; 47, 5a; and *HWTS* 27, 6a ff.; *TCTC* 279, Ch'ing-t'ai 1(934)/5/*ping-wu* and Ch'ing-t'ai 2(935)/4/*kuei-wei*.

When Han Chao-yin was promoted Chief Minister in 4th/935, another Military Secretary, Liu Yen-hao, was appointed. Liu Yen-hao was a younger brother of the empress; *CWTS* 69, 10b-11a. The more important man in the Secretariat, however, was the Assistant Military Secretary, Liu Yen-lang;

Han Chao-yin did not stay long at the court, but in the succeeding reign of Shih Ching-t'ang, the founder of the Chin dynasty, the experiment of having a bureaucrat to be in charge of the Military Secretariat was repeated. In Intercalary 11th/936, Sang Wei-han, the emperor's ex-secretary, was appointed Chief Minister and Military Secretary at the same time. Sang Wei-han was the first of a new generation of examination graduates from the lesser families to have reached the highest position in the empire. He was the son of a reception officer (*k'o-chiang*) from Lo-yang who had served the ex-Huang Ch'ao officer, Chang Ch'üan-i. He passed the *chin-shih* examinations in 4th/925 after which he began to work in the provinces and soon became secretary to Shih Ching-t'ang. In 936, he devised the strategy which destroyed the Later T'ang. For this, he was entrusted with the post of Military Secretary.[15]

Shih Ching-t'ang extended the experiment further by making another Chief Minister Military Secretary as well. The second man, Li Sung, was another new bureaucrat, this time from Ho-pei. Li Sung had risen from being a very junior provincial secretary to be a secretary of Li Ts'un-hsü's heir apparent, Prince Li Chi-chi, and later became an administrator of the Salt and Transport Commission. He then had six years' service with the Military Secretariat, including two years as Scholar of the Tuan-ming Hall. These years in the Secretariat made him eminently qualified for the dual appointment.[16]

The appointments of Sang Wei-han and Li Sung to the Military Secretariat had deprived the emperor's ex-retainer officers as well as the other palace commissioners of an office which had been their privilege for almost twelve years (923-936, excepting the period 5th/934-12th/935). These two appointments put the palace commissioners on the defensive for the first time. The senior palace commissioner Liu Ch'u-jang, who had done valuable service on the battlefield, resented Sang Wei-han's power. In 10th/938, less

CWTS 46, 10a; 47, 5b and 11a; 69, 11a-b; *HWTS* 27, 4a-10a; also *TCTC* 279, Ch'ing-t'ai 2(935)/9/*chi-yu*.

[15] *CWTS* 89, 1a-9a; Chang Ch'i-hsien, *Lo-yang Chin-shên Chiu-wên Chi*, 2, 5b-6a; also *TCTC* 280, T'ien-fu 1(936)/5/*chia-wu*.

[16] *CWTS* 108, 1a-4a and *HWTS* 57, 1a-5a.

than two years after the appointments were made, Liu Ch'u-jang was able to force the emperor to dismiss Sang Wei-han and appoint him instead. He was able to do this with the help of the Chief Commander of the Emperor's Personal Army (the *shih-wei ch'in-chün tu chih-hui shih*). The emperor was most reluctant to do so and at the first opportunity dismissed him and abolished the office of Military Secretary altogether. The functions of the Secretariat were then placed under the control of the Imperial Secretariat (*chung-shu shêng*), that is, in the hands of one of the Chief Ministers.[17]

This was a setback to the palace commissioners, but it was only temporary. By this time, the commissioners had begun to play a new role through the powerful organ of the Emperor's Personal Army. The Emperor's Personal Army (*shih-wei ch'in-chün*) had been established by Li Ssŭ-yüan in 926 as a large force which was to be permanently at his side and which, if necessary, he could personally lead to battle against any revolt. The Army was initially established in order to cope with the special circumstances in Lo-yang in 4th/926. It consisted chiefly of the section of Li Ts'un-hsü's armies which had followed Li Ssŭ-yüan from Ho-pei. Two other sections of the imperial armies had to be dealt with, one under Chu Shou-yin who had been commander of Li Ts'un-hsü's armies at Lo-yang, and the other under Jên Huan who had just brought the large Shu expeditionary army back from Szechuan. Li Ssŭ-yüan had no difficulty in reorganizing the latter army under his own command after making Jên Huan one of his Chief Ministers. But the army under Chu Shou-yin probably had to be left in his command for Li Ssŭ-yüan appointed him Controller of the Six Armies and the Guards (*p'an liu-chün chu-wei shih*) and governor of Lo-yang.[18]

There were, therefore, two sets of commands, one under the Chief Commander (*tu chih-hui shih*) of the Emperor's Army and the other under the Controller. But by the end of 926, Li Ssŭ-yüan

[17] *CWTS* 108, 2a-b; 94, 9b-10a; 78, 4b; and *HWTS* 47, 12b-13a. *Wu-tai Shih Tsuan-wu*, 3, p. 34-35, has a lengthy discussion of the dismissal of Sang Wei-han and the appointment of Liu Ch'u-jang and notes internal discrepancies in the *HWTS*.

[18] *CWTS* 74, 5a-b.

was able to send Chu Shou-yin away from Lo-yang and appoint his thirteen-year-old son, Prince Li Ts'ung-hou, as Controller and metropolitan governor. The post of Assistant Controller was given to Shih Ching-t'ang, the Chief Commander of the Emperor's Army and also the emperor's son-in-law, who was appointed to help the boy prince. In this way, the two sections of the imperial armies were united.[19]

Chu Shou-yin, however, had been sent to K'ai-fêng as governor to deal with the mutinous garrison there. He probably left Lo-yang with a considerable force and his success at K'ai-fêng gave him control of another large army. This was far from desirable from the court's point of view and in 10th/927 a pretext was found for the emperor to lead his Personal Army against Chu Shou-yin.[20] The quick success of Li Ssŭ-yüan gave him the control of the only remaining independent army in Ho-nan.

The total imperial force was then divided between Lo-yang and K'ai-feng for over a year. The Controller Li Ts'ung-hou and his Assistant Shih Ching-t'ang, shared the army command. In 4th/928, Shih Ching-t'ang was replaced by K'ang I-ch'êng who was also made the Chief Commander of the Emperor's Army at Lo-yang while Li Ts'ung-hou was appointed governor of K'ai-fêng. After 4th/929, the armies were brought together again when prince Li Ts'ung-jung replaced his younger brother as Controller and was also appointed governor of Lo-yang.[21]

The division of the imperial armies has been considered in some detail in order to show the position of the Chief Commander and

[19] *CWTS* 74, 5b; 38, 2a and 3b; 75, 4b. T. Hori, 'Gōdai Sōshu ni okeru Kingun no hatten', *Tōyō Bunka Kenkyujo Kiyo*, 4, pp. 96-106 and H. Kikuchi, 'Gōdai Kingun ni okeru Jiei Shingun Shi no seiritsu', *Shien*, 70, p. 74.

[20] *CWTS* 38, 12a; 74, 5b. There is evidence that Li Ssŭ-yüan and his advisers forced Chu Shou-yin to rebel (in T'ien K'uang, *Ju-lin Kung-i*, 2 (*hsia*), p. 43, also quoted by the re-compilers of the present edition of the *CWTS* 74, 9a-b. *K'ao-chêng*), but the *TCTC* and the *HWTS* follow the version in the *CWTS* (*TCTC* 276, T'ien-ch'êng 2(927)/10/*i-yu* ff. and *HWTS* 51, 2b).

A large section of the imperial armies had been left at K'ai-fêng (see memorial of 8th/926; *TFYK* 484, 21a) and regiments of it had mutinied in 926 (*CWTS* 36, 6a-b; *TCTC* 275, T'ien-ch'êng 1(926)/6/*ting-yu*). It is thus likely that Chu Shou-yin had brought a large force with him in order to take office in K'ai-fêng and that after taking over, he had a considerable army.

[21] *CWTS* 39, 5a; 40, 3a. T. Hori, *op. cit.*

the comparatively passive role he played under the emperor and his immediate family. There was still no sign that the Chief Commander was becoming a powerful political figure, nor was there evidence that the palace commissioners were playing any part in the imperial armies. The important turning point came some years later in 933. In 11th/933, Prince Li Ts'ung-jung, then Controller of the Six Armies and the Guards and governor of Ho-nan, attempted a *coup d'état*. But the Chief Commander, K'ang I-ch'êng, supported the palace commissioners Chu Hung-chao, Mêng Han-ch'iung and Fêng Pin and turned the Emperor's Army on the prince. The superiority of the Army over the active force of the Six Armies and Guards at the disposal of Li Ts'ung-jung was clearly demonstrated. Although the prince had acquired for his retainer force two regiments of the Emperor's Army, the Army still had the advantage of being stationed in the palace grounds while the units under the prince, as governor of Lo-yang, seem to have been scattered around the capital.[22]

After the failure of the attempted *coup d'état*, the Controller's office was merged with that of the Chief Commander, and all the armies at Lo-yang came under one command. More significant, the Chief Commander had co-operated, although somewhat unwillingly, with the palace commissioners in power and had shown what a key political figure he had become.

Another opportunity to demonstrate the power of the man who controlled the Emperor's Army followed soon after. On Li Ssŭ-yüan's death, Li Ts'ung-hou, who had been a Controller of the Six Armies, was put on the throne. A young man not yet twenty years old, he was dominated by the palace commissioners.[23] The excessive power of these commissioners was resented by various governors in the provinces as well as by the commanders of the Emperor's Army. Thus, when the governor of Ch'i (in Kuan-chung), Prince Li Ts'ung-k'o, refused to be transferred and revolted, the commanders were secretly sympathetic. The revolt did not seem dangerous at first as none of the other governors

[22] *CWTS* 44, 9a-b; 51, 4a-b; 66, 4b-5a and 7a; 72, 7a; *HWTS* 27, 2b-3a; *TCTC* 278, Ch'ang-hsing 4(933)/11/*wu-tzŭ* to *kuei-ssŭ*, *passim*.

[23] See note 13 above.

between Ch'i and Lo-yang supported it. But what had been certain isolation and defeat for Li Ts'ung-k'o was transformed into victory when several of the commanders of the Emperor's Army sent against him were successfully bribed to join his cause. There followed the surrender of other units of the Army, including finally the Chief Commander himself as well as the commander of the troops left to police the capital. Within twelve days, the Emperor's Army had placed a new emperor on the throne and turned the tables on the palace commissioners.[24]

The important feature of the events of 933-934 was the vulnerability of the palace commissioners. They were not, like the eunuchs in Li Ts'un-hsü's reign, completely without military backing. From time to time, senior commissioners had been appointed governors of important provinces and had been in charge of some imperial regiments there.[25] Some of them had even been able to get the support of the highest imperial commanders for a short period. Nevertheless, they were vulnerable because they had no real control of the Emperor's Army which had emerged as the most powerful organization in the empire.

But from 930-933, there were the first signs of a new role for the palace commissioners. One of them was sent as a cavalry supervisor with the expeditionary armies against governors in Szechuan in 930-931. In 933, the Commissioner of the Palace Parks (*kung-yüan shih*) was sent as an army supervisor with the armies ordered against the governor of Hsia province (north of Kuan-chung). Early in 934, the emperor Li Ts'ung-hou also sent supervisors with the sections of the Emperor's Army despatched against his adopted brother in Ch'i province.[26] However, there was

[24] *CWTS* 45, 5b-8b; 46, 3b-4b; 66, 5a-b and 7a-b; 72, 7a-b; *TCTC* 278, Ch'ing-t'ai 1(934)/1/*jên-wu* and *chi-hai*; Intercalary 1st month; 279, Ch'ing-t'ai 1(934)/2/*chi-mao* ff. and 3/*i-mao* ff. to *wu-ch'ên*.

[25] The most significant appointments were those of Chu Hung-chao to be governor of Ch'i during the Shu campaigns (*CWTS* 41, 2b and 66, 4b), of Fêng Pin to the great Ping province (*CWTS* 41, 8a) and of Fan Yen-kuang to Chên province twice (*CWTS* 39, 4b-5a; 44, 8a; and 97, 2a).

[26] Chang Yen-po, the Commissioner of Palace Reception (*k'o-shêng shih*, see note 8 above), was appointed Cavalry Supervisor in the Shu campaign (*CWTS* 97, 5b). An Infantry Supervisor was also appointed for that campaign; he was not a palace commissioner but probably one of the intermediate

probably little the commissioners could have gained from accompanying the expeditionary armies. All the three campaigns were unsuccessful and the new emperor Li Ts'ung-k'o (934-936) who also employed them in this function was no more successful in his wars.[27] But the direct experience the commissioners had of the Emperor's Army and the relations they had established with its officers may have made it easier for the commissioners in the Chin dynasty (936-946) to gain considerable military authority.

I have discussed above the experiment with bureaucrats in the highest palace commission, the Military Secretariat, after 934, and the resentment shown against them by Liu Ch'u-jang, a senior palace official who had started in Li Ts'un-hsü's palace service in 923. This was in 938, the first two years of the Chin dynasty. But even in this struggle, it was with the help of the Chief Commander of the Emperor's Army, Yang Kuang-yüan, that Liu Ch'u-jang was able to force the removal of the bureaucrat Sang Wei-han from the Military Secretariat (pp. 157-158).

This co-operation of the two men in 938 was the beginning of closer relations between the commanders of the Emperor's Army and a number of palace commissioners. The co-operation had been initially brought about by the circumstances in which Shih Ching-t'ang founded the Chin dynasty in late 936. An important factor in Shih Ching-t'ang's success had been the surrender of Yang Kuang-yüan and his officers with the largest section of the Emperor's Army of Later T'ang.[28] Because of this support, Yang Kuang-yüan was

officials between the palace and the administrative offices at the time (Li Yen-hsün, *CWTS* 94, 15b).

The Commissioner of Palace Parks in 933 was An Ch'ung-i (*CWTS* 44, 3a and *TCTC* 278, Ch'ang-hsing 4(933)/3/*kuei-wei*). One of Li Ts'ung-hou's Supervisors was Wang Ching-ch'ung (see note 8 above and *TCTC* 279, Ch'ing-t'ai 1 (934)/3/*kêng-shên*).

Supervisors had been appointed for expeditionary armies earlier on but not from among the palace commissioners (see Chang Ch'ien-chao in *TCTC* 276, T'ien-ch'êng 3(928)/4/*jên-yin*.

[27] Li Ts'ung-k'o sent his senior Commissioner of Palace Attendants Liu Yen-lang to supervise the Infantry Commander of the Emperor's Army in 9th/936 (*TCTC* 280, T'ien-fu 1(936)/9/*chi-yu*). Also in *CWTS* 106, 9b-10a, Chang P'êng, an ex-monk, is described as having become a *kung-fêng kuan* in Li Ts'ung-k'o's palace and then employed as an Army Supervisor.

[28] *CWTS* 48, 10b-11a; 97, 6b; *TCTC* 280, T'ien-fu 1(936)/Intercalary 11th/*chia-tzŭ*.

appointed Chief Commander of the new Emperor's Army, an appointment similar to Li Ssŭ-yüan's appointment of Chu Shou-yin as Controller of the Six Armies and Guards in 926. Shih Ching-t'ang did not really trust Yang Kuang-yüan and, in the first major campaign of the Chin dynasty (against the governor of Wei who controlled another section of the Army), he sent Liu Ch'u-jang to him to 'join in discussions on military affairs'.[29]

The emperor had also, like Li Ssŭ-yüan, introduced his provincial staff and retainer officers into the palace and into the Emperor's Army. The difference was that in addition to making his Provincial Commander, Liu Chih-yüan, Cavalry Commander of the Army, he appointed a reception officer (*k'o-chiang*) Ching Yen-kuang to be Infantry Commander. Previous to 936, a reception officer would normally have gone into the palace service (see Table VIII). Ching Yen-kuang's appointment was obviously exceptional because another reception officer (a *tien-k'o*) Li Shou-chên became a palace commissioner first before he was given commands in the Emperor's Army.[30]

The appointments of Ching Yen-kuang as Infantry Commander and of Liu Ch'u-jang to observe the Chief Commander gave the palace commissioners who had been colleagues of these two men an indirect connexion with the Army. This connexion gave them a new source of power and compensated them for the loss of control over the policy-making organ, the Military Secretariat. In relation to imperial government, the new function of the palace officials could help tighten imperial control of the Army and satisfactorily bridge the gap between the military and the administrative.

[29] *CWTS* 94, 9b. Also *TCTC* 281, T'ien-fu 3(938)/10/after *wu-tzŭ*.

[30] *CWTS* 76, 1b. In 99, 2a-b, Liu Chih-yüan is called Chief Commander of the Emperor's Army. Ching Yen-kuang, *CWTS* 88, 1a-b; Li Shou-chên, *CWTS* 109, 5a.

Apart from the earlier reception officers in Table VIII, there was the *k'o-chiang* of Li Ts'ung-k'o (934-936), Fang Hao, who was appointed Commissioner of Palace Attendants at first and finally Military Secretary; *CWTS* 96, 6b and *HWTS* 27, 5b. In *CWTS* 46, 7a, Fang Hao is called a 'personal officer' (*ch'in-chiao*).

But in the Chin, another reception officer was to go through the palace commissions before becoming a commander of the Emperor's Army. This was Li Yen-t'ao who had started his career as a retainer; *CWTS* 88, 4a-b.

The importance of the palace officials was derived from the need of the emperors since the Liang dynasty for a class of men to replace the T'ang eunuchs and be loyal to the throne. These men had to be distinct from the traditional bureaucrats who tended to remain aloof from the emperors. They also had to be more reliable than the professional army officers who were often no more than mercenaries. Since the Liang, there had grown an increasing number of such men. Each emperor, with his experience of provincial government, had brought members of his staff (from among both the *ya-chün* and the *ya-li*) to his palace. And the families of the palace officials as well as those of the governors, prefects and army commanders provided a steady supply of fresh talent into the palace service as long as a career there gave opportunities both for wealth and power.

It was not, however, until the Chin dynasty that the responsibilities of the palace officials were sufficiently broadened for these men to have supervisory powers over both the army and the bureaucracy and that a group can actually be defined.[31] In the following tables, the careers of twenty-one of the most senior palace commissioners of the Chin known in our sources by name have been considered. They include Commissioners of Palace Attendants, of Inner and Outer Reception and those of Finance who were not of bureaucrat origins. Most of them did not remain palace officials throughout their careers, but their part in other offices was possible chiefly because of their experience and connexions in the palace.[32]

Firstly, there is the distribution of their careers before the foundation of Chin.

[31] For the palace officials before the Chin, note their introduction in the Liang and their partial replacement by eunuchs under Li Ts'un-hsü (see Chapter Four). Li Ssŭ-yüan's re-employment of non-eunuchs in the palace is dealt with earlier in this chapter.

[32] The careers of the following twenty-one men have been considered (references from *CWTS* unless otherwise stated):

1. Liu Sui-ch'ing (96, 5b-6b)
2. Yüan I (no biography; see 59, 9b; 37, 4b; 48, 8a; 83, 7b; 102, 3b; 110, 8a; 111, 1a and 2a; 112, 7a and 9b; 113, 9a; 115, 7b).
3. Yang Yen-hsün (90, 10b; *HWTS* 47, 8a-9a).
4. Liu Ch'u-jang (94, 8b-10b; *HWTS* 47, 11b-14a).

TABLE IX[33]

1. *Those who had already been at the court*		11
a. from families of Liang governors	2	
b. from Li Ts'un-hsü's provincial staff	5	
c. from Li Ssŭ-yüan's provincial staff	2	
d. earlier career not known	2	
2. *Those in Shih Ching-t'ang's personal service*		8
a. reception and garrison officers	4	
b. retainers and domestic stewards	3	
c. relative by marriage	1	
3. *Origins unknown*		2

It can be seen that as many as half of the highest officials were men who had served in the palace through several reigns.

In the following table, there are shown the careers of the same twenty-one men during the Chin after their service with the palace commissions. The emphasis is on the variety of their later careers and several of them are considered more than once.

5. Ch'ên Ssŭ-jang (*Sung Shih*, 261, 4b-5b).
6. Kao Han-yün (94, 12a-13b; important differences from biography in *TFYK* 374, 24a-b).
7. Liu Shên-chiao (106, 1b-4a; *HWTS* 48, 11a-13a).
8. Ti Kuang-yeh (129, 2a-3b; *HWTS* 49, 1a-2a; see Table VIII and note 8 above).
9. Wang Ching-ch'ung (46, 14a; 48, 4a; 80, 3a; biography in *HWTS* 53, 1a-3b).
10. Ting Chih-chün (no biography; see 80, 3a and *TCTC* 275, T'ien-ch'êng 2(927)/1/after *kêng-wu*).
11. Su Chi-yen (no biography; see 44, 3b; 47, 10b; 77, 2b).
12. Li Shou-chên (109, 5a-9b; *HWTS* 52, 6b-11a).
13. Liu Chi-hsün (96, 7b-8a).
14. Chou Huai (95, 7a-8a).
15. Mêng Ch'êng-hui (96, 7a-b).
16. Chiao Chi-hsün (*Sung Shih*, 261, 6b-7b).
17. Li Yen-t'ao (88, 4a-5a).
18. Li Ch'êng-fu (90, 16b-17a).
19. Chang Ts'ung-ên (*Sung Shih*, 254, 4b-5a).
20. Tung Yü (no biography; see 81, 7b; 83, 2a; and *TFYK* 511, 16a).
21. Sung Kuang-yeh (no biography; see 76, 18b; 80, 8a; 83, 7b).

[33] See note 32. In the table, 1(a) were nos. 1 and 2 in note 32; 1(b) were nos. 3 to 7; 1(c) were nos. 8 and 9; 1(d) were nos. 10 and 11; 2(a) were nos. 12 to 15; 2(b) were nos. 16 to 18; 2(c) was no. 19; the two whose origins are unknown were nos. 20 and 21.

TABLE X[34]

1. Commanders or Supervisors of the Emperor's Army (the Supervisors were officially still palace commissioners)		6
2. Governors or deputy governors (including men who had been Army Supervisors, or were at the same time commanders)		9
3. Defence Commissioners or prefects (including a palace commissioner who had been an Army Supervisor)		5
4. Others		7
a. sinecure office at court or with the Imperial Guards	2	
b. died in office (as palace commissioners)	2	
c. not known	3	

Here, more than one in four of the palace officials were actively involved with the Emperor's Army. As many as fourteen men were sent to the provinces, probably in order to restrict the influence of their neighbouring governors or, if they were merely prefects, that of their own governors.

Finally, the careers of the nine of the twenty-one men who are known to have survived the fall of Chin and the succeeding dynasties may be included here to illustrate their continued influence in affairs at the court.

It can be seen that there was some continuity not only in the service of these men with the palace commissions but also in their relations with the imperial armies.

TABLE XI[35]

1. Taken out of China by Khitans		1
2. Those who died during the Han (947-950)		3
a. governors (who revolted and were killed)	2	
b. defence commissioners	1	

[34] The six connected with the Emperor's Army were nos. 4, 5, 9, 12, 17 and 19 in note 32. The nine who were governors or deputy governors were nos. 3, 4, 12, 13, 14, 16, 17, 18 and 19.

The five defence commissioners or prefects were nos. 1, 5, 7, 8 and 21. Of the others, the two who held sinecure offices at the court were nos. 9 and 11; the two who died in office were nos. 6 and 15; and the three whose later careers are not known were nos. 2, 10 and 20.

[35] The nine men who are known to have survived after 946 were nos. 2, 5, 7, 8, 9, 12, 16, 17, and 19 in note 32. Li Yen-t'ao (no. 17) was taken north by the Khitans, Li Shou-chên (no. 12) and Wang Ching-ch'ung (no. 9) revolted

3. Those who lived to serve the Chou	5
a. as palace commissioner	1
b. as palace commissioner and then governor	1
c. as army commander and governor (at same time)	2
d. sinecure office	1

(Of the three men whose careers are known in the Sung, two held only sinecure offices while the third continued as a governor and married his daughter to the heir apparent of the Sung founder, Chao K'uang-yin).

During the reign of the second Chin emperor, Shih Ch'ung-kuei (942-946), the Emperor's Army dominated events. Its Chief Commander, Ching Yen-kuang, was actually able to dictate the policy of the court concerning the Khitans. The Chin founder had been set on the throne with Khitan support for the price of sixteen prefectures along the northern and north-eastern borders, regular tributes of cash and silks and various privileges within the Chin empire. Shih Ching-t'ang's submissiveness to the Khitans was resented by both the governors and the army officers. One of the first policy decisions advised by Ching Yen-kuang was that the young Shih Ch'ung-kuei should assert his independence of the Khitans.[36]

This decision angered the Khitans and led to a disastrous war which ended four years later in the downfall of the dynasty. But the immediate effect of the war was to further strengthen the Emperor's Army and give greater power to the Army commanders and Super-

during the Han and were killed and Liu Shên-chiao (no. 7) died as a distinguished defence commissioner in 949.

Of those who lived to serve the Chou, Ti Kuang-yeh (no. 8) was palace commissioner and Yüan I (no. 2) was a palace commissioner and then governor. Ch'ên Ssŭ-jang (no. 5) and Chiao Chi-hsün (no. 16) were both commanders in various expeditionary armies as well as governors, and Chang Ts'ung-ên (no. 19) held a sinecure office at the court.

The last three men (nos. 5, 16 and 19) lived on until the Sung. Chiao Chi-hsün and Chang Ts'ung-ên held only sinecure posts while Ch'ên Ssŭ-jang married his daughter to the Sung emperor's son.

[36] *CWTS* 88, 1b-2a; *TCTC* 283, T'ien-fu 7(942)/end of year and T'ien-fu 8(943)/9/after *wu-tzŭ*. A Tun-huang manuscript of a letter from the Chin to the Khitans about this time is discussed in Yang Lien-shêng's article, 'A "Posthumous Letter" from the Chin emperor to the Khitan emperor in 942', *Harvard Journal of Asiatic Studies*, pp. 418-428.

For the resentment against the submissiviness to the Khitans, see *TCTC* 282, T'ien-fu 6(941)/6/*wu-wu*.

visors. Although Ching Yen-kuang was removed from office for being defeated in battle in a war he had precipitated himself, his Deputy Commander and a Cavalry Commander continued to exercise the influence of the Army in the court. They were Li Shou-chên and Li Yen-t'ao, both previously palace commissioners.[37]

After successfully crushing the rebellion of the governor of Ch'ing, Li Shou-chên was given the governor's mansion at K'ai-fêng which, as if to reflect his new wealth and influence, he rebuilt and extended and made the largest in the capital. In his extravagance, he was following in the steps of Ching Yen-kuang whose house in K'ai-fêng occupied a whole ward in the city and in Lo-yang was supreme south of the Lo river.[38] As for Li Yen-t'ao, he exercised his power closer to the throne and, together with 'intimate officials' (*chin-ch'ên*), 'promoted and appointed generals and ministers' without consulting the court.[39] The only man who opposed the excessive influence of the two ex-palace officials was Sang Wei-han, the Chief Minister who had been re-appointed head of the Military Secretariat when this commission was established again in 6th/944. But Li Shou-chên and Li Yen-t'ao joined forces with the emperor's brother-in-law, Fêng Yü, who was the other Military Secretary, and had him removed in 12th/945. Li Shou-chên was then able to treat the new Military Secretary, Li Sung, with contempt.[40]

The junior palace officials also seem to have played their part in drawing the palace and the Army together. By 939-941, they had already been sent with armed forces to deal with mutinies and invasions along the borders.[41] Their responsibilities increased

[37] Nos. 12 and 17 in note 32 above. For Ching Yen-kuang's defeat and removal from office, see *CWTS* 82, 6b and 88, 2a-b.

[38] *CWTS* 109, 5b-6a describes Li Shou-chên's newly acquired wealth; *TFYK* 454, 18a has details of Ching Yen-kuang's great wealth which are omitted in *CWTS* 88, 2b-3a.

[39] *CWTS* 88, 4b; *TCTC* 284, K'ai-yün 2(945)/2/*ping-shên*.

[40] *CWTS* 109, 6b; *TCTC* 285, K'ai-yün 2(945)/12/*ting-hai*. The exceptional power of Fêng Yü is described in *CWTS* 89, 13a-b and *TCTC* 285, K'ai-yün 2(945)/8/*ping-yin*.

[41] *CWTS* 78, 3b; 79, 4a and 8b; *TCTC* 282, T'ien-fu 4(939)/3rd month and T'ien-fu 6(941)/1/*ping-yin*.

in importance, and when the governor of Ch'ing province rebelled in 12th/943, a team of twenty-six palace attendants (*kung-fêng kuan* and *tien-chih*) was sent along the Huang Ho from Ho-yin (north of Lo-yang) to the sea and ordered to patrol these areas.[42]

A new group of versatile officials had gathered round the throne. It consisted of men with experience of military administration and others with special administrative skills. These men filled the gap between the bureaucrats and the soldiers, but there does not appear to have been a stable basis for them to survive as a distinct group. A few of them were drawn towards the professional army and what might have been a new military aristocracy. But it was the bureaucracy which tended to absorb the abler palace officials and their descendants, attracting them with its respectability and its rich and enduring traditions.

The bureaucrats of this period did not directly challenge the power of the palace officials. An incident in 7th/926 shows a common attitude of the bureaucrats. A palace guards officer (*tien-chih*) was killed by An Ch'ung-hui the Military Secretary outside the gates of the Censorate office and the Chief Censor, Li Ch'i, was forced to report the matter. Li Ch'i, however, was afraid of An Ch'ung-hui and went to discuss the incident with him before submitting the report. Eventually, Li Ch'i memorialized about the killing, but 'the meaning of (his) words were equivocal and (he) dared not speak directly of the crime'.[43] An Ch'ung-hui was able to accuse the dead officer of having insulted him and to point to the killing as a warning to those 'within and without' (*chung-wai*, that is, both the palace staff and the bureaucrats).

The aloofness of the bureaucrats from active politics at the court has already been noted. There were exceptions to the rule, but in the early years of this period, 926-946, such activity was by no

[42] *CWTS* 82, 3b. For *kung-fêng kuan* and *tien-chih*, see Chap. 4, note 15.

[43] *TFYK* 521, 3b-4a. In *TCTC* 275, T'ien-ch'êng 1(926)/7th month, where Li Ch'i is said to have 'reported' the incident (*i-wên* 以聞), Hu San-shêng comments that Li Ch'i was afraid of An Ch'ung-hui and did not dare to submit a 'memorial of accusation' (*ho-chou* 劾奏).

means safe. The Chief Minister, Jên Huan (926-927), who was outspoken in his criticism of An Ch'ung-hui, was removed from office and then executed. It was no less precarious to support one group of powerful palace officials. The Chief Minister, Chao Fêng (929-931), who had spoken in defence of An Ch'ung-hui did not remain long in office either after the latter's execution.[44]

In the field of imperial finance, the bureaucrats were similarly subdued. In 4th/926, the Commission of State Finance was abolished and the three economic offices (the *san-ssŭ*, that is, the Board of Finance, the Bureau of Public Revenue and the Salt and Transport Commission) were left in the control of one of the Chief Ministers who was appointed the *p'an san-ssŭ* (Chief Executive of the Three Offices).[45] After only thirteen months, however, the Three Offices were placed in the hands of one of the palace officials, Chang Yen-lang, a finance expert who had been in Li Ssŭ-yüan's service before he came to the throne. In 8th/930, a new commission was actually created to control the Three Offices under a palace commissioner (the *san-ssŭ shih*). This commission was essentially the same as that for State Finance and the finance experts who were the first two commissioners, Chang Yen-lang and Mêng Ku, were men in the tradition of Chao Yen of Liang and K'ung Ch'ien of the previous reign. It is significant that the new commission was established on the recommendation of the Military Secretariat and against the advice of the Chief Ministers.[46]

[44] Jên Huan, *CWTS* 67, 11b-13b; also 36, 9a; 37, 4b-5a; and *TCTC* 275, T'ien-ch'êng 2(927)/5/end of month.

Chao Fêng, *CWTS* 67, 6b-8a and *HWTS* 28, 12b-18b; also *TCTC* 277, Ch'ang-hsing 1(930)/9/*chia-hsü* and Ch'ang-hsing 2(931)/2/*hsin-ch'ou*. Chao Fêng did, however, try to save Jên Huan from death, but his failure left him no less a supporter of An Ch'ung-hui; *CWTS* 67, 7a and *TCTC* 276, T'ien-ch'êng 2(927)/10/*wu-tzŭ*.

[45] The Offices were left in the hands of the aristocrat Tou-lu Ko only for fifteen days; *CWTS* 35, 12a and 36, 2a (also see *infra*, p. 111, for the Chief Minister appointed Commissioner of State Finance in 11th/923 and removed soon afterwards for taking illegal loans). Jên Huan was then made *p'an san-ssŭ* and he retained this post for a year; *CWTS* 36, 2a and 38, 8a; 67, 13a.

Also see *TCTC* 275, T'ien-ch'êng 1(926)/5/*ping-ch'ên* and T'ien-ch'êng 2(927)/5/end of month.

[46] *CWTS* 41, 8b-9a; 149, 7b-8a; *HWTS* 26, 7b-8b.

Chang Yen-lang; *CWTS* 69, 8a-b and *HWTS* 26, 7b. Mêng Ku; *TFYK* 483,

The bureaucrats also failed to retain full control of the finance offices in the reigns of Li Ts'ung-k'o (934-936) and Shih Ching-t'ang (936-942). Early in each reign, a Chief Minister or various high bureaucrat officials controlled the Three Offices, only to lose that control to finance experts not of bureaucrat origins.[47] This loss of control occurred in spite of the fact that the two emperors were sympathetic to the bureaucrats and important advances were made in bureaucratic influence in the government during their reigns.

Nevertheless, the decade 926-936 was important for the recovery of the bureaucrats. A decisive factor was that there was no satisfactory alternative to the form of government they provided. The governors and army officers who came to power in the ninth century had emphasized personal relationships in the organizations they controlled and there were the beginnings of a new ruling class of army families, a new military nobility with its retainer service. But a government based on such personal ties was essentially unstable. The group of palace officials which the retainer service of Chu Wên and Li Ts'un-hsü had produced had great supervisory powers but had nothing to match the traditions of the bureaucracy which gave it stability.

Two aspects of the bureaucracy's survival are reflected in the following table which shows the distribution and origins of the bureaucrats for the years 926-936. It has been based on the backgrounds of forty-three men in three branches of the bureaucracy, the Censorate, the Department of Affairs of State and the Imperial Secretariat.

29a-b; *CWTS* 69, 7a. Chao Yen and K'ung Ch'ien have been considered in Chapter Four.

[47] During the reign of Li Ts'ung-k'o, the Three Offices were placed first in the Chief Minister Liu Hsü's control. But after the dismissal of Liu Hsü six months later, the imperial finances were again administered by the finance expert Chang Yen-lang (see note 46 above). *CWTS* 89, 12a-b; 69, 8b-10b; *TCTC* 279, Ch'ing-t'ai 1(934)/7/*hsin-hai*; 9/*wu-yin*; and 12/*i-hai*.

During the reign of Shih Ching-t'ang, the Three Offices were for a month in the hands of Chou Huai, one of his provincial officers, before being placed under various bureaucrats—Fêng Tao in charge of the Salt and Transport Commission, Lung Min of the Board of Finance and Wang Sung of the Bureau of Public Revenue. After 938, however, the Offices were re-united under the finance expert Liu Shên-chiao. They were not returned to bureaucrat

TABLE XII[48]

	Censor	Vice-Pres.* *li-pu*	Vice-Pres.* *hu-pu*	Sec.,+ Imp. Sec.	Total
T'ang and Liang courtiers	4	6	5	4	19
Exam. graduates of Liang	1	—	2	1	4
Ho-pei literati who served Liang	—	—	1	2	3
Anti-Liang bureaucrats	—	1	—	—	1
Northern literati (after 923)	5	2	4	—	11
Uncertain	2	1	2	—	5
Total	12	10	14	7	43

* Vice-President of Civil Office (*li-pu*) and of Finance (*hu-pu*)
+ Secretary of the Imperial Secretariat

control until 7th/944. *CWTS* 95, 7a-8a; 76, 5b-7a; 106, 2a; 83, 2a; *HWTS* 48, 12a; *TCTC* 280, T'ien-fu 1(936)/12/*kêng-tzŭ*; 281, T'ien-fu 2(937)/1/*i-ch'ou*.

[48] A. The twelve vice-presidents of the Censorate were as follows (references are from the *CWTS* unless otherwise stated):

4 T'ang and Liang courtiers:
Ts'ui Chü-chien (*HWTS* 55, 23a-b; *TFYK* 459, 32a).
Lu Wên-chi (127, 1a-2b; *HWTS* 55, 5a-10b).
Liang Wên-chü (92, 4a-b).
Liu Tsan (68, 7a-8b).

1 Liang examination graduate:
Lu Shun (128, 7b-8b).

5 Northern literati:
Chang Chao (*Sung Shih* 263, 1a-4b).
Chang P'êng (106, 9b-10a).
Lü Ch'i (92, 2b-3b; *TFYK* 729, 17a-b).
Lü Mêng-ch'i (no biography, see 89, 11b; 36, 6b; 39, 8b; 43, 1a).
Lung Min (108, 9a-11a).

2 of uncertain origins:
Hsü Kuang-i (no biography, see 40, 3b; 41, 10b).
Ts'ui Yen (no biography, see 42, 9b; 44, 2b).

B. The ten vice-presidents of the Ministry of Civil Office (thirteen are known by name but three of them became head of the Censorate later on and are included in sub-section A above):

6 T'ang and Liang courtiers:
Chang Wên-pao (68, 6a-b) Ts'ui I-sun (69, 6b-7a).
Liu Yüeh (68, 3a-b) Wang Ch'üan (92, 9a-10a).
Lu Chan (93, 5a) Yao I (92, 1a-2b).

1 anti-Liang bureaucrat from the T'ang court:
Li Tê-hsiu (60, 9a).

2 Northern literati:
Han Yen-yün (92, 10a-b) Yo Tsung-chih (71, 4a-b).

The large number of bureaucrats who had served through the Liang to the end of the Chin is remarkable evidence of the continuity which they provided in imperial government. This continuity also ensured the survival of bureaucratic traditions. The other feature is the swift rise to high office of the eleven provincial literati who had come to the court after 923. They provided fresh blood to the civil service and augmented the supply of bureaucrats produced by traditional methods of selection. The careers of some

1 of uncertain origins:
Wên Nien (no biography, see 37, 6b; 38, 14a).

C. The fourteen vice-presidents of the Ministry of Finance (nineteen are known by name but five held posts in the Censorate or the Civil Office later on — in A and B above):

5 T'ang and Liang courtiers:
Kuei Ai (68, 5b; also 38, 4b).
Li I (92, 10b-11b).
Ma Kao (71, 5a-b; *HWTS* 55, 18b-22b).
P'ei Hao (92, 6a-b; *HWTS* 57, 15a-16a).
Yang Ning-shih (128, 4a-6a).
2 Liang examination graduates:
Jên Tsan (no biography, see 128, 8a; 30, 3a; 36, 6a; 40, 5a and 7a; 42, 7a; 44, 4a-b, 8a and 9b).
Ts'ui T'o (93, 5b-6b).
1 Ho-pei literati who served the Liang:
Chao Fêng (67, 6b-8a; *HWTS* 28, 12b-18b).
4 Northern literati:
Fêng Tao (126, 1a-12b) Liu Hsü (89, 11a-13a)
Li Sung (108, 1a-4a) Shih Kuei (92, 4b-6a).
2 of uncertain origins:
Ch'êng Sun (96, 9a; also 38, 11b; 43, 11a; 46, 14a)
Yen Chih (no biography, see 38, 7a; 40, 5a; 41, 10b; 41, 13a).

D. The seven secretaries of the Imperial Secretariat (eighteen are known by name but eleven later held posts in the three offices already considered — in A, B and C above):

4 T'ang and Liang courtiers:
Fêng Ch'iao (no biography, see 68, 4a-b; 9, 2b; 30, 3a; 42, 8b; *TFYK* 475, 20b).
Li Yü (67, 8a-11b).
Lu Tao (92, 7a-8a).
Tou Mêng-cheng (68, 4b-5a).
1 Liang examination graduate:
Ho Ning (127, 5a-7a).
2 Ho-pei literati who had served Liang:
Ch'ên Ngai (68, 6b-7a) Wang Yen (131, 4b-5b).

of the eleven men also testify to the relaxing of bureaucratic standards.[49]

The ideal of a bureaucratic empire received fuller recognition in Li Ssŭ-yüan's reign, although bureaucrats were still unable to dominate affairs at the court. By the end of the reign and in the decade following 933, there was obvious imperial favour for them. This was largely because of the more important role they had begun to play in the control of the provinces.

Two examples of this role in the provinces show the greater confidence the bureaucrats had begun to feel about themselves. In 933, a nephew of Li Ssŭ-yüan who was governor of Chên province ordered three of his officials to investigate a property dispute in a local merchant's family. The officials accepted bribes from one of the parties in the dispute and executed the defendant. The matter came to the notice of the Censorate which ordered two of the bureaucrats appointed by the court to the province, the assistant governor and the secretary, to review the case. The corruption in the governor's office was revealed and the three men concerned executed. Only intervention from a favourite concubine of the emperor saved the governor from being dismissed.[50]

This was the first recorded example of successful bureaucrat criticism in the provinces since the Huang Ch'ao rebellion. The emperor's exclamation that his nephew's actions made him ashamed to meet his court officials underlines his part in raising the morale of the bureaucrats.[51]

The increased confidence of the bureaucrats can be illustrated further by their resolute stand against the governor of the border province of Ching in 942. The governor, Chang Yen-tsê, an ex-

[49] Several of these eleven men probably would not have reached the ranks of the bureaucracy if the governors they served had not become emperors. Examples were Chang P'êng (106, 9b-10a), Han Yen-yün (92, 10a-b), Shih Kuei (92, 4b-6a) and Yo Tsung-chih (71, 4a-b) (also in note 48 above).

[50] *CWTS* 123, 8a-9a and 44, 2b. More details in Sun Kuang-hsien, *Pei-mêng So-yen*, 20, 1a-2a.

The three officials were probably a senior administrator, a military deputy and the governor's own executive official. The *Pei-mêng So-yen* and *CWTS* 44, 2b, agree about the men concerned, but *CWTS* 123, 9a, has a different version in that the same three men are said to have held other posts.

[51] *CWTS* 123, 9a.

army commander of Turkish origins who had allied himself by marriage to the imperial family as well as to that of the most powerful governor at the time, had killed the provincial secretary, Chang Shih, in 941. The next year, Chang Shih's father reported the killing and there was a great outcry about it among the bureaucrats at the court. The governor was recalled and actually demoted in rank. A posthumous title was conferred on Chang Shih, his father given a pension, his brother and his son appointed to minor provincial posts, his property returned and his family compensated to the extent of 100,000 cash. This was a great triumph for the bureaucrats who had made an issue of Chang Shih's fate. An interesting epilogue to the affair was the governor's respect for the literati when he was later again appointed a governor.[52]

This trend towards stronger bureaucrat influence has already been noted in the earlier discussion on the post of Military Secretary in the reigns of Li Ts'ung-k'o and Shih Ching-t'ang (pp. 156-158). The recovery of the bureaucracy had been partly at the expense of the palace service but, more significant, it was also partly because of the attitude of some of the palace officials towards the bureaucrats. At least two of the twenty-one palace commissioners considered above (Table IX) introduced their sons into the civil service. In the Sung dynasty, Kao Han-yün's son was to become a junior metropolitan governor (*K'ai-fêng shao-yin*) and Liu Ch'u-jang's son rose to high office in the ministries in the Department of Affairs of State.[53] A remarkable example was the family of Hou I, the farmer's son who had risen from being a soldier to be a governor. One of his sons who followed him around as a member of the provincial staff was eventually taken into the palace as a minor commissioner, and a grandson became a *chin-shih* graduate in the Sung. Another son was allied in marriage to Chao P'u, the Chief Minister who dominated the Sung court.[54]

[52] *CWTS* 98, 5b-6b and *TFYK* 449, 16b-17a; 460, 40a. Also see *CWTS* 80, 9b; 96, 8a-9a; *TCTC* 283, T'ien-fu 7(942)/1/*jên-wu* and 4/*chi-wei*: *Sung Shih* 262, 6a.

[53] Kao Han-yün's son, *CWTS* 94, 13b; Liu Ch'u-jang's son, *CWTS* 94, 10b and *Sung Shih* 276, 1a-2a.

[54] *Sung Shih* 254, 1a-2b and 3a.

There was also the earlier example of Sang Wei-han. He was the son of a provincial reception officer. His father could have become a palace official and so could he. But he had 'a small talent for letters' and his father's governor was sympathetic to his aspirations and pulled the right strings for him.[55] He was a *chin-shih* in 925 and eleven years later became the first Chief Minister and Military Secretary of the Chin empire.

Sang Wei-han was the outstanding product of the late T'ang provincial organization. He was the forerunner of many more men of similar background who were to swell the ranks of the bureaucracy. His own talents and the perspicacity of his father's governor had, however, saved him one step in the rise to the highest offices at the court. That step was the palace service which provided others with the experience of imperial government and an introduction to the highest political circles. In time, the versatility of the palace officials not only distinguished them as a group, but also enriched the outlook and broadened the activities of new generations of bureaucrats.

The palace officials had taken over the functions of the eunuchs of the ninth century. Their success as the trusted men of the Wu-tai emperors was one of the main contributions of the *chieh-tu shih* system to the new imperial power and characterized the early half of the tenth century. Furthermore, it was in the interests of such a group of men to support a strong central government, and their support was one of the factors in the decline of provincial power in this period.

[55] Chang Ch'i-hsien, *Lo-yang Chin-shên Chiu-wen Chi*, 2, 5b-6a. Also *CWTS* 89, 1a-9a.

CHAPTER SEVEN

The Decline of the Provinces and the Emergence of a New Structure of Power 926-947

After the Huang Ch'ao rebellion, the relationship between the court and the provinces had been determined by the fact that each governor had the resources to declare himself independent of central authority and could hope for enough support from some of his fellow governors to remain independent. Provincial power had grown so strong that the T'ang dynasty never recovered its authority, and it took two generations of two new imperial houses to re-establish control over North China.

This control was by no means perfect, as can be seen in the part played by some of the governors in the sudden fall of the imperial house of Li Ts'un-hsü. But in the course of the twenty years 907-926, the number of provinces which could support independent governors was greatly reduced and even more so was the number of governors who had the resources to defy the central government. At the beginning of 926, there only remained a few strong provinces in Ho-pei and Kuan-chung, one in Shan-nan and potentially two in the newly conquered territories of Shu.[1]

[1] In Ho-pei, Yu and Ting provinces were the strongest provinces while Chên and Wei could possibly support independent governors. In Kuan-chung, Ching, Ch'i, and Yen provinces were under hereditary governors (and north of Kuan-chung, there were Hsia and Ling provinces governed by a Li and a Han family respectively).

In southern Shan-nan, the governor of Ching had declared his independence. In Shu, I (Ch'êng-tu) and Tzŭ provinces were potentially dangerous to Li Ssŭ-yüan because large units of the expeditionary army to Shu had been left behind under the control of the governors of these provinces.

The fact that Li Ssŭ-yüan ascended the throne in 926 after rebelling against his emperor, however, made relations more difficult between the court and the provinces. Having been one of Li Ts'un-hsü's governors, Li Ssŭ-yüan was faced with the task of re-establishing imperial authority in an empire governed largely by his colleagues. Because these governors had been his colleagues, they gained in status with regard to the new court and Li Ssŭ-yüan was forced to bargain for the support which some of them could give him. If this support was not forthcoming at a reasonable price—for example, more honours and privileges or transfer to a wealthier or more strategic province—then Li Ssŭ-yüan had to resort to force.

Fortunately for him, provincial power at that time was not comparable to that in the early years of the century, and it was eventually possible for him to gain control over most of the provinces of Li Ts'un-hsü's empire. This was helped by the fact that when Li Ts'un-hsü died there were no governors for five provinces. The governors of another seven had been killed in the course of the upheaval following the rebellion. Three other governors whom Li Ssŭ-yüan did not trust were in provinces close to the capital (Lo-yang) and could thus be easily removed.[2] Therefore, at the beginning of his reign, there were fifteen vacancies to fill mainly with his relatives and with various army officers who had

[2] Four of the five provinces did not have governors because Li Ts'un-hsü had executed the governors just before his death. The governors were Chu Ling-tê of Sui in Szechuan (*CWTS* 63, 9a-10a), Chu Ling-hsi of Hsü$_3$ in Ho-nan (*Ibid.*), Li Ts'un-ngai of Fu in Kuan-chung (*CWTS* 34, 1b) and K'ang-Yen-hsiao of Shan who had rebelled in Szechuan in 2nd/926 (*CWTS* 74, 3a-4b). The fifth province was probably left vacant after the governor's transfer in 1st/926. This was Hua province in Ho-nan (*CWTS* 34, 2a).

The seven governors who were killed during Li Ssŭ-yüan's revolt were the four brothers of Li Ts'un-hsü who had nominally governed P'u, Yün, Chin and Hsing provinces (*HWTS* 14, 18b-21a), and Yüan Hsing-ch'in of Sung (*CWTS* 70, 3a), Li Ts'un-ching of T'ung (*TCTC* 275, T'ien-ch'êng 1(926)/4/ before *hsin-ch'ou*) and Chang Hsien of Ping (also viceroy of the Northern Capital, T'ai-yüan; *CWTS* 69, 3a-b).

The three governors close to the capital who were removed were Shih Ching-jung of Hua in Kuan-chung (*TCTC op. cit.*), Tuan Ning of Têng (*CWTS* 73, 4b) and Chu Shou-yin of Yen whose appointment as governor of Lo-yang kept him under Li Ssŭ-yüan's control (*CWTS* 74, 5b).

supported him in his revolt.[3] Of the twenty provinces still outside his direct control, seven were situated in the midst of his other provinces and were taken over by the end of 926.[4] The remaining thirteen were situated close to the borders. Four of them, however,

[3] Of the fifteen governors who filled the vacancies, two were Li Ssŭ-yüan's relatives and nine his supporters. Three were Li Ts'un-hsü's governors who were either transferred from their own provinces or were re-employed. Of these three, Huo Yen-wei was also a supporter of Li Ssŭ-yüan. The fifteenth vacancy was filled by Liang Han-yung who was one of the leading commanders of the expeditionary army to Shu and had returned with Jên Huan in 4th/926. (The references below are from *CWTS* unless otherwise stated):

Li Ssŭ-yüan's relatives

Li Ts'ung-k'o (46, 2b)
Shih Ching-t'ang (75, 4a-b).

His supporters

Chao Tsai-li (90, 1b)
Fang Chih-wên (91, 1b)
Fu Yen-ch'ao (56, 11a-b)
Liu Chung-yin (no biography; see 35, 12a; 36, 3b where Shan (陝) was probably an error for Fu (鄜); see also 38, 9b).
Liu Yen-tsung (61, 7b)
Mi Chün-li (no biography; see 36, 2b and 3a).
T'ao Ch'i (no biography; see 36, 3b and *TCTC* 274, T'ien-ch'eng 1(926)/3/*hsin-ssŭ*).
Wang Ssŭ-t'ung (65, 5b).
Wang Yen-ch'iu (64, 3b-4a).

Others

An Ch'ung-yüan (90, 9b; 34, 8b-9a; 36, 7b).
Huo Yen-wei (64, 2a).
Li Shao-wên (59, 11a).
Liang Han-yung (88, 9b-10a).

[4] The seven provinces taken over by the end of 926 were Ch'ing in Ho-nan, Wei and Ts'ang in Ho-pei, Yün and Lu in Ho-tung, An in Shan-nan and Pin in Kuan-chung. The governors of these provinces were all transferred and more reliable men were appointed in their place. In one case, however, it was not the governor who could not be trusted but some of the provincial commanders. It was necessary to send a member of the imperial family with a strong central force to take over the province from the local garrison. The governor who was transferred was Chao Tsai-li, one of the men who had supported Li Ssŭ-yüan (see note 3 above).

The other six governors who were transferred were as follows (references are from the *CWTS*):

Fu Hsi (59, 4b).
Kao Hsing-kuei (65, 4a-b).
K'ung Ching (64, 7b)
Liu Ch'i (64, 8a-b).
Mao Chang (73, 1b).
Wang Ching-k'an (no biography; see 34, 7a and 37, 6b).

were also taken over by 928.[5] His success encouraged Li Ssŭ-yüan to be more aggressive. After a large-scale campaign in 928-929, he was rewarded with the capture of Ting, the last independent province of Ho-pei.[6] By early 930, he had replaced another four border governors.[7] Only Ching province on the Yangtse, I and Tzŭ provinces in Shu and Hsia province north of Kuan-chung continued to defy him until his death in 11th/933.[8]

Li Ssŭ-yüan's achievement was considerable for a man who had usurped the throne. Although he was unable to preserve his predecessor's empire intact, he was successful in consolidating control over the Ho-pei, Kuan-chung and Shan-nan regions. This he had done with Ho-nan as his administrative and economic base and Ho-tung, the home of the tribal imperial power, as the strategic centre.

An important feature of Li Ssŭ-yüan's success was his willingness to concede a measure of autonomy to the governors. He had himself as a governor felt the weight of increasing central control under Li Ts'un-hsü's government and he knew what the main sources of irritation were. When he became emperor he promptly executed the Commissioner of State Finance and prohibited central finance officials from interfering with provincial accounts. He also abolished the system of provincial Army Supervisors.[9] But the concessions were not excessive and the essentials for administrative control were left as they were. A few months later

[5] Of the governors of these four provinces, Chang Yün (*CWTS* 90, 6a) and Liu Hsün (*CWTS* 61, 6a-b) were recalled, Chang-Ching-hsün (*CWTS* 61, 7a) was transferred, and Chang T'ing-yü (*CWTS* 65, 5a) died in office.

[6] *CWTS* 54, 6b-8b, the biography of the governor of Ting, Wang Tu. Also see *CWTS* 39, 5b to 40, 1b, *passim*; and *TCTC* 276, T'ien-ch'êng 3(928)/4/*kuei-ssŭ*, ff. to T'ien-ch'êng 4(929)/2/*kuei-ch'ou*.

[7] All the four governors were comparatively young men who had inherited their respective provinces from their fathers. They were Li Chi-yen and Li Chi-ch'ang (*CWTS* 132, 5a-6b and 6b-7a), Han Ch'êng (*CWTS* 132, 9b) and Kao Yün-t'ao (*CWTS* 132, 8b).

[8] The governors of Ching were Kao Chi-hsing and his son Kao Ts'ung-hui (*CWTS* 133, 1a-2b and 2b-4a). The governor of I was the founder of Later Shu, Mêng Chih-hsiang (*HWTS* 64A, 1a-16a) and that of Tzŭ was Tung Chang (*CWTS* 62, 5b-8a). The governor of Hsia was the Tangut tribesman Li Jên-fu (*CWTS* 132, 10a-b).

[9] *WTHY* 24, pp. 290-291; *CWTS* 35, 12a-b and *TFYK* 160, 12a-b; also *TCTC* 275, T'ien-ch'êng 1(926)/4/*kêng-tzŭ*.

when he had reorganized the imperial armies and established his Personal Army, Li Ssŭ-yüan felt strong enough to define his position in relation to the provinces he could control. In 8th/926, there were two important documents addressed to the governors which illustrate some aspects of his provincial policy. The documents also have special interest because they mark the limits of Li Ssŭ-yüan's administrative reforms.

The first document was the edict of 10/8th/926.[10] It was mainly concerned with regulating some of the privileges of the governors. The first section distinguished between the provincial officials appointed by the court and those recommended by the governor himself and ordered that the governor's own staff should accompany him on transfers and follow him out of office when he was dismissed. In this way, a governor's friends or protégés could be prevented from holding independent office. As a new governor to the province could be better persuaded to accept a court-chosen staff, the court could expect that when all the governors had been either replaced or regularly transferred a fresh set of officials consisting of men more likely to be loyal to the central government would have been built up.[11]

[10] *WTHY* 25, pp. 301-302; *CWTS* 37, 1a-2a and *TFYK* 61, 11b-12a. The *WTHY* dates the edict as 11/8th/926 while the *CWTS* dates it as *chia-wu*/8th which is 10/8th. The *TFYK* gives only the month. I have followed the *CWTS* here.

[11] *WTHY* 25, p. 301, has the fullest text for this section of the edict. It has an introduction which is also in *TFYK* 61, 11a, but it has been omitted in *CWTS* 37, 1a. After the introduction, however, the *TFYK* text is similar to that of the *CWTS* and a little different from that of the *WTHY*. The text of the *WTHY* reads as follows (it is abbreviated in *CWTS* and *TFYK* except for two sentences in the middle):

'The practice in recent years has been different from (that) in the past. Although a governor's establishment was transferred, the administrators continued in their original posts.

(In the *TFYK*, the last sentence reads, "Although a governor's establishment has already been transferred . . ." The *CWTS* has the same wording but has in error *sui* 隨 instead of *sui* 雖).

'From now on, those (the administrators) who have been appointed by the court shall not be transferred together with their governor.

(In the *TFYK*, the second half of the sentence reads: ". . . (they) may not be transferred by the governor". This makes little sense in the context. The *CWTS* text for the same half of the sentence, however, may be read ". . .

The second section dealt with four aspects of the problem of recommending provincial and prefectural staff. The first emphasized the relative privileges of senior governors, junior governors and superior prefects (defence and militia commissioners) and showed how the court had scaled down the position of the senior governors when compared with that of the others. The second aspect was that the governors and superior prefects were required to submit details of the careers of their nominees. The third concerned the right of the ordinary prefects to nominate their staff. These prefects were prohibited from directly memorializing to the throne about their nominations. This order is interesting because it suggests that by this time there were matters on which the prefects could approach the court without going through the provincial government. Lastly, the abuses of privileges were dealt with. Governors and prefects often made false claims and excessive demands for their nominees and the edict called for the reform of a practice which 'corrupted the law'.[12]

The edict was followed two weeks later, on 23/8th/926, by another which was devised by the Military Secretariat.[13] The second document dealt with the violations of administrative regulations in the provinces. The chief abuse, which was an important source of a governor's wealth, was the levying of additional taxes in various forms and under many pretexts. In order to restrict the malpractices, the officials of the basic administrative units, the counties (*hsien*) and the garrison-towns (*chên*), were ordered to reject requests made by their governors or prefects for extra taxes. In this way, Li Ssŭ-yüan's court showed its determination to re-assert its authority in local government.[14]

(they) are not concerned with the governor's transfer". This is due to the difference of one word in the three texts, hsi 係 in *WTHY*, *hsü* 許 in *TFYK* and *chi* 計 in *CWTS*).

'If (they) have been appointed to their posts at the request of (the governor) himself, (they) must follow (him) away and their work will also come to an end if the (governor's) office is discontinued.'

[12] *WTHY* 25, p. 301-302; *CWTS* 37, 1b-2a; *TFYK* 61, 11b-12a.

[13] *CWTS* 37, 2a-b and *TFYK* 65, 17b-18b. The *CWTS* text is greatly abbreviated when compared with that in the *TFYK*.

[14] In *TFYK* 65, 18a, the section on this reads,

Another threat to imperial authority took the form of the illegal recruitment of men of all classes, including criminals and bandits, to be the governor's armed retainers. This recruitment had been carried out in spite of the fact that the governors were permitted to form their guards from men of the imperial regiments. It was done in order to circumvent the check which the court had hoped to maintain on the number of men the governors had in their private service. It is probable that the illegally recruited men were then employed as unofficial staff to supervise the provincial officials and to enforce demands which the officials might refuse to grant.[15]

'(When) the various *hsien* and *chên* receive special despatches (those sent with the official tallies?) from the *chou*, (the *hsien* and *chên* officials) should act accordingly if the principles of the demands are just (but) are prohibited from secretly complying with the despatches if they concern the levying of additional taxes from the people. Hereafter, if some information (of such irregularities) is acquired by inquiry, the officials of the place(s) involved will be the first to be punished.'
The text in *CWTS* 37, 2b has the first sentence in an abbreviated form and omits the second sentence altogether.

[15] *TFYK* 65, 17b and *CWTS* 37, 2b. As with the section in note 14 above, the *CWTS* text is an abbreviated one, but there are important differences from the *TFYK* text. Firstly, the *CWTS* text seems to refer to the guards (*ya-tui* 牙隊) of both the governors and the prefects (*chieh-tu shih ch'ih shih* 節度使刺史), but the *TFYK* text refers only to the governors, that is, to the prefects who were also *chieh-tu shih* (the *chieh-tu ch'ih-shih* 節度刺史). I think it is probable that only the governors were involved in the illegal recruitment of men and that, in the context, the *TFYK* text is correct. There is no evidence that ordinary prefects dared to recruit illegally to strengthen their guards.

Other differences between the two texts are noted in the following translation which is based on the *TFYK*:
'The governor has been permitted to select men from the (imperial) regiments for his (provincial) guards. (These men) were then issued with food and clothing from the official departments.

(The *CWTS* text has *chieh* 結, "arrange for" instead of *chi* 給, "issue". *Chieh* is probably a copyist's error.)

'Extremely large numbers of men have already been (selected). Now (? *ju-chin* 如今 instead of *ju* 如) that it is known that there has been further enlistment which has caused disturbances, it is immediately advised that a thorough investigation be made.

(From the context, *ju* 如, "if" by itself does not make sense. I suggest that

An additional abuse connected with another level of recruitment was that 'members of powerful families (the *yu-li hu*) practised bribery in their various localities hoping to be put in charge of affairs'.[16] This was specially deplored by the court because strong local loyalty to a governor might encourage him to be independent of central control.

The document ended with a warning that if the governors and prefects continued to violate the regulations mentioned, the people were allowed to report them and be rewarded if their reports were confirmed by investigation. Although the warning was conventional, there was throughout the statement a new note of confidence in the government's ability to enforce the law in the provinces. This can be contrasted with Li Ssŭ-yüan's passive policy four months earlier before he was certain of his control over the imperial armies of his predecessor.

The two documents also show the limitations of administrative reforms in that the issues mentioned in both of them remained dominant in Li Ssŭ-yüan's reign and the various regulations continued to be violated from time to time by individual governors. It is, however, possible that the policy of reforms was effective in most provinces for a few years after 926, and that it was Li Ssŭ-yüan's later military reverses which made it more difficult for him to maintain the policy. There seems to have been a correlation

chin 今, "now" followed *ju* in the original text. The sentence is abbreviated in the *CWTS* and reads, "Inquiries (show that) there is still the enlistment (of more men)", which seems to confirm that the present *TFYK* text is wrong in having *ju* by itself.)

'Various kinds of men, most of whom had gone into hiding because (they had) committed crimes, have been at the prefectural office (of the governor?) to offer to be retainers (*yüan-sui* 元隨) of the governor. (These men) ask for tasks (which) oppress the people.'

(In the *CWTS*, the first sentence reads, 'Various kinds of men, most of whom had fled from justice for their crimes, have given their names to the prefectural office (to be considered) as retainers of the governor'. It is possible that in the *TFYK* text the word *ming* 名, 'name', is missing.)

[16] *TFYK* 65, 17b. Also in *CWTS* 37, 2b, but *CWTS* omits the clause in the *TFYK* which says, 'From now on, the people are allowed to report (on such matters)'.

between the failure to pursue further reforms and the failure of the campaigns against Shu (Szechuan) in 930-931.

This correlation can be seen in the example of the appointment of senior provincial officials which was the main theme of the edict of 10/8th/926 discussed above. On 9/5th/928, the court went further than the early edict and fixed the number of annual nominations each governor could make. It was also decided that the future appointments of the two senior administrators (the two *p'an-kuan*) should be left to the court. But in 7th/931, four months after the last provinces in Szechuan were lost, the number of annual nominations per governor was reconsidered and increased. A year later, in 7th/932, a memorial was submitted which showed that the administrators who were not chosen by a governor himself were often prevented from performing their duties by the governor's staff, and that some of the governors still nominated their administrators as they pleased. The regulations of 9/5th/928 seemed to be no longer effective by this time. What was more important was that the court did not think it wise to do anything about the criticisms and the memorial was not heeded.[17]

There was in fact no notable progress in administrative reforms in the last years of Li Ssŭ-yüan's reign nor was there any in the fifteen years after his death. Li Ssŭ-yüan's young son, Li Ts'ung-hou, was on the throne for only five months while the usurper, Li Ts'ung-k'o, was faced with serious disaffection in his armies from the beginning of his reign. A stronger rule was possible after Shih Ching-t'ang, the founder of the Chin, had brought the imperial armies together again firmly under his control in 9th/938. But he paid greater attention to measures which strengthened the Emperor's Army, and he and his nephew Shih Ch'ung-kuei were both content with the degree of administrative con-

[17] The regulations of 9/5th/928 are preserved in the form of a memorial from the Imperial Secretariat; *CWTS* 39, 6a. The revised regulations of 7th/931 are preserved as an edict; *CWTS* 42, 6b. The memorial of 7th/932 is preserved only in *TFYK* 475, 25a.

For the events leading to the loss of all the provinces in Szechuan, see *CWTS* 41, 10a-13a and *TCTC* 277, Ch'ang-hsing 1(930)/9/*kuei-hai* to *kêng-yin*; 11/*chia-hsü* to *chia-shên*; 12/*jên-ch'ên* to *jên-tzŭ*; Ch'ang-hsing 2(931)/1/*kuei-yu*; 2/*chi-ch'ou*, *chia-wu* and *ting-ssŭ*; 3/*chi-wei*, *jên-hsü*.

trol they had inherited from the successors of Li Ssŭ-yüan.

Nevertheless, there was a consistent provincial policy during the whole period. Two aspects of the policy stand out. Firstly, the court continued with the policy of keeping the resources of the governors to the minimum. The Chin court was particularly successful in this and in 11th/938 was able to cut up Wei province, the bane of central government for 180 years, into three small parts. Wei Chou became a subsidiary capital with a viceroy-governor who had jurisdiction only over Wei province. The other two provinces which were created also reduced the size of the neighbouring province of Chên. In 8th/944, another province was created with its capital at Ch'an Chou, one of the most strategic crossings on the Huang Ho, and, consequently, both the provinces of Hsiang in Ho-pei and of Yün in Ho-nan were reduced in size.[18] The policy was applied in a different way to the three rebellious provinces of An, Hsiang and Ch'ing (the first two in Shan-nan and the third in the eastern end of Ho-nan). After crushing the rebellions the court abolished the provinces. An, Hsiang and Ch'ing Chou were then made defence prefectures under the control of the emperor's trusted courtiers.[19]

The second aspect of the policy that stands out was the bureaucratic supervision of provincial and local government, especially of the work of those officials who had customarily been directed by the governor's personal staff. In practice this supervision was not very successful but it was maintained as the ideal throughout the period, and its importance lay in that it inspired the bureaucrats to have greater confidence in themselves. An example of this new confidence can be seen in the way Wan T'ing-kuei, the assistant governor of Ching province, took over control of the province when the governor was dying in early 939. With the help of the secretary, Li Shêng, he was able to prevent the governor's family and retainer officers from seizing control of the government and to preserve order until the arrival of the new governor. His achievement was all the more significant because the governor was

[18] *CWTS* 77, 10a-b; 83, 3a. Also *TCTC* 281, T'ien-fu 3(938)/11/*hsin-hai* and 284, K'ai-yün 1(944)/8/*kuei-hai*.

[19] *CWTS* 79, 4b; 81, 6a and 83, 6b.

a senior Turkish officer of great influence and his retainers had been accustomed to interfering in the provincial administration.[20] Another example of bureaucrat confidence in the provinces has already been considered. This was the affair of the provincial secretary who had been murdered by his governor (see Chapter Six, pp. 174-175). Although the bureaucrats were unable to achieve full control of the provincial governments, they had become more successful in keeping a check on provincial power.

Administrative reforms and constant supervision by the Court played their part in the decline of provincial power in that they helped to make permanent the gains achieved by military pressure. But the decline is better seen in terms of the increase in central military power and its effect on the kind of role the governors were able to play in imperial politics.

The most important development in central power was the rise of the emperor's 'private army' (*ssŭ-ping*) at the expense of the 'army of the state' (*kuo-ping*). This development was due to the policy initiated by Li Ssŭ-yüan whose approach to the empire was conditioned partly by his predecessor's failure to control the imperial armies and partly by his own experience of the provincial 'governor's guards' (*ya-chün*). The principle behind his military policy was that at no time should there be an army outside the metropolitan territories stronger than the Emperor's Personal Army. This was a defensive policy which could not win new territories and even lost him some of the border provinces. But it was designed to provide security at the centre and, by so doing, to help consolidate imperial power over the more accessible areas of the empire. The policy was comparatively successful and laid the foundations for the integration of Ho-pei and Kuan-chung with Ho-nan later on.

The Emperor's Army was Li Ssŭ-yüan's answer to the unstable relations between the court and the provinces which his usurpation had brought about. But he did not foresee that the Army would become a source of instability at the capital. It has been noted that the Chief Commander of the Army had begun to play a part in the

[20] *CWTS* 88, 15b-16a and *TFYK* 454, 10b-11b.

imperial succession even before Li Ssŭ-yüan's death in 11th/933. Early in the following year, the Army played a more decisive role when some of its officers placed the usurper Li Ts'ung-k'o on the throne.[21] But, as the support for Li Ts'ung-k'o had been purchased by promises of rewards and was not based on either personal loyalty to himself or his effective control of the Army, relations with the governors became difficult again. The disputed succession had lost Li Ts'ung-k'o all the remaining provinces in Shu (those in south Shensi)[22] and the other governors, most of whom had been his fellow-officers under Li Ssŭ-yüan, were indifferent to his claims to the throne. In the years 934-936, Li Ts'ung-k'o tried to make the Army once more the instrument of imperial security. His failure to do so can be seen in the campaign against Shih Ching-t'ang in 936 and this failure gave a new lease of power to several governors.

When Li Ts'ung-k'o became emperor, he had appointed five of the army officers and prefects who had supported him to widely scattered provinces in order to separate the older governors from each other.[23] In time, he was able to transfer or recall all the governors except the two who were imperial relatives. These two were Shih Ching-t'ang of Ping province, the son-in-law of Li Ssŭ-yüan, and Chao Tê-chün of Yu province, the father of another son-in-law.[24]

The two governors commanded border defence units, but

[21] *CWTS* 45, 5b-8b; 46, 3b-4b.

[22] The provinces were lost to the 'empire' of Later Shu which was founded by Mêng Chih-hsiang the governor of Ch'êng-tu three months before Li Ts'ung-k'o usurped the throne; *TCTC* 278, Ch'ing-t'ai 1(934)/1/*chi-ssŭ*. The provinces were those of Liang and Yang; *TCTC* 279, Ch'ing-t'ai 1(934)/4/ before *jên-shên*.

[23] Of the five men, Yang Ssŭ-ch'üan (*CWTS* 88, 11a), Yin Hui (*CWTS* 88, 11b) and An Shên-ch'i (*CWTS* 47, 2b-3a) had surrendered units of the Emperor's Army to Li Ts'ung-k'o at Ch'i Chou while An Ts'ung-chin (*CWTS* 45, 8b) showed his support at Lo-yang. The fifth man, Hsiang-li Chin (*CWTS* 90, 17b), was a superior prefect along the western border who had been one of the first to join Li Ts'ung-k'o's cause.

The five men were scattered, in Pin in Kuan-chung, in Ying in Ho-tung, in Hsing in Ho-pei, in Hsiang in Shan-nan and in Shan in Ho-nan.

[24] Shih Ching-t'ang; *CWTS* 75, 1a-7a. Chao Tê-chün; *CWTS* 98, 8b-9a. Chao Tê-chün's son (in fact, an adopted son) was Chao Yen-shou; *op. cit.*, 11a.

neither of them was likely to be a serious threat to Li Ts'ung-k'o as long as the main Emperor's Army supported him. But the loyalty of the Army had been shaken since 934 by Li Ts'ung-k'o's inability to fulfil his promises of generous cash rewards on ascending the throne. Thus, two weeks after Shih Ching-t'ang rebelled at Ping Chou in 5th/936, the Army regiments stationed at Wei Chou mutinied. A large expeditionary force had to be sent to deal with the mutiny and 20,000 men were tied up at Wei Chou for two critical months while Shih Ching-t'ang arranged to bring in the Khitan armies to support him. Several other imperial units along the borders also mutinied and went over to Shih Ching-t'ang. In 9th/936, the section of the Emperor's Army sent against Shih Ching-t'ang was defeated and then surrounded outside Ping Chou by the Khitans. At this point, Li Ts'ung-k'o made the mistake of sending the bulk of the Army remaining with him out of the capital under the control of his two strongest governors, Chao Tê-chün of Yu and Fan Yen-kuang who had re-captured Wei Chou from the mutineers. The two governors distrusted each other and neither made any effort to relieve the surrounded army. Instead, Chao Tê-chün began to bargain for Khitan support for himself.[25]

The emperor had only a fourth section of the Army left with him and this was inadequate for his own defence. The situation at the capital can be best seen through the desperate edicts of 10th/936 ordering the formation of a new army to defend the emperor. It was ordered that from each unit of seven families one soldier should be produced and armed. There was also a scheme to supply the army with horses. But in the face of the great opposition aroused by these edicts, only five thousand men and two thousand horses were received.[26] By this time, two of the three sections of the Emperor's Army outside the capital had submitted

[25] *CWTS* 48, 4a-10b; 75, 7a-9a; 69, 11a; 70, 9a-b; 97, 2a-b; 98, 9a-10b. Also *TCTC* 279, Ch'ing-t'ai 1(934)/4/after *i-hai* and *jên-ch'ên*; 280, T'ien-fu 1(936)/5/*chia-wu*, *wu-shên* and *kuei-ch'ou*; 9/*hsin-ch'ou*, *chia-ch'ên* and *kêng-hsü*; 10/*kuei-yu*; and 11/*kêng-yin*.

[26] *WTHY* 12, p. 159; *CWTS* 48, 9b. Also *TCTC* 280, T'ien-fu 1(936)/10/*jên-hsü* and *K'ao-i* for that date which corrects the *CWTS* with a reference to *the Veritable Records of Fei-ti* (Li Ts'ung-k'o).

The emperor's relations with his officials and the status of these men can

to Shih Ching-t'ang and the Khitans. No further resistance could be offered and Shih Ching-t'ang marched into Lo-yang soon afterwards as the first Chin emperor.

Shih Ching-t'ang's first concern was to re-unite under his control the large section of the Emperor's Army under Fan Yen-kuang the governor of Wei province. Before he could achieve this, however, he had to go through eighteen months of great uncertainty. The sections of the Army he had under him were not entirely reliable and in the months 6th-7th/937 there were two dangerous mutinies both taking place about a hundred miles of his new capital at K'ai-fêng. Although he succeeded in crushing both of them, it did not make his task of defeating Fan Yen-kuang at Wei Chou any easier. The prolonged siege of Wei Chou affected his prestige among the other governors. In 9th/938 he was finally forced to negotiate with Fan Yen-kuang and guarantee the safety of the rebel governor's family and supporters.[27] All the sections of the Emperor's Army were thus finally re-united and the new Army was reorganized under the command of his trusted officers.

both be seen in the following excerpts from the edict on supplying horses to the new army in the *WTHY*:
'In the various provinces, prefectures, counties and garrison-towns, all officials above (and including) the county secretaries, the (governor's) chief executive officers and the training officers may each keep one riding horse. As for the literati and the commoners in the villages who own horses, their horses whether male or female are all to be compulsorily loaned, no matter how influential (these people) may be . . .
'The governors, the defence and the militia commissioners and the prefects (may keep) their own horses (but) apart from this, (they) are not to take advantage (of the edict) to seize (the horses of others).
'The officers now garrisoning various places, excepting those sent to battle and those accompanying the emperor, may each keep five of their horses if they are commanding officers, two if they are junior commanding officers and one if they are the heads of regiments . . .
'All personnel accompanying the emperor below and including civil and military officials (*pai-kuan* 百官), officers in charge of armies and palace commissioners who originally had horses (before they came to office?) are free to present (the horses to the emperor) as they wish. (They) may not seize privately owned horses under cover (of this edict).'

[27] *CWTS* 77, 6a-7b; 97, 2b-3b; and *TCTC* 281, T'ien-fu 3(938)/9/*i-ssŭ*.

For the mutinies of 6th-7th/937, see *CWTS* 76, 14b-15b; 97, 5a-b; 91, 13b-14a; and *TCTC* 281, T'ien-fu 2(937)/6/after *ting-wei* and 7/before *chia-yin*.

In the years which followed, Shih Ching-t'ang quietly bore the criticisms and even insults of the Khitans as well as those of his governors. He concentrated on strengthening the Emperor's Army and gave its officers great honours and privileges. He also employed the 'intimate officials' of the palace service as Supervisors in the Army.[28] By 941 he was confident enough to deal with the insubordinate governors of both Chên and Hsiang provinces. The two comparatively easy victories he had there reflect the extent of the recovery of imperial power.[29]

Shih Ching-t'ang did not live long enough to enjoy the fruits of his patience. He died in 6th/942, but the confidence of the Emperor's Army which he had done much to revive took a turn he had never expected or desired. The Chief Commander of the Army, Ching Yen-kuang, in whose hands he had left his heir and the future of the empire, decided soon after Shih Ching-t'ang's death to assert a greater degree of independence of the Khitans. This precipitated the Khitan war which ended disastrously for the dynasty and for the Army which Shih Ching-t'ang had rebuilt.[30]

Although the decision to be independent of the Khitans had brought disaster to the dynasty, it made a significant contribution to later history. The war of 943-946 forced the court to drain the resources of the empire for the use of the imperial forces and this had an important effect on provincial power. The region of central and southern Ho-pei was the most affected. The Ho-pei provinces were so exhausted that they could no longer be threats to the central government. The war concentrated more power than had ever been possible before in the central government and particularly in the Emperor's Army and the men appointed to command it as an expeditionary force. Tu Ch'ung-wei, an uncle of the emperor, was trusted with full control of almost the entire Emperor's Army. When he surrendered to the Khitans in 12th/946, the whole empire was at their mercy.[31]

[28] See Chapter Six, discussion before and after Table X.

[29] *CWTS* 80, 4b-6a and 81, 5a; 98, 4a-b and 5a; *TCTC* 282, T'ien-fu 6(941)/11/*ting-ch'ou* and 12/*jên-ch'ên*, ff.; 283, T'ien-fu 7(942)/1/*ting-ssŭ* and 8th month.

[30] See Chapter Six, note 36.

[31] *CWTS* 85, 3a, ff.; 109, 2b-3a; *TCTC* 285, K'ai-yün 3(946)/12/*ping-yin* to *kuei-yu*.

There followed an interregnum of five months when North China was ruled by the Khitan emperor. During this period, the great Emperor's Army was disarmed and its horses confiscated. As for the governors in Ho-nan and Ho-pei, three were killed, one preferred suicide, four were taken to Khitan territory and the other twelve collaborated with the enemy. In Kuan-chung, one submitted to the Shu empire in Szechuan and another killed himself, while six others paid court to the Khitans. Only one governor of the remoter provinces stayed aloof. Of the four governors in Ho-tung, only Liu Chih-yüan of Ping did not go to the Khitan court.[32]

In the final count, two governors out of thirty-three were free to lead an opposition. The first of the two was Shih K'uang-wei of Ching (in Kuan-chung). As an uncle-in-law of the Chin emperor, he had a claim to lead such an opposition, but four of the five prefectures in his province were inhabited mainly by Tibetan and Tangut peoples over whom he had only nominal authority. Although the province could be easily defended, it could also be

[32] Of the governors in Ho-nan and Ho-pei, Huang-fu Yü (*CWTS* 95, 1b-2a) committed suicide and Liang Han-chang (*CWTS* 95, 4b), Ching Yen-kuang (*CWTS* 88, 3a-b) and Sang Wei-han (*CWTS* 89, 7b) were killed. The three boy princes who were nominal governors were taken away with Li Yen-t'ao (*HWTS* 17, 13b-15b; *CWTS* 88, 4b-5a). The twelve who submitted to the Khitans were as follows (references from *CWTS* unless otherwise stated):

Ho-pei	*Ho-nan*
Chang Yen-tsê (98, 6b-7b)	An Shên-ch'i (123, 5a)
Fang T'ai (94, 4a-b)	Fêng Tao (126, 5b)
Li Yin (106, 5a-b)	Fu Yen-ch'ing (*Sung Shih*, 251, 4a-6a)
Tu Ch'ung-wei (109, 2b-3a)	Kao Hsing-chou (123, 3a)
Wang Ching (*Sung Shih*, 252, 1a-2a)	Li Shou-chên (109, 7a-b)
Wang Chou (106, 1b)	Li Ts'ung-min (123, 9b)

Of the governors in Kuan-chung, Ho Chien (*CWTS* 94, 5a-b) surrendered to Shu while An Shên-hsin (*CWTS* 123, 7b), An Shên-yüeh (no biography, see *CWTS* 85, 2a), Chiao Chi-hsün (*Sung Shih*, 261, 6b-7b), Chou Mi (*CWTS* 124, 8b), Kuo Chin (*CWTS* 106, 8a) and Liu Chi-hsün (*CWTS* 96, 7b-8a) submitted to the Khitans. Chao Tsai-li killed himself (*CWTS* 90, 2a-b). Only Shih K'uang-wei of Ching (*CWTS* 124, 7a) stayed away from the Khitan court.

In Ho-tung, Chang Ts'ung-ên (*Sung Shih*, 254, 4b-5a), Hou I (*Sung Shih*, 254, 1a-2b) and Liu Tsai-ming (*CWTS* 106, 6a-b) went to pay court to the Khitan emperor. Liu Chih-yüan merely sent his officers (*CWTS* 99, 3b-4b).

cut off by the Khitans from the resources of the Wei valley.[33]

The other governor, Liu Chih-yüan, was better placed to resist the Khitans. Ping was the only province which had been left with all its resources intact for more than sixty years. It was the strategic refuge of the Turkish imperial house and the governor of Ping was expected to be one of the chief defenders of the throne. Liu Chih-yüan had been governor there for five and a half years and, as commander of the northern defences, he had been allowed a larger army than was customary for governors. His nine prefectures were, however, surrounded on three sides by the Khitans and his army was not strong enough to offer battle on several fronts at the same time. Although he succeeded in resisting the Khitan emperor's demand for his personal attendance at the court, he felt obliged to send tribute. He also made no attempt to save the captured Chin emperor.[34]

It was soon apparent that the Khitans could not cope with the empire they had not expected to conquer. They did not have the numbers to garrison the provinces so that when lawlessness grew beyond control, they had to re-arm some units of the Chin army and send them to deal with it. Liu Chih-yüan was aware that many of the Chin officers resented their new masters and was encouraged by this to set himself up as the leader of the resistance against the Khitans. He declared himself emperor in 2nd/947 and his action was followed quickly by mutinies led by these officers first at Shan, then at Chin and Lu provinces. When the provinces were taken over by these officers, Liu Chih-yüan was offered two routes south from Ping Chou into Ho-nan.[35] He was also helped by bandit gangs which attacked the environs of Lo-yang.

In Ho-pei other imperial units revolted against the Khitans at

[33] *CWTS* 124, 7a; *TCTC* 286, T'ien-fu 12(947)/1/after *i-wei*.

[34] *CWTS* 99, 3a-5a; and 85, 6a-b; *TCTC* 286, T'ien-fu 12(947)/1/after *i-mao*; and 2/*chia-hsü*.

Liu Chih-yüan is said to have set off to save the Chin emperor, but this was four days *after* he had been proclaimed emperor at Ping Chou. It is doubtful if Liu Chih-yüan was sincere in his show of loyalty; he was known to have disliked the emperor.

[35] *CWTS* 99, 4b-5b; 125, 1a-b and 2b; *Sung Shih* 252, 2a-b and 8a-b; *TCTC* 286, T'ien-fu 12(947)/2/*kêng-wu*, *kêng-ch'ên* and after *hsin-ssŭ*.

Ch'an Chou at a strategic Huang Ho crossing, and bandits almost held Hsiang Chou which would have threatened the Khitans' best route home. In Mêng province, a dramatic mutiny offered to Liu Chih-yüan a clear road to Lo-yang.[36] The main Khitan army began to withdraw from Ho-nan in 4th/947 in order to avoid the continental summer and the decisive event which Liu Chih-yüan could not have hoped for took place—the Khitan emperor died suddenly in Ho-pei, and the choice of his successor had to be decided at the capital in Manchuria. A military vacuum was thus created which Liu Chih-yüan marched south to fill. In 6th/947, he entered K'ai-fêng.[37]

Liu Chih-yüan became leader of the empire mainly because he had the only effective army in the only province which was strategically situated to threaten the Khitans. But a more important factor than his control of Ping province was the lack of any alternative leadership which could have been offered by the men who had led the Emperor's Army. These men had been discredited by their defeat in the Khitan war and by their collaboration with the enemy. In any case, the bulk of their Army had been divided into several parts and disarmed by the time the Khitans returned north.

The Han dynasty founded by Liu Chih-yüan ended after only three and a half years. Its short duration has made it an historical oddity and historians have paid it little of the attention it deserves. The dynasty has a claim to importance because, during its short course, provincial power in North China declined below the point where it could be a threat to imperial authority. As a corollary to this, the provinces were entirely dominated by the Emperor's Army which had emerged as the basis of a new structure of power. Ping province in Ho-tung was an important exception, and it was possible for the Han court to be successfully maintained there after the fall of the dynasty at K'ai-fêng in 11th/950. The strength of the province was the result of a policy of the Turkish imperial houses (of Later T'ang, Chin and Han). Ping province had been

[36] *CWTS* 99, 5b-9a; *Sung Shih* 252, 6a-b; *TCTC* 286, T'ien-fu 12(947)/2/*ting-ch'ou* and *kuei-wei* 4/after *ting-mao*.

[37] *CWTS* 99, 9b and 100, 1a-2a; *TCTC* 286, T'ien-fu 12(947)/4/*ping-tzŭ*, ff. and 287, 5/*i-yu*; 6/*ping-ch'ên* and *chia-tzŭ*.

deliberately preserved as a bastion and a refuge. Although its survival for twenty-eight years against the Chou emperors and the founder of the Sung was helped throughout by Khitan support, it served its purpose well and its provincial resources were in sharp contrast with those of other provinces.[38] This contrast, in fact, emphasizes the extent the other provinces had been weakened by imperial policy in the preceding decades.

The weakness of the governors was fortunate from Liu Chih-yüan's point of view for the imperial resources had been much reduced after the Khitan war and occupation. As it was, the only resistance to the new court was offered by Tu Ch'ung-wei, the commander-in-chief of the Chin expeditionary armies who was also governor of Wei province. He refused to recognize Liu Chih-yüan's claim to the throne and for five months defended Wei Chou with the remnants of the Chin army that he had with him. The resources of his province were by this time extremely limited and he could not have survived for long without help. He had hoped for Khitan backing and for the support of other Chin commanders, but neither was forthcoming. Instead, the three Chin officers and an ex-governor who had removed the Khitan-appointed governors of Chên, Hsing, Hsiang and Ts'ang provinces (in Ho-pei) all chose to support Liu Chih-yüan.[39] Tu Ch'ung-wei was finally forced to surrender. The campaign against him had not only further exhausted the provinces of southern Ho-pei, but also showed the extent these provinces had become militarily integrated with the metropolitan territories of Ho-nan.[40]

The Han Emperor's Army was largely rebuilt out of the Chin army units which had been recalled from their respective provinces. After the defeat of Tu Ch'ung-wei, the units of the Chin army

[38] Liu Ch'ung, a cousin of Liu Chih-yüan, was left as governor of Ping in 947. When the Han was overthrown in 11th/950, he declared himself emperor at Ping Chou. His dynasty is known as Pei Han or Tung Han (Northern or Eastern Han). *CWTS* 135, 12b-14b and *HWTS* 70, 1a-3a.

[39] *CWTS* 100, 3a and 6b-7b; 106, 8b-9b; 125, 4b-5a; *Sung Shih* 252, 1a-b and 254, 5a-b; *TCTC* 287, T'ien-fu 12 (947)/6/*kêng-ch'ên*; Intercalary 7/*hsin-ssŭ* and 8/*kêng-yin*.

[40] *CWTS* 109, 3b-4b. *TCTC* 287, T'ien-fu 12(947)/Intercalary 7/*kêng-wu*; 9/*chia-hsü*, 10/*wu-hsü* and *ping-wu*; 11/*ping-ch'ên* to *ting-ch'ou*.

which he had led were also absorbed into the new Army. When Liu Chih-yüan died in 1st/948, there remained outside of imperial control only the provincial guards of two governors in Kuan-chung. His successor, Liu Ch'êng-yu, recalled the two governors and sent a section of the Emperor's Army to escort their guards to the capital. Owing to the incompetence of the imperial officers, one group of guards seized Ch'ang-an and rebelled. The rebel force then sought the leadership of the governor of P'u, Li Shou-chên, who had been the last Chief Commander of the Emperor's Army to be appointed by the Chin and Tu Ch'ung-wei's deputy at the time of the surrender to the Khitans in 946. Li Shou-chên answered the call and his decision encouraged the imperial garrison at Ch'i Chou to mutiny and join him. The rebels also received support from the state of Shu (Szechuan). But the imperial armies were able to keep the rebels apart and to drive off the Shu reinforcements. Although prolonged sieges of P'u Chou, Ch'i Chou and Ch'ang-an were necessary before the rebellion was finally crushed, there is no evidence that the rebels were likely to succeed.[41] In fact, the rebellion was the last the Kuan-chung region could support in the tenth century and its failure helped the integration of that region with metropolitan Ho-nan.

A measure of the Han court's control over the provinces was its ability to appoint not only bureaucrats to the provincial government but also army officers to supervise the governor's personal staff. The latter were officers attached to the imperial finance departments who were sent to the provinces as executive officers, examining officials of provincial finance and even the governor's adjutants (*yüan-ts'ung tu ya-ya*, *k'ung-mu kuan* and *nei chih-k'o* respectively).[42] These appointments were unprecedented and caused

[41] *CWTS* 109, 7b-9a and 9b-12a; *HWTS* 53, 1a-6b; *TCTC* 288, Ch'ien-yu 1(948)/3/*kuei-yu* and *ting-ch'ou*; 4/*hsin-ssŭ* and *wu-tzŭ*, ff.; 6/*i-yu*; 8/*jên-wu* and *chi-hai*; 10/*wu-yin*, ff.; 12/*jên-wu*, ff.; Ch'ien-yu 2(949)/1/*wu-shên*; 4/*kuei-mao*; 5/*ping-wu*, ff.; 7/*chia-ch'ên* and *chia-yin*.

Many governors and court officials were secretly in touch with Li Shou-chên during the rebellion but they probably confined themselves to moral support as there is no evidence that Li Shou-chên received any material help. *Sung Shih* 249, 4a-5a; *TCTC* 288, Ch'ien-yu 2(949)/7/*jên-hsü*.

[42] *CWTS* 110, 14a and 103, 12b. These appointments were made in addition

great resentment in the provinces. But the court had ensured the governor's acceptance of these officers by interfering with his authority in another way. Units of the Emperor's Army under independent officers were sent from time to time to patrol the provinces. These officers were called patrol commissioners (*hsün-chien shih*) and were given special responsibilities for border defence and for policing districts terrorized by bandits. In this way, they reduced the governor's military authority and indirectly helped to increase the court's control over the governor's yamen.[43]

Various aspects of the decline of provincial power have been considered. There remains to be seen the effect of this decline on the relationship between the court and the provinces. In the following table, it seems clear that a more stable relationship had emerged after 947. The table is based on the careers of the new governors appointed in each reign. Most of these governors lived

to those of bureaucrats to the orthodox provincial offices (the latter according to the regulations of 11/1st/948; *CWTS* 100, 9b and *WTHY* 25, p. 303).

[43] On the use of patrol commissioners, see *CWTS* 102, 3a and 5a-b; 103, 13a; 105, 1b-2b; 129, 6a-b; *HWTS* 53, 1a-2a; *Sung Shih* 252, 3b-4a; 255, 1a-b; 272, 9b-10a.

Patrol commissioners had long been employed to supervise police affairs in metropolitan provinces, but it was not until the last few years of the Chin that they were appointed to supervise the governors and the provincial troops; see *CWTS* 125, 2b; *Sung Shih* 252, 1a-b and 8a-b. Also see *TCTC* 284, K'ai-yün 1(944)/4/*ting-wei* for the use of such commissioners to command special militia troops.

Chu Wên had used a patrol commissioner for Lo-yang; *CWTS* 73, 3b. Li Ts'un-hsü appointed a commissioner for Wei Chou were the provincial army was very strong; *CWTS* 61, 8a; 94, 6a; *TCTC* 274, T'ien-ch'êng 1(926)/2/*jên-ch'ên*. (The commissioners were called *tu hsün-chien shih* or, as in *TCTC* 269, Chên-ming 1(915)/6/*kêng-yin*, *tu hsün-an shih*). Another commissioner was also appointed for the Northern Capital, T'ai-yüan; *CWTS* 56, 10b.

Under Li Ssŭ-yüan, T'ien Wu is said to have been appointed patrol commissioner of Hsiang province in 927; *CWTS* 90, 16a. This was the year in which Li Ssŭ-yüan ordered the Hsiang governor to command an expeditionary force to capture Ching province on the Yangtse. T'ien Wu was at that time a commander in one of the Six Armies (in the Yü-lin 羽林 Army), and his appointment might have been one of the reasons why the governor Liu Hsün was so easily removed in the same year for failing against Ching Chou; *CWTS* 61, 6a-b; *TCTC* 275, T'ien-ch'êng 2(927)/2/*jên-yin*; 5/*kêng-wu*; 6/*jên-ch'ên*. But there is no evidence that other patrol commissioners of this type were appointed until the Chin.

on into the succeeding reign and remained as governors when a lineal successor ascended the throne. But when a new imperial house was founded, the new court was bound for its own safety to replace as many of the previously appointed governors as possible with men of its own choice. On the other hand, when the authority of the new court was guaranteed by a strong central army, it was not essential to replace the governors quickly.

TABLE XIII[44]

	(1) 923-926	(2) 926-933	(3) 934-936	(4) 936-942	(5) 942-946	(6) 947-948	(7) 948-950	(8) 951-953	(9) 954-959
A. Total no. of new governors	28	61	18	34	19	17	9	17	18
B. No. who died during the reign	5	15	—	6	2	—	—	2	2
C. No. who survived into the succeeding reign	23	46	18	28	17	17	9	15	16
D. No. who survived as governors in the 1st three years of the succeeding reign	9	26	6	20	4	12	6	11	13
(i) % of total survivors	39	57	33	71	24	70	67	73	81

[44] The table is based on the following references (in *CWTS* unless otherwise stated). The abbreviation 'n.b.' stands for 'no biography'. The names of the governors are placed in the following order (cf. table): B. for those who died during the reign; C. for those who survived into the succeeding reign but were killed, recalled or forced to retire; D. for those who survived as governors in the first three years of the succeeding reign.

(1) New governors appointed in 923-926 (reign of Li Ts'un-hsü):

B

1 Chu Ling-hsi (n.b.; 63, 9a-10a)
2 K'ang Yen-hsiao (74, 1b)
3 Kuo Ch'ung-t'ao (57, 4a)
4 Li Ts'un-hsien (53, 9b)
5 Li Ts'un-ngai (*HWTS* 14, 19a)

C

6 Chang Hsien (69, 3a-b)
7 Chang T'ing-yü (65, 5a)
8 Ch'ang Ts'ung-chien (94, 1b)
9 Chu Shou-yin (74, 5a)
10 Li Shao-wên (59, 11a)
11 Li Ts'un-chi (*HWTS* 14, 20b)
12 Li Ts'un-ching (n.b; 33, 8b)
13 Li Ts'un-ch'üeh (*HWTS* 14, 20b)
14 Li Ts'un-pa (*HWTS* 14, 19b)
15 Li Ts'un-wo (*HWTS* 14, 20a)
16 Mao Chang (73, 1a-b)
17 Shih Ching-yung (55, 10b)
18 Wang Chêng-yen (69, 5a)
19 Yüan Hsing-ch'in (70, 1b)

D

20 An Yüan-hsin (61, 3a-b)
21 Chang Ching-hsün (61, 7a)
22 Chao Tê-chün (98, 8b)
23 Hsia Lu-ch'i (70, 4a)
24 K'ung Hsün (*HWTS* 43, 10a)
25 Liu Hsün (61, 6a-b)
26 Lu Chih (93, 2a-b)
27 Mêng Chih-hsiang (*HWTS* 64A, 1b)
28 Tung Chang (62, 5b)

---

(2) New governors appointed in 926-933 (reign of Li Ssu-yüan)

B

1 An Ch'ung-hsü (n.b; 41, 7b; 42, 5a; 66, 3a-b)
2 An Ch'ung-hui (66, 3a-b)
3 An Shên-t'ung (61, 2a)
4 Chang Tsun-hui (61, 9b)
5 Hsi-fang Yeh (61, 9a-b)
6 Kao Hsing-kuei (65, 4b)
7 Li Ts'ung-jung (51, 4a-b)
8 Liu Yen-tsung (61, 7b)
9 Mêng Ku (69, 7b)
10 Mi Chün-li (n.b; 36, 2b; 41, 11a)
11 Po Wên (n.b; 42, 4b; 44, 4b and 6a)
12 Sun Chang (61, 10a)
13 Sun Yüeh (69, 8a)
14 T'ao Ch'i (n.b; 36, 3b; 38, 10a; 39, 10a)
15 Wang Yen-ch'iu (64, 4a-b)

C

16 An Ch'ung-pa (61, 5a)
17 Chang Wên (59, 10a)
18 Chao Fêng (67, 7b)
19 Ch'ên Kao (n.b; 39, 4a; 40, 4a; 42, 1b; 46, 13b)
20 Chou Chih-yü (64, 9a-b)
21 Chu Hung-chao (66, 4b)
22 Fêng Pin (*HWTS* 27, 2b)
23 Fu Yen-ch'ao (56, 11a-b)
24 K'ang I-ch'êng (66, 6b)
25 K'ang Ssŭ-li (70, 7b)
26 Li Ch'êng-yüeh (90, 12b)
27 Li Tsan-hua (n.b; 43, 5a; 44, 7b; 76, 4a)
28 Li Ts'ung-hou (45, 1a-b)
29 Liang Han-yung (88, 10a)
30 Liu Chung-yin (n.b; 35, 12a; 38, 9b; 41, 7a; 42, 3a; 44, 8b; 46, 12b)
31 So Tzu-t'ung (65, 8b)
32 Wang Ching-k'an (n.b; 34, 7a; 37, 6b; 39, 3b; 44, 8a)
33 Wang Ssŭ-t'ung (65, 5b)
34 Wang Wan-jung (n.b; 44, 7a; 46, 16a)
35 Yo Yen-ch'ou (66, 8a)

D

36 An Ts'ung-chin (*HWTS* 51, 22a-b)
37 Chang Ch'ien-chao (74, 7a-b)
38 Chang Ching-ta (70, 8b-9b)
39 Chang Wan-chin (88, 15a)
40 Chang Yen-lang (*HWTS* 26, 7b)
41 Chao Tsai-li (90, 1b-2b)
42 Chao Yen-shou (98, 11a)

43 Fan Yen-kuang (97, 2a)
44 Fang Chih-wên (91, 1b)
45 K'ang Fu (91, 6a-b)
46 Kao Hsing-chou (123, 2b)
47 Li Chin-ch'üan (97, 12a-b)
48 Li Chou (91, 9b)
49 Li Tê-ch'ung (90, 15b)
50 Li Ts'ung-chang (88, 12a-b)
51 Li Ts'ung-k'o (46, 2a-3b)
52 Li Ts'ung-min (123, 8a)
53 Li Ts'ung-wen (88, 14a)
54 Sha Yen-hsün (n.b; 41, 12a; 47, 10b; 95, 9a)
55 Shih Ching-t'ang (75, 4b-9b)
56 Sun Han-shao (53, 7a-b)
57 Ti Chang (75, 10a-b)
58 Wang Chien-li (91, 4a-b)
59 Yang Han-chang (n.b; 40, 4a; 48, 10a)
60 Yang Han-pin (n.b; 39, 4a; 76, 4a)
61 Yang Kuang-yüan (97, 6b)

(3) New governors appointed in 934-936 (reign of Li Ts'ung-k'o)

C

1 Chang Ch'êng-yu (n.b; 46, 11b and 12b)
2 Chang Wu (n.b; 47, 5b)
3 Chang Yen-ch'i (n.b; 48, 3b)
4 Han Chao-yin (n.b; 47, 12a; 76, 2b)
5 Hsiang-li Chin (90, 17b)
6 Li Ch'ung-mei (*HWTS* 16, 3a)
7 Li Yen-shun (n.b; 47, 10b; 76, 13b)
8 Liu Yen-hao (69, 11a)
9 Sung Shên-ch'ien (n.b; 47, 11a; 48, 3b; 76, 2b)
10 Tung Wên-ch'i (n.b; 47, 2b; 94, 15a)
11 Yang Ssŭ-ch'üan (88, 11a)
12 Yin Hui (88, 11b)

D

13 An Shên-ch'i (123, 4a-b)
14 An Shu-ch'ien (123, 11b)
15 Fêng Tao (126, 4a; 5b)
16 Huang-fu Yü (95, 1a-b)
17 Liu Ching-yen (*HWTS* 47, 30a)
18 Ma Ch'üan-chieh (90, 4a)

(4) New governors appointed in 936-942 (reign of Shih Ching-t'ang)

B

1 An Ch'ung-jung (98, 1a)
2 Chou Huai (95, 7b)
3 Fu Yen-jao (91, 13b)
4 Lu Shun-mi (95, 7a)
5 Shih Ch'ung-hsin (87, 2b)
6 Shih K'uang-han (88, 8b-9a)

C

7 Li Huai-chung (124, 9a)
8 Liu Ch'u-jang (94, 10a-b)
9 Liu Sui-ning (n.b; 76, 3b; 78, 4a)
10 Ma Wan (106, 7a)
11 Sang Wei-han (89, 2b-3a)
12 Ting Shên-ch'i (n.b; 79, 10b; 84, 5b)
13 Wang T'ing-yin (88, 7b-8a)
14 Yang Yen-hsün (90, 11b)

D

15 An Shên-hsin (123, 7a-b)
16 An Shên-hui (123, 6a-b)
17 Chang Yen-tsê (98, 5b; 6b)
18 Ching Yen-kuang (88, 1b)
19 Chou Mi (124, 8b)
20 Fêng Hui (125, 6a)
21 Fu Yen-ch'ing (*SS* 251, 4a-b)
22 Ho Chien (94, 5a)
23 Hou I (*SS* 254, 1a-b)
24 Kuo Chin (106, 8a)

25 Li Shou-chên (109, 5b)
26 Liu Chih-yüan (99, 2b)
27 P'an Huan (94, 3a-b)
28 Shih Ch'ung-kuei (81, 1b)
29 Shih Pin (*HWTS* 17, 10b-11a)
30 Sung Yen-yün (123, 12b)
31 T'ien Wu (90, 16a-b)
32 Tu Ch'ung-wei (109, 1a-4b)
33 Wang Chou (106, 1a-b)
34 Wang Ling-wên (124, 8a)

---

(5) New governors appointed in 942-946 (reign of Shih Ch'ung-kuei)

B

1 Li Ch'êng-fu (90, 17a)
2 Liang Han-chang (95, 4b)

C

3 An Shên-yüeh (n.b; 84, 3a; 85, 2a; 102, 3b)
4 Chang Ts'ung-ên (*SS* 254, 4b)
5 Chao Ying (89, 10a)
6 Fang T'ai (94, 4a)
7 Hsüeh K'o-yen (n.b; 84, 3a; 100, 5b)
8 Li Chien-ch'ung (129, 6a)
9 Li Yen-t'ao (88, 4b)
10 Li Yin (106, 5a)
11 Liu Chi-hsün (96, 7b)
12 Liu Tsai-ming (106, 6a)
13 Shih Ch'ung-jui (*HWTS* 17, 13b)
14 Shih Yen-hsü (*HWTS* 17, 14a)
15 Shih Yen-pao (*HWTS* 17, 14a)

D

16 Che Ts'ung-yüan (125, 9a-b)
17 Chiao Chi-hsün (*SS* 261, 6b)
18 Shih K'uang-wei (124, 7a)
19 Wang Ching (*SS* 252, 1a-b)

---

(6) New governors appointed in 947-948 (reign of Liu Chih-yüan)

C

1 Liu Chu (107, 12a)
2 Liu Hsin (105, 1b-2b)
3 Pai Tsai-jung (106, 9b)
4 Shih Hung-chao (107, 1a-b)
5 Wang Shou-ên (125, 3a)

D

6 Chang Yen-wei (123, 11a)
7 Ch'ang Ssŭ (129, 1a-b)
8 Chao Hui (125, 1b)
9 Hou Chang (*SS*, 252, 8a-b)
10 Hsüeh Huai-jang (*SS* 254, 5b-6a)
11 Kuo Ts'ung-i (*SS* 252, 3b)
12 Liu Ch'ung (135, 13a)
13 Mo-jung Yen-ch'ao (130, 5b-7b)
14 Pai Wên-k'o (124, 9b-10a)
15 Wang Chi-hung (125, 5a)
16 Wang Yen (*SS* 252, 2a-b)
17 Wu Hsing-tê (*SS* 252, 6a-b)

---

(7) New governors appointed in 948-950 (reign of Liu Ch'eng-yu)

C

1 Hu Yen-k'o (*SS* 254, 5a-b)
2 Li Hung-hsin (*SS* 252, 5a-b)
3 Liu Ch'êng-pin (*HWTS* 18, 5a-b)

D

4 Kuo Wei (110, 5b)
5 Liu Hui (129, 5a)
6 Li Hung-i (*SS* 252, 6a)
7 Liu Tz'ŭ (124, 4b)
8 Sung Yen-wo (*SS* 255, 3a-b)
9 Wang Jao (125, 10a-b)

In this table, the careers of the new governors appointed in each reign who survived into the succeeding reign or reigns have been examined in order to see how many of the men were retained as governors for more than three years. (The period of three years has been chosen because it was the average reign of the nine emperors considered here and because the governors whom the court wished to recall would normally have been recalled before the end of three years). The percentage of those who continued as governors for that period of time is then compared with the percentages for the governors of the other reigns who were simi-

(8) New governors appointed in 951-954 (reign of Kuo Wei)

B

1 Ho Fu-chin (124, 3b)
2 Wang Yin (124, 2a-b)

C

3 Cheng Jên-hui (123, 10a-b)
4 So Wan-chin (n.b; 113, 1a and 8b)
5 Ts'ao Ying (129, 4a)
6 Wang Chin (124, 6a)

D

7 Ch'ai Jung (114, 1b)
8 Chang To (*SS* 261, 9b)
9 Han T'ung (*SS* 484, 1b)
10 Kuo Ch'ung-wei (*SS* 255, 1a-b)
11 Li Yün (*SS* 484, 3b)
12 Pai Ch'ung-tsan (*SS* 261, 3b)
13 T'ien Ching-hsien (*SS* 261, 10b)
14 Wang Jên-hao (*SS* 261, 4a)
15 Wang Yen-ch'ao (*SS* 255, 6a-b)
16 Yo Yüan-fu (*SS* 254, 9a-b)
17 Yüan I (n.b; 113, 9a; 115, 7b)

---

(9) New governors appointed in 954-959 (reign of Ch'ai Jung)

B

1 Pai Yen-yü (124, 10b)
2 Shih Yen-ch'ao (124, 6b)

C

3 Chao Chao (*SS* 254, 11a)
4 Li Ch'ung-chin (*SS* 484, 6b)
5 Li Yen-chün (129, 4b)

D

6 Chang Yung-tê (*SS* 255, 7b-8a)
7 Chao K'uang-yin (*SS* 1, 2a-b)
8 Ch'ên Ssŭ-jang (*SS* 261, 4a-5a)
9 Han Ling-k'un (*SS* 251, 1a-b)
10 Hsiang Hsün (*SS* 255, 4b-5a)
11 Li Chi-hsün (*SS* 254, 8a-b)
12 Li Wan-ch'üan (*SS* 261, 10a-b)
13 Mo-jung Yen-chao (*SS* 251, 2a-b)
14 Shih Shou-hsin (*SS* 250, 1a-b)
15 Wang Ch'üan-pin (*SS* 255, 10b)
16 Wang Hui (*SS* 261, 10b)
17 Yang T'ing-chang (*SS* 255, 2a-b)
18 Yüan Yen (*SS* 261, 8b)

---

larly re-employed. It is valid to consider the percentages for governors who lived on into the reign of a lineal successor of their emperor to represent a normal rate of re-employment. According to D(i), columns (2) and (4) which concern the reigns of two emperors with lineal successors (Li Ssŭ-yüan and Shih Ching-t'ang), this normal rate of re-employment can be said to have been between 57 % and 71 % or roughly between 55 % and 75 %. The figures are confirmed in D(i), columns (6) and (8) for the reigns of two other emperors with lineal successors (Liu Chih-yüan and Kuo Wei) where the figures are 70 % and 73 % respectively.

In sharp contrast to these figures, the percentages for reigns before 947 which were each followed by the foundation of a new imperial house are all below 50 % and vary between 24 % and 39 % (see D(i), columns (1), (3) and (5)). It is suggested that these lower percentages reflect the unstable relations between the court and the provinces which prevailed at the time. The governors appeared to each new court to be potential threats and it was thought necessary to recall them as soon as possible.

The equivalent percentage figures for governors who remained as governors under new imperial houses after 947, however, are very high. According to D(i), columns (7) and (9), during the transitions from the Han to the Chou and from the Chou to the Sung, the figures are 67 % and 81 % respectively. The former figure is within the range of the normal rate mentioned above, while the latter is even higher. If it is taken into consideration that in the years after 947 the provinces were smaller in size and poorer in resources than they had ever been and that central military power was greater, then these figures suggest that a more stable relationship between the court and the provinces had emerged. The two imperial houses of Chou and Sung had both been set up by *coup d'états* supported by the bulk of the Emperor's Army while the governors had to be content to play a passive role. The figures in D(i), (7) and (9) may even suggest that more governors survived because they had become less important in imperial politics.[45]

[45] *CWTS* 103, 5a, ff.; 110, 6b, ff.; *Sung Shih* 1, 2b, ff.; *TCTC* 289, Ch'ien-yu 3(950)/11/*ping-tzŭ*, ff.; *Hsŭ TCTC Ch'ang-pien*, chüan 1, *passim*.

The more stable relationship between court and provinces after 947 was, in fact, a corollary to the appearance of a new structure of power based on the Emperor's Army. In the following table, the employment of commanders and officers of the Army as new governors can be seen to have become increasingly important after 947.

TABLE XIV[46]

	(1) 926-933	(2)* 933-936	(3) 936-942	(4) 942-946	(5) 947-948	(6) 948-950	(7) 951-954	(8) 954-959
A. Total no. of new governors	61	21	34	19	17	9	17	18
B. Commanders and other officers of Emperor's Army	8	4	9	4	8	4	5	11
C. % of commanders and officers employed	13	19	27	21	47	44	29	61

* The reigns of Li Ts'ung-hou (933-934) and Li Ts'ung-k'o (934-936) (see note 46).

[46] The table has been based on the references given in note 44 (2) to (9) except for column (2)* where the two reigns of Li Ts'ung-hou and Li Ts'ung-k'o have been considered together. Li Ts'ung-hou appointed only three new governors in his brief reign of four months and two of them were commanders of the Emperor's Army. Li Ts'ung-k'o, on the other hand, appointed eighteen new governors in two and a half years and only two of them were commanders of the Army. If the figures are compared, it can be seen that the percentage of commanders appointed in Li Ts'ung-hou's reign, 67 % (2 out of 3), is a figure far above those for the reigns immediately preceding and succeeding his, that is, 13 % in Li Ssŭ-yüan's reign (C, column (1)) and 11 % in Li Ts'ung-k'o's reign (2 out of 18). If the percentages for two other reigns in the following decade are taken into consideration (27 % and 21 % in C, columns (3) and (4) respectively), it can be seen that the appointments in Li Ts'ung-hou's reign were not representative of the period. I have thus considered the three years between Li Ssŭ-yüan's death and the foundation of the Chin by Shih Ching-t'ang as one period. The percentage figure for the commanders of the Army for this period is then 19 % (C, column (2)*) which fits in roughly with the trend for the twenty years 926-946.

The following were the commanders and officers of the Emperor's Army who were appointed governors (for detailed references, see note 44):

(1) nos. 24, 31, 35, 36, 38, 54, 55 and 59 in note 44 (2).

The percentage figures at the foot of the table clearly show the developments since 926. A finer point not brought out in the table is that most of the post-947 commanders of the Army continued as commanders after their appointment as governors. They spent little time in their provinces, being mainly at the capital or on patrol or with the emperors on the battlefield. The provinces were administered in their absence by a court-chosen or at least a court-approved staff consisting chiefly of bureaucrats. Thus, when these commanders were on active duty, they not only extended imperial authority in the provinces, but also left their own provinces to be better controlled by the central government.[47]

The overwhelming influence of the Emperor's Army had changed the structure of power which had been based on the numerous *chieh-tu shih* in North China after the Huang Ch'ao rebellion. In the sixty years from the end of the rebellion to the fall of Chin, the governors had dominated the struggle for imperial power. The successful governors who had become emperors had modelled their courts on their provincial governments and the provincial organization had been reproduced on an enlarged scale tentatively at first during the Liang and then more extensively during the reign of Li Ssŭ-yüan. By the end of the Chin dynasty, the three groups of men in the provincial organization, the bureaucrats, the *ya-li* and the *ya-chün* officers, had found their place in imperial government as the court bureaucrats, the palace officials and the officers of the Emperor's Army.

During the Chin, the Emperor's Army had been successfully

(2) An Yen-wei and Chang Ts'ung-pin (*CWTS* 45, 3a); and nos. 3 and 13 in note 44 (3)
(3) nos. 3, 7, 10, 18, 23, 24, 25, 26 and 32 in note 44 (4)
(4) nos. 2, 9, 10 and 19 in note 44 (5)
(5) nos. 2, 3, 4, 8, 9, 15, 16, and 17 in note 44 (6)
(6) nos. 2, 6, 7 and 9 in note 44 (7)
(7) nos. 2, 5, 9, 10 and 13 in note 44 (8)
(8) nos. 3, 4, 6, 7, 9, 11, 12, 13, 14, 15 and 18 in note 44 (9).

[47] *Sung Shih* 1, 2a-b; 250, 1a-b; 251, 1a-b and 2a-b; 254, 8a-b and 11a; 255, 1a-b, 7b-8a and 10b; 261, 8b and 10a-b; 484, 1b and 6b. The development was specially important during the reign of Ch'ai Jung (954-959); *CWTS* 114-119, *passim*.

developed to check the power of the governors, and later, its commanders began to interfere directly with affairs at the court. The Khitan war of 943-946 helped the Chin policy of military centralization, but this policy put even more power in the hands of the commanders of the Army. By the time of the Han dynasty, the Emperor's Army had superseded the governors as the dominant force in the empire and had become the chief source of instability. The climax of the Army's power came in 12th/950 when it put the man who was commanding it on the throne. This commander was Kuo Wei who had no claim whatsoever to be emperor apart from the fact that the bulk of the Army was under his control at the time.[48]

The great power of the Army during the Chou and early in the Sung is beyond the scope of this study. It must be emphasized, however, that the two Chou emperors Kuo Wei and Ch'ai Jung were forced to attempt far-reaching reforms of the Army in order to check its power. The reforms included the establishment of a new Palace Corps (the *tien-ch'ien chün*) which was directly led by the emperor.[49] Ch'ai Jung died before his work was completed, and consequently his son was defenceless against Chao K'uang-yin the Commander of the Palace Corps who founded the Sung. The control of the Army and the Palace Corps remained the chief concern of Chao K'uang-yin himself and a permanent solution cannot be said to have been found until after his death.[50]

The thirty years after 947 were the years when North China appeared as one large 'province' faced with other hostile 'provinces'

[48] *CWTS* 103, 6a-13b; 110, 6a-14b; *TCTC* 289, Ch'ien-yu 3(950)/11/*ping-tzŭ, ting-ch'ou, kêng-ch'ên, hsin-ssŭ, kuei-wei, chia-shên, i-yu* and *ting-hai*; 12/*chia-wu, hsin-hai, jên-tzŭ* ff., *kêng-shên*; Kuang-shun 1(951)/1/*ting-mao*.

[49] The Palace Corps existed during the Han dynasty (*CWTS* 102, 8a), but did not become important until the Chou when the units of the palace guards were finally strengthened by select troops from the Emperor's Army and from various provincial garrisons; *CWTS* 114, 14a and *WTHY* 12, p. 157. See also T. Hori, 'Gōdai Sōshu ni okeru Kingun no hatten', *Tōyō Bunka Kenkyujo Kiyō*, 4, pp. 116-127.

[50] For the boy-emperor who succeeded Ch'ai Jung, see *CWTS* 120, 1a ff.; and for the foundation of the Sung, see *Sung Shih* 1, 2b ff. and *Hsü TCTC Ch'ang-pien*, chüan 1, *passim*. The problems of reforming the Palace Corps and the Emperor's Army are considered in T. Hori, *op. cit.*, pp. 127 ff.

in Central, West and South China. This large 'province' was the result of the integration of the thirty small provinces which existed at the end of the Huang Ch'ao rebellion. The process of integration had taken more than sixty years and the important changes in the structure of power brought about in the course of it formed the background of the eventual reunification of China.

Appendix

THE ALLIANCE OF HO-TUNG AND HO-PEI IN WU-TAI HISTORY

Traditional Chinese historians have often dismissed the dynasties of Later T'ang, Chin and Han as those of weak foreign (Sha-t'o Turk) rule. This has been a convenient approach towards the Wu-tai period because it is easy to blame barely literate Turks for the dynastic failures. And more important, this attitude has made it easier to praise the Chinese dynasties of Chou and Sung for their progress after 954 towards the reunification of China. In fact, in order to give the Sung founders the credit for re-establishing the Confucian state, the historians have tried to disassociate the Sung from the Wu-tai as much as possible. This has, I believe, made it very difficult for us to understand the power structure of the Wu-tai as well as that of the Sung.[1]

In my study of the Wu-tai, it has become clear to me that there was great continuity in this period of Chinese history. Neither violent peasant rebellions nor foreign invasions were decisive in determining the development of new institutions or new power groups. After a hundred years of disorder in North China, it was finally the long struggle to succeed the T'ang dynasty between 875 and 923 which brought about some permanent changes. In this struggle, two groups of men were clearly better placed and organized than all others to establish the new dynasty. The two were the group led by Chu Wên and his sons and that led by the Sha-t'o Turk Li K'o-yung and his son Li Ts'un-hsü. In this struggle, Chu Wên led the remnants of the Huang Ch'ao rebels and the armies of North China south of the Huang Ho (that is, mainly those of Honan and Shantung). As for the Sha-t'o Turk aristocrats, they led the forces of 'Restoration'. In the name of the T'ang dynasty, they gathered all professed Loyalists into their provincial organization in the Ho-tung region (Shansi). But neither of the two groups could gain an advantage over the other or even feel secure as long as it did not control the independent provinces of the Ho-pei region (Hopei). These provinces had been independent for 150 years and cherished their power to undermine any form of imperial authority. Until they could be conquered

[1] Western writings have also tended to over-emphasize the problem of 'Turkic' conquest during the Wu-tai. A recent example is Professor Eberhard; see his *Conquerors and Rulers*, pp. 89-102.

and their armies absorbed or won over as allies, Chu Wên and Li K'o-yung could not break the deadlock in their own struggle.

Chu Wên was initially more successful from 898-900. He gained the support of the Wei provincial army (Southern Hopei) and forced the leaders of Chên and Ting provinces (Central Hopei) to accept his leadership. But he failed to subdue the powerful governor of Yu (Northern Hopei, capital at modern Peking). Nevertheless, his partial success made him confident enough to dethrone the T'ang emperor and establish the Liang dynasty in 907. Even as Chu Wên ascended the throne, the Ho-pei situation changed. A new governor took over in Northern Hopei and soon threatened Chu Wên's allies in Chên and Ting provinces. These allies began to look for help from Li Ts'un-hsü. Within three years, Chu Wên's position in Ho-pei had become so precarious that, in spite of two bouts of illness in 909 and 910, he decided in 911 and in 912 to lead his armies personally to Ho-pei. His failure merely worsened his health and was to lead to his murder by his son when he returned to Lo-yang.

Li Ts'un-hsü conquered Yu province in 913, allied himself with the governors of Chên and Ting provinces and in 915 was offered Wei province by the mutinous hereditary garrison. From then on, the Ho-pei military and administrative personnel nominally identified themselves with the cause of T'ang 'Restoration'. By 923, when Li Ts'un-hsü finally overthrew the Liang, the Sha-t'o Turk forces of Ho-tung (Shansi) were the senior partners in an alliance which had fought together for at least eight difficult years, and as long as thirteen years, along the Huang Ho. Table XV following briefly illustrates this.

The alliance itself was never a stable one. When the T'ang was 'restored' south of the Huang Ho, Li Tsun-hsü as emperor was generous to the defeated Liang generals and officials and gave no privileges to his Ho-pei allies. As a result of this, there was considerable unrest in Ho-pei and in 926 a section of the Wei provincial army mutinied. This was followed by a series of mutinies and acts of defiance in Ho-pei which ended by putting Li Ssŭ-yüan on the throne. From the events of 2nd-4th/926, it is clear that the Ho-pei armies felt that they had not been dealt with fairly and that Li Ssŭ-yüan could use his popularity with the Ho-pei forces to take the throne.[2] They had backed Li Ssŭ-yüan in order to secure a share of the victory in 923, not to challenge the leadership of the Sha-t'o Turks. After 926 the Ho-pei armies were gradually integrated with the Turkish and other Chinese troops of the imperial armies and Ho-pei power was whittled away along with that of the other provinces. But as junior partners in the 923 victory, Ho-pei men succeeded in gaining considerable power and influence in the imperial court and in the

[2] *TCTC*, 274, T'ien-ch'eng 1(926)/2/*chi-ch'ou* to 3/*jên-wu*; *CWTS*, 34, 3a-10a; 35, 7a-9b; *HWTS*, 5, 9b-10a and 6, 3b-4a.

TABLE XV

The Ho-pei governors, 883-923[3]

Provinces	Independent	Allied with Chu Wên	Allied with Ho-tung
Yu	to 895 897-913	—	895-897 after 913*
Ting	to 892	900-910	892-900 after 901
Chên	to 900 921-922	900-910	910-921 after 922*
Wei	to 891	891-992 912-915†	after 915*

* Period when provincial troops fought as part of Li Ts'un-hsü's armies.
† Period when governed by LIANG generals.

palace armies. The following Table XVI shows the origins of 161 men who held key appointments in the Emperor's Army and in the Palace Commissions from 926 to 960. As I have shown elsewhere in this study, the Army and the Commissions formed the backbone of Wu-tai central power. The four columns (a)-(d) represent

(a) the chief commanders in the *shih-wei ch'in-chün*
(b) the *shu-mi shih* (military secretaries)
(c) the *hsüan-hui shih*, both North and South; the *k'o-shêng shih*, both Inner and Outer; and the *san-ssŭ shih* (finance commissioner)
(d) the secretaries to the *shu-mi shih* (both the *Tuan-ming tien hsüeh-shih* and the *shu-mi yüan chih hsüeh-shih*)

In the final column (e), I have counted the number of different individuals for each region in each dynasty, but not more than once if they appear in more than one of the columns (a) to (d). It should be noted that while Ho-pei men were Chinese, Ho-tung men include Sha-t'o, T'u-chüeh, Uighur and T'u-yü-hun tribesmen as well as Chinese. As for 'Ho-nan', it is meant to cover the rest of Wu-tai North China, that is, the large area which includes the modern provinces of Honan, Shantung, Central Shensi and most of Hupei.

[3] The chart is based on the material for the Ho-pei wars in *CWTS*, chüans 1-10, 25-29; *TCTC*, chüans 255-272; *HWTS*, chüans 1-5.

TABLE XVI

The Ho-pei element in the Wu-tai power structure, 926-960

	Commanders, Emperor's Army	Military Secretaries	Other palace commissioners	Commission Secretaries	Total
	(a)	(b)	(c)	(d)	(e)
Later T'ang[4] 926-937					
Ho-tung	10	4	3	—	14
Ho-pei	2	2	9	7	16
Ho-nan	—	2	5	1	6
Not known	3	2	3	2	9
Chin[5] 937-946					
Ho-tung	10	1	3	1	13
Ho-pei	5	3	7	6	18
Ho-nan	2	1	6	3	11
Not known	—	—	3	1	4
Han[6] 947-950					
Ho-tung	13	—	2	1	15
Ho-pei	4	3	3	—	9
Ho-nan	1	—	1	—	2
Not known	2	—	3	2	7
Chou[7] 951-960					
Ho-tung	6	3	4	1	11
Ho-pei	7	4	5	5	18
Ho-nan	1	1	4	3	7
Not known	—	—	—	1	1
Total 926-960					
Ho-tung	39	8	12	3	53
Ho-pei	18	12	24	18	61
Ho-nan	4	4	16	7	26
Not known	5	2	9	6	21

[4] In this note and notes 5, 6 and 7, the sources are from the *CWTS* unless otherwise stated.

Footnote

[4] (a) *Ho-tung*

An Ts'ung-chin (*HWTS* 51, 15b-17b)
An Yen-wei (91, 7b-8a)
Chang Ch'ien-chao (74, 6b-7b)
Chang Ts'ung-pin (97, 4b-5a)
Fu Yen-jao (91, 13a-14a)
K'ang I-ch'êng (66, 6b-7b)
Li Ts'ung-chang (88, 12a-13a)
Shih Ching-t'ang (75, 1a-6a)
So Tzŭ-t'ung (65, 8a-b)
Yo Yen-ch'ou (66, 7b-8a)

Ho-pei

Huang-fu Yü (95, 1a-2b)
Liu Tsai-ming (106, 5b-6b)

Not Known

Chang Yen-ch'i (48, 3b)
Sha Yen-hsün (41, 12a)
Yang Han-chang (39, 2a)

(b) *Ho-tung*

An Ch'ung-hui (66, 1a-4a)
Chu Hung-chao (66, 4a-5b)
Fêng Pin (*HWTS* 27, 2a-3a)
Liu Yen-hao (69, 10b-11a)

Ho-pei

Chao Yen-shou (98, 11a-13a)
Fan Yen-kuang (97, 1a-4b)

Ho-nan

Fang Hao (96, 6b-7a)
K'ung Hsün (*HWTS* 43, 7a-8b)

Not Known

Chao Ching-i (39, 6b)
Han Chao-yin (46, 8b; 10a)

(c) *Ho-tung*

Chu Hung-chao, see (b) above
Fêng Pin, see (b) above
Liu Yen-hao, see (b) above

Ho-pei

Chang Tsun-hui (61, 9b-10a)
Chao Yen-shou, see (b) above
Fan Yen-kuang, see (b) above
Hsüeh Jên-ch'ien (128, 6b-7a)
Li Yen (70, 5a-6b)
Liu Ch'u-jang (94, 8b-10b)
Liu Hsü (89, 11a-13a)
Mêng Ku (69, 7a-b)
Yang Yen-hsün (90, 10b-11b)

Ho-nan

Chang Yen-lang (69, 8a-10b)
Chang Yen-po (97, 5b)
Fang Hao, see (b) above
Li Chuan-mei (93, 2b-4b)
Liu Yen-lang (69, 11a-b)

Not Known

Li Jên-chü (*HWTS* 26, 9b-10b)
Mêng Han-ch'iung (Eunuch, 72, 6b-7b)
Wang Mei (46, 8b)

(d) *Ho-pei*

Chao Fêng (67, 6b-8a)
Fêng Tao (126, 1a-12a)
Li Ch'ien-hui (*TFYK* 154, 8b-9a)
Li Sung (108, 1a-4a)
Liu Hsü, see (c) above
Lü Ch'i (92, 2b-3b)
Mêng Ku, see (c) above

Ho-nan

Li Chuan-mei, see (c) above

Not Known

Han Chao-yin, see (b) above
Hsüeh Wên-yü (48, 1a)

Footnote

5 (a) *Ho-tung*

An Shên-ch'i (123, 4a-6a)
Hou I (*SS* 254, 1a-2b)
Kuo Chin (106, 7b-8a)
Li Huai-chung (124, 9a)
Li Yen-t'ao (88, 4a-5a)
Liang Han-chang (95, 4a-5a)
Liu Chih-yüan (99, 1a-3b)
Pai Fêng-chin (95, 5a-6a)
Tu Ch'ung-wei (109, 1a-5a)
Yang Kuang-yüan (97, 5b-9b)

Ho-pei

Fêng Hui (125, 5b-7a)
Kao Hsing-chou (123, 1a-4a)
Li Ch'iung (94, 10b-12a)
Li Yin (106, 5a-b)
T'ien Wu (90, 16a-b)

Ho-nan

Ching Yen-kuang (88, 1a-4a)
Li Shou-chên (109, 5a-9b)

(b) *Ho-tung*

Chang Ts'ung-ên (*SS* 254, 4b-5a)

Ho-pei

Fêng Yü (*HWTS* 56, 3b-4b)
Li Sung, see 4(d) above
Liu Ch'u-jang, see 4 (c) above

Ho-nan

Sang Wei-han (89, 1a-9a)

(c) *Ho-tung*

Chang Ts'ung-ên, see (b) above
Chou Huai (95, 7a-8a)
Li Yen-t'ao, see (a) above

Ho-pei

Kao Han-yün (94, 12a-13b)
Liu Chi-hsün (96, 7b-8a)
Liu Ch'u-jang, see 4(c) above
Liu Shên-chiao (106, 1b-4a)
Mêng Ch'êng-hui (96, 7a-b)
Wang Ching-ch'ung (*HWTS* 53, 1a-3a)
Yang Yen-hsün, see 4(c) above

Ho-nan

Chiao Chi-hsün (*SS* 261, 6b-7b)
Li Ch'êng-fu (90, 16b-17a)
Li Shou-chên, see (a) above
Liu Sui-ch'ing (96, 5b-6b)
Ti Kuang-yeh (129, 2a-3b)
Yüan I (83, 7b)

Not Known

Sung Kuang-yeh (76, 18b)
Ting Chih-chün (80, 3a)
Tung Yü (83, 2a)

(d) *Ho-tung*

Pien Kuang-fan (*SS* 262, 15b-16b)

Ho-pei

Fêng Yü, see (b) above
Li Sung, see 4(d) above
Lü Ch'i, see 4(d) above
Ssŭ-t'u Hsü (128, 10b-11b)
Wu Ch'êng-fan (92, 6b-7a)
Yin P'êng (89, 13b-14a)

Ho-nan

Ho Ning (127, 5a-7a)
Li Ku (*SS* 262, 1a-3b)
Yen K'an (*SS* 270, 1a-2a)

Not Known

Wu Chüan (76, 4a)

Footnote

[6] (a) *Ho-tung*

Chang To (*SS* 261, 9b-10a)
Kuo Ch'ung-wei (*SS* 255, 1a-2a)
Li Hung-chien (107, 8b)
Li Hung-hsin (*SS* 252, 5a-b)
Li Hung-i (*SS* 252, 6a)
Li Wan-ch'üan (*SS* 261, 10a-b)
Liu Hsin (105, 1b-2b)
Pai Ch'ung-tsan (*SS* 261, 3b-4a)
Pai Tsai-jung (106, 8b-9b)
Shih Yen-ch'ao (124, 6a-b)
So Wan-chin (103, 9b)
T'ien Ching-hsien (*SS* 261, 10b)
Yen Chin-ch'ing (107, 9b-10a)

Ho-pei

Liu Tz'ŭ (124, 4a-5b)
Ts'ao Ying (129, 3b-4a)
Wang Yen-ch'ao (*SS* 255, 6a-7b)
Wang Yin (124, 1a-3a)

Ho-nan

Shih Hung-chao (107, 1a-5b)

Not Known

Fan Ai-nêng (103, 9b)
Shang Hung-ch'ien (100, 9a-b)

(b) *Ho-pei*

Kuo Wei (110, 1a-10b)
Wang Chün (130, 1a-5b)
Yang Pin (107, 5b-7a)

(c) *Ho-tung*

Hu Yen-k'o (*SS* 254, 5a-b)
Yen Chin-ch'ing, see (a) above

Ho-pei

Li Hui (129, 4b-5a)
Wang Chang (107, 7a-8b)
Wang Chün, see (b) above

Ho-nan

Wu Ch'ien-yü (*SS* 271, 2a-b)

Not Known

Hsüeh K'o-yen (100, 5b)
Wang Hao (99, 7a)
Wang Ts'ung-chang (100, 2a)

(d) *Ho-tung*

Nieh Wên-chin (107, 10a-b)

Not Known

Han Tso (99, 8b)
Wang Tu (100, 5b)

[7] (a) *Ho-tung*

Chang To, see 6(a) above
Chang Yung-tê (*SS* 255, 7b-10b)
Han T'ung (*SS* 484, 1a-4a)
Kuo Ch'ung-wei, see 6(a) above
Mo-jung Yen-chao (*SS* 251, 2a-3a)
Yüan Yen (*SS* 261, 8b-9a)

Ho-pei

Chao K'uang-yin (*SS* 1, 1a-2b)
Han Ling-k'un (*SS* 251, 1a-2a)
Kao Huai-tê (*SS* 250, 7a-8b)
Li Chi-hsün (*SS* 254, 8a-9a)
Li Ch'ung-chin (*SS* 484, 10a-14a)
Ts'ao Ying, see 6(a) above
Wang Yin, see 6(a) above

Ho-nan

Chang Ling-to (*SS* 250, 10a)

(b) *Ho-tung*

Chêng Jên-hui (123, 9b-10b)
Ti Kuang-yeh, see 5(c) above
Wu Yen-tso (*SS* 257, 1a-b)

From the table, it is clear that the Ho-tung officers, whether Chinese or non-Chinese, dominated the Emperor's Army (64 % of those whose origins are known) and the Ho-pei men dominated the various commissions (50 %, 46 % and 64 % respectively of those whose origins are known). In the total at the bottom of column (e), it can be seen that the 114 Ho-tung and Ho-pei men comprised 81 % of all those whose origins are known. And of this high proportion, the Ho-pei men formed 53 % (that is, 61 out of 114). When it is borne in mind that 'Ho-tung' covers Chinese as well as non-Chinese tribesmen and that 'Ho-nan' comprises the modern provinces of Honan, Shantung, Shensi and Hupei, the proportion of officers from Ho-pei, at most one-fourth the size of the other 'regions', is indeed remarkable. This high proportion shows that the alliance which won the war in 923 was meaningful throughout the Wu-tai. Ho-pei men played their rightful part in the efforts to rebuild a new order in the empire. It is not surprising that the four men who finally made this possible, Kuo Wei the founder of Chou and his adopted son Ch'ai Jung and the two Chao brothers who founded the Sung dynasty, were all originally from Ho-pei.

Ho-pei

Fan Chih (*SS* 249, 1a-3a)
Wang Chün, see 6(b) above
Wang Jên-hao (*SS* 261, 4a-b)
Wei Jên-p'u (*SS* 249, 6a-7a)

Ho-nan

Wang P'o (128, 1a-4a)

(c) *Ho-tung*

Chêng Jên-hui, see (b) above
Li Yen-chün (129, 4a-b)
Ti Kuang-yeh, see 5(c) above
Wu Yen-tso, see (b) above

Ho-pei

Chang Mei (*SS* 259, 1a-b)
Tsan Chü-jun (*SS* 262, 3b-4a)
Wang Jên-hao, see (b) above
Wang Tsan (*SS* 274, 1a-b)
Yang T'ing-chang (*SS* 255, 2a-3a)

Ho-nan

Ching Fan (127, 8a-b)
Hsiang Hsün (*SS* 255, 4b-6a)
Li Ku, see 5(d) above
Yüan I, see 5(c) above

(d) *Ho-tung*

Wang P'u (*SS* 249, 4a-5a)

Ho-pei

Chang Mei, see (c) above
Pien Kuei-tang (*SS* 262, 11a-b)
Tou I (*SS* 263, 4b-6a)
Ts'ao Han (*SS* 260, 1a-2b)
Wei Jên-p'u, see (b) above

Ho-nan

Ching Fan, see (c) above
Wang P'o, see (b) above
Yen K'an, see 5(d) above

Not Known

Ch'ên Kuan (110, 15a)

Notes on the Sources

Most of the sources for Wu-tai history which have been preserved are official compilations or works based on official documents. Contemporary works by individual writers were numerous but most of them were lost after the eleventh century. Early and middle Sung historians had consulted some of them, but it is rarely possible for us today to tell what material had been used in the histories they wrote. Some parts of the contemporary works have also survived in encyclopedias like the *T'ai-p'ing Kuang-chi* and in anecdotal collections made during the Sung. This material is exceedingly difficult to use today as its origins often cannot be clearly determined and little or nothing is known of the authors. In any case, the anecdotal character of the works has not made them essential for this study. They have been merely used, where possible, to show whether a part of the main official account might have been taken from a private source.

Such contemporary works are listed in well-known catalogues like the *Ch'ung-wên Tsung-mu*, the *Chung-hsing Shu-mu* and the *Mi-shu Shêng Hsü-pien Ssŭ-k'u Ch'üeh-shu-mu*; they are also to be found in bibliographies like the *Chün-chai Tu-shu Chih*, the *Chih-chai Shu-lu Chieh-t'i*, the *Shih Lüeh* and the *T'ung Chih*. Lists have also been compiled in the *Sung Shih* Monograph on Bibliography and in the *Wên-hsien T'ung-k'ao*. In Ch'ing times, when there was a revival of interest in the Wu-tai, three further list were produced: Hsü Chiung's in *Wu-tai Shih-chi Pu-k'ao* (chüans 22-24); Ch'ên Chan's in *Hsü T'ang Shu*, chüan 19; and Ku Huai-san's *Pu Wu-tai Shih I-wên Chih* now published in the Supplement to the Twenty-five Histories (*Nien-wu Shih Pu-pien*). In the few instances in this study where a contemporary private account of an event has been utilized, a discussion of the work concerned is made in the notes.

Of the large number of contemporary writings, the works of two men deserve a special note here: the *T'ung-lu* in 65 chüans by Fan Chih and *Chin-ch'ao Hsien-fan Chi* in 4 chüans attributed to him and the *Pei-mêng So-yen* in 20 chüans by Sun Kuang-hsien. Both the works of Fan Chih contributed important material to the history of the Wu-tai. The *T'ung-lu* included fresh material on the neglected reign of Liang Mo-ti (913-923) while the *Hsien-fan Chi* was a first-hand account of the Khitan victory and interregnum (946-947) and was probably the most important source for that troubled year. Unfortunately, neither of the works has survived. We owe our knowledge of the value of *T'ung-lu* through the library catalogue, the *Ch'ung-wên Tsung-mu* (2, p. 49) and that of the *Hsien-fan Chi* through the *Tzŭ-chih T'ung-chien K'ao-i*.

The *Pei-mêng So-yen* of Sun Kuang-hsien has a different kind of importance. Most of this collection has been preserved and some of its material concerning contemporary North China can be usefully compared with accounts in the official history, the *Chiu Wu-tai Shih*. Sun Kuang-hsien lived through the whole period of the Wu-tai in the Middle Yangtse region, in the so-called state of Nan P'ing (modern Central Hupei). After Nan P'ing fell to the Sung in 963, he served the Sung as a prefect. He died five years later and his writings possibly reached the Imperial Library by 972 when the editors of the official *Wu-tai Shih* started work. His is a valuable source when it is borne in mind that in the period after 930 when relations between Ching province (or Nan P'ing) and North China had improved, Sun Kuang-hsien had contacts with the official world of the northern capitals of Lo-yang and K'ai-fêng.

The chief source used for this study is the official history of the Five Dynasties, the *Chiu Wu-tai Shih* in 150 chüans, compiled more than thirteen years after the end of the Chou dynasty. It was compiled largely from the official records prepared for each reign of the Wu-tai emperors, the Veritable Records (*Shih-lu*). Since these Veritable Records had been mainly edited from original documents, the value of the *Chiu Wu-tai Shih* as a collection of historical material can be seen to be very great. I have, in an article (*Asia Major*, London, 1957) on history-writing during the Five Dynasties, shown the background and the limitations of the Veritable Records and other official works of the Wu-tai and the probable effect they had on the compilation of the *Chiu Wu-tai Shih*. The editors of the history seem to have confined themselves largely to re-editing the official records, that is, to correcting the discrepancies and re-wording and cutting short some of the details.

In my article, I also considered the reconstructed text of the *Chiu Wu-tai Shih* now available to us. The eighteenth-century scholars who rescued the text from the Ming encyclopedia, the *Yung-lo Ta-tien*, have left us at least three slightly different editions. I have used here, not the final approved palace edition, but the edition which has retained the source-references at the end of each preserved text. These notes have made quite clear which parts of the present *Chiu Wu-tai Shih* had come from the original that was copied into the Ming encyclopedia. This is the Ssŭ-pu Ts'ung-k'an edition of the Po-na pên Twenty-four Histories.

The *Chiu Wu-tai Shih* deals largely with the history of North China. This bias for the north has been considered its weakest point, but it suits this study admirably. Further, although the bureaucrat editors of the Sung included probably more material on the bureaucrats than was due, they also included a great amount of information about the careers of army officers and upstart courtiers and about the events in which the bureaucrats played little part. The many omissions in the work were quickly noticed and two sets of supplementary material appeared soon afterwards. These were the *Wu-tai Shih Ch'üeh-wên* in 2 chüans by Wang Yü-ch'êng and the *Wu-tai Shih Pu* in 5 chüans by T'ao Yüeh. The two works have been partially recovered from the *Yung-lo Ta-tien* encyclopedia in the eighteenth century and have now been included as commentaries to the present editions of the *Chiu Wu-tai Shih*.

The standard history of the Wu-tai period, the well-known *Wu-tai Shih-chi* (also known as *Hsin Wu-tai Shih*) in 74 chüans by Ou-yang Hsiu has been useful. It is more readable and concise than the *Chiu Wu-tai Shih* which it replaced in the Standard Canon. But Ou-yang Hsiu was often too much concerned with style and the correct moral tone of early Sung Neo-Confucianism. As a result, his judgement on Wu-tai soldiers and statesmen was usually stereotyped according to fixed patterns of praise and blame. The work deserves its place as a literary and philosophical classic, but it has to be read with great care as history. Read together with the *Chiu Wu-tai Shih* and the last 40 chüans of the *Tzŭ-chih T'ung-chien* of Ssŭ-ma Kuang, however, it gives an extra dimension to Wu-tai history.

The section on bureaucratic and military institutions in the *Chiu Wu-tai Shih* is notably small—10 chüans of Monographs appended at the end. For a fuller picture of legal and institutional history, we must turn to the *Wu-tai Hui-yao* in 30 chüans edited by Wang P'u. Wang P'u, who was the Chief Minister of the Chou dynasty and remained at this post in the first years of the Sung, compiled this work on his own initiative and submitted it to the Sung emperor in 961. He was at the time also the Supervisor of National History in charge of the compilation of the Veritable Records of Chou Shih-tsung (954-959) and thus had access to the imperial archives. It is not known whether he depended on the available sets of Veritable Records and other edited collections of imperial edicts and memorials for the text of his documents or actually used the originals. If the originals had been still preserved in the archives, it is likely that he would have seen them. Whatever the sources he used, the texts were probably as close to the originals as they could have been at the time. The texts contained in the *Wu-tai Hui-yao* are fuller than those in the *Chiu Wu-tai Shih* and there are many edicts and memorials not found in the latter work at all. But the editor had chopped up some of the texts and arranged them according to subject headings modelled on those of the *T'ang Hui-yao*. He had also abridged or paraphrased some of the other texts.

The fact that the Sung was a great dynasty has caused this collection to be considered as one which rounded off the bureaucratic progress of an era. This would place a wrong emphasis on the work. Wang P'u could not have predicted the success of the Sung. He compiled the documents as a continuation of the *Hui-yao* of the T'ang dynasty and, by bringing the *Hui-yao* up to date, intended primarily to facilitate reference to bureaucratic precedents in a period of confusion. The contents show that the selection was guided by what the editor thought was important information to the bureaucrats. The limitations of the *Wu-tai Hui-yao* as historical material are thus clear. The Wu-tai was a period which was dominated by military men and new groups of officials not of literati origins. But these men were hardly dealt with except when bureaucratic controls were tentatively or successfully extended to them. From this collection, it would be easy to over-estimate the influence of the bureaucrats. Nevertheless, as the powerful figures of the period were inarticulate, even the indirect references to them have been valuable, especially if the documents throw light on the relations between them and the bureaucrats.

The arrangement of material in the *Wu-tai Hui-yao* is unlike that of the Monographs in the standard histories. The *Chiu Wu-tai Shih* has a select number of texts in 10 chüans and the later history, the *Wu-tai Shih-chi*, has a supplementary 3 chüans, but neither set of Monographs was found satisfactory by later scholars. In the 18th century, before the *Chiu Wu-tai Shih* was recovered, the 3 chüans in the *Wu-tai Shih-chi* were all that remained of Wu-tai institutions in the standard works. This aroused the historian Hsü Chiung to compile an addendum in 24 chüans, the *Wu-tai Shih-chi Pu-k'ao*. Although this contains little that is original, the new arrangement of material makes it a useful reference work. It draws on many non-official writings of the Sung, but largely re-classifies the material in the *Wu-tai Hui-yao* and augments it with more information from the other important collection of official documents of the period, the *Ts'ê-fu Yüan-kuei*.

The *Ts'ê-fu Yüan-kuei* is a different kind of collection altogether. It was compiled about half a century after the *Wu-tai Hui-yao* and was in the tradition of the great Sung encyclopedias at the end of the tenth century. It is an encyclopedia of general history with a new classification of the surviving official records in the imperial libraries. The large stock of T'ang and Wu-tai records available can be deduced by the preponderance of documents and biographical information for the two periods. This preponderance makes the collection valuable for this study. Although the mass of the material can be found in the *Chiu Wu-tai Shih* and the *Wu-tai Hui-yao*, there are notable exceptions, some of which have been collected by Hsü Chiung, some by the scholars who reconstructed the *Chiu Wu-tai Shih*, and others by P'êng Yüan-jui in his commentary to Ou-yang Hsiu's *Wu-tai Shih-chi* (published 1828). Where the material also appears in other collections, the *Ts'ê-fu Yüan-kuei* provides valuable texts for purposes of collation.

Three other Sung encyclopaedias, the *T'ai-p'ing Yü-lan*, the *T'ai-p'ing Kuang-chi* and the *T'ai-p'ing Huan-yü Chi*, all contain material on the Wu-tai. The *T'ai-p'ing Yü-lan* has quotations from the *Chiu Wu-tai Shih* and quotes the latter work as if the history of each of the five dynasties was a complete work in itself. In this way, it provides more texts for purposes of collation. The *T'ai-p'ing Kuang-chi* has been mentioned earlier as containing some anecdotal material while the *T'ai-p'ing Huan-yü Chi* gives valuable geographical data. A fourth encyclopedia, the *Wên-yüan Ying-hua*, also provides important historical material for the last decades of T'ang.

Three later collections have also been valuable for this study. The first is the thirteenth-century encyclopedia, the *Wên-hsien T'ung-k'ao*, important portions of which have been collected by Hsü Chiung in the *Wu-tai Shih-chi Pu-k'ao*. The second is the nineteenth-century collection of T'ang prose, the *Ch'üan T'ang Wên*, which includes Wu-tai writings. And finally, the great collection of various kinds of inscriptions by Wang Ch'ang, the 160-chüan *Chin-shih Ts'ui-pien*.

The bias of official records or even official collections is not always possible to correct, especially when there are so few surviving non-official sources for the Wu-tai. The more obvious editorial comments have helped to show some of the principles behind the selection of material, but the work of editing was often the last of a long process of official sifting and weeding. The mammoth task of questioning the origins of every fact and every story has not always been possible. I have only been able to clear up some points which are important for the argument of this study and explained them in the notes. For the chronological framework and the historical narration, I have depended largely on the Basic Annals of the *Chiu Wu-tai Shih* and on the last 40 chüans of the *Tzŭ-chih T'ung-chien*.

Select Bibliography

a. Early Chinese Works.

Chih-kuan Fên-chi 職官分紀, in 50 ch., by Sun Fêng-chi 孫逢吉, preface dated 1092, *Ssŭ-k'u Chên-pên* edition, 1934-35.

Chin-shih Ts'ui-pien 金石萃編, in 160 ch., by Wang Ch'ang 王昶 (1725-1806), 1805.

Ch'ing-i Lu 清異錄, in 2 ch., by T'ao Ku 陶穀, ca. 960, 1920.

Chiu T'ang Shu 舊唐書, in 200 ch., edited by Liu Hsü 劉昫 and others, completed 945. *SPPY* edition, 1927-36.

Chiu Wu-tai Shih 舊五代史, in 150 ch., edited by Hsüeh Chü-chêng 薛居正 and others, completed 974. *SPTK* edition, 1935. (Also consulted Ms. copy in microfilm, A 319-320, in the Chinese Library of the University of Cambridge, and the *SPPY* edition.)

Ch'un-ming T'ui-ch'ao Lu 春明退朝錄, in 3ch., by Sung Min-ch'iu 宋敏求, preface dated 1076, *TSCC* edition, 1935-7.

Ch'ung-wên Tsung-mu 崇文總目, in 5 ch., compiled by Wang Yao-ch'ên 王堯臣 and others, completed 1041, re-edited by Ch'ien Tung-yüan 錢東垣, edition of the Basic Sinological Series.

Ch'üan T'ang-Wên 全唐文, in 1,000 ch., compiled about 1814 by Tung Kao 董誥 and others, Undated edition.

Chün-chai Tu-shu Chih 郡齋讀書志, in 5 ch., by Ch'ao Kung-wu 晁公武, 1151, *SPTK* edition, 1935.

Ho tung Hsien-shêng Chi 河東先生集, in 16 ch., by Liu K'ai 柳開, edited by Chang Ching 張景 whose preface is dated 1000. *SPTK* edition, 1935.

Hsin T'ang Shu 新唐書, in 225 ch., by Ou-yang Hsiu 歐陽修 and Sung Ch'i 宋祁 and others, 1060. *SPPY* edition 1927-36.

Hsin Wu-tai Shih 新五代史, in 74 ch., by Ou-yang Hsiu and annotated by Hsü Wu-tang 徐無黨, edition of P'êng Yüan-jui

彭元瑞 and Liu Fêng-kao 劉鳳誥 with additional commentaries, including the complete text of the *Chiu Wu-tai Shih*, 1828.

Hsü T'ang Shu 續唐書, in 70 ch., by Ch'ên Chan 陳鱣, 1814. *TSCC* edition, 1935-7.

Hsü Tzŭ-chih T'ung-chien Ch'ang-pien 續資治通鑑長編, in 520 ch., by Li T'ao 李燾, completed 1174, Chekiang Shu-chü edition, 1881.

Ju-lin Kung-i 儒林公議, in 2 ch., by T'ien K'uang 田況 (1003-61). *TSCC* edition, 1935-7.

Jung-chai Wu-pi 容齋五筆, in 74 ch., by Hung Mai 洪邁 (1123-1202). *SPTK* edition, 1935.

Kuei-yüan Pi-kêng Chi 桂苑筆耕集, in 20 ch., by Ts'ui Chih-yüan 崔致遠, ca. 900, *SPTK* edition, 1935.

Lo-yang Chin-shên Chiu-wên Chi 洛陽搢紳舊聞記, in 5 ch., by Chang Ch'i-hsien 張齊賢, completed 1005, *Chih-pu Tsu-chai Ts'ung-shu* edition.

Mêng-ch'i Pi-t'an 夢溪筆談, in 26 ch., by Shên Kua 沈括, ca. 1086, with commentary (*chiao-chêng* 校證) by Hu Tao-ching 胡道靜, Shanghai, 1956.

Nan-pu Hsin-shu 南部新書, in 10 ch., by Ch'ien I 錢易, ca. 1016, *TSCC* edition, 1935-7.

Nien-êr Shih Cha-chi 廿二史劄記, in 36 ch., by Chao I 趙翼, 1795, *SPPY* edition, 1927-36.

Ou-yang Wên-chung Kung Wên-chi 歐陽文忠公文集, in 158 ch., by Ou-yang Hsiu (1007-72), *SPTK* edition, 1935.

Pei-mêng So-yen 北夢瑣言, in 20 ch., with 4 ch. of *i-wên* 逸文, by Sun Kuang-hsien 孫光憲, ca. 960, *Yün-tsu-tsai-k'an Ts'ung-shu* edition, 1899.

Pu Wu-tai Shih I-wên Chih 補五代史藝文志, in 1 ch., by Ku Huai-san 顧櫰三, *Êr-shih-wu Shih Pu-pien* edition, 1937.

Shih-lin Yen-yü 石林燕語, in 10ch., by Yeh Mêng-tê 葉夢得, ca. 1136, *Pai Hai* edition, ca. 1600.

Ssŭ-k'ung Piao-shêng Wên-chi 司空表聖文集, in 10 ch., by Ssŭ-k'ung T'u 司空圖 (837-908), *SPTK* edition, 1935.

Sung-ch'ao Shih-shih 宋朝事實, in 20 ch., by Li Yu 李攸, 12th century, Basic Sinological Series edition, 1935.

Sung Hui-yao Chi-kao 宋會要輯稿, in 200 *ts'ê*, Shanghai, 1936 — *Chih-kuan* 職官 section.

Sung Shih 宋史, in 496 ch., edited by T'o-t'o 托托 in 1343-1345, *SPPY* edition, 1927-36.

T'ai-p'ing Huan-yü Chi 太平寰宇記, in 200 ch., by Yo Shih 樂史, completed about 980, 1803 edition.

T'ai-p'ing Kuang-chi 太平廣記, in 500 ch., by Li Fang 李昉 and others, completed 978, *Wên-yu T'ang Shu-fang* edition (reprint of a Ming edition), 1934.

T'ai-p'ing Yü-lan 太平御覽, in 1,000 ch., by Li Fang and others, completed 983, *SPTK* edition, 1935.

T'ang Chih-yen 唐摭言, in 15 ch., by Wang Ting-pao 王定保, ca. 955, *TSCC* edition, 1935-7.

T'ang Fang-chên Nien-piao 唐方鎮年表, in 8 ch., by Wu T'ing-hsieh 吳廷燮, *Êr-shih-wu Shih Pu-pien* edition, 1937.

T'ang Hui-yao 唐會要, in 100 ch., by Wang P'u 王溥, 961, *TSCC* edition, 1935-7.

T'ang-shih Lun-tuan 唐史論斷, in 3 ch., by Sun Fu 孫甫 (998-1057), *Yüeh-ya T'ang Ts'ung-shu* edition, 1853.

T'ang Ta Chao-ling Chi 唐大詔令集, in 130 ch., by Sung Min-ch'iu 宋敏求, 1070, *Shih-yüan Ts'ung-shu* edition, 1916.

Ts'ê-fu Yüan-kuei 册府元龜, in 1,000 ch., by Wang Ch'in-jo 王欽若 and Yang I 楊億, completed by 1013, edition of Li Ssŭ-ching 李嗣京, 1642.

Tu-shih Fang-yü Chi-yao 讀史方輿紀要, in 130 ch., by Ku Tsu-yü 顧祖禹 (1631-92), Shanghai, 1955.

Tu T'ung-chien Lun 讀通鑑論, in 30 ch., by Wang Fu-chih 王夫之, *SPPY* edition, 1927-36.

Tung-tu Shih-lüeh 東都事略, in 30 ch., by Wang Ch'êng 王偁, completed 1186, Huai-nan Shu-chü edition, 1883.

Tzŭ-chih T'ung-chien 資治通鑑, in 294 ch., by Ssŭ-ma Kuang 司馬光, 1085, *SPPY* edition (1927-36) and punctuated and collated edition of 1956, both with *K'ao-i* and Hu San-shêng's 胡三省 commentary.

Tzŭ-chih T'ung-chien K'ao-i 資治通鑑考異, in 30 ch., by Ssŭ-ma Kuang, *SPPY* and 1956 editions both included in the *Tzŭ-chih T'ung-chien*. Also separate *SPTK* edition, 1935.

Wên-hsien T'ung-k'ao 文獻通考, in 348 ch., by Ma Tuan-lin 馬端臨, completed before 1319, *T'u-shu Chi-ch'êng* edition 1901.

Wên-yüan Ying-hua 文苑英華, in 1,000 ch., by Li Fang and Sung Po 宋白, completed by 987, edition of 1567.

Wu-tai Ch'un-ch'iu 五代春秋, in 2 ch., by Yin Chu 尹洙 (1001-46), *Ch'an-hua An Ts'ung-shu* edition, 1887.

Wu-tai Hui-yao 五代會要, in 30 ch., by Wang P'u 王溥, 961, *TSCC* edition, 1935-7.

Wu-tai Shih-chi Pu-k'ao 五代史記補考, in 24 ch., by Hsü Chiung 徐炯, *Shih-yüan Ts'ung-shu* edition, 1916.

Wu-tai Shih-chi Tsuan-wu 五代史記纂誤, in 3 ch., by Wu Chên 吳縝, ca. 1090, *TSCC* edition, 1935-7.

Wu-tai Shih Ch'üeh-wên 五代史闕文, in 1 ch., by Wang Yü-ch'êng 王禹偁, ca. 1000, *Ch'an-hua An Ts'ung-shu* edition, 1887.

Wu-tai Shih-hua 五代詩話, in 12 ch., by Wang Shih-chên 王士禎 and revised by Chêng Fang-k'un 鄭方坤, 1748, *Yüeh-ya T'ang Ts'ung-shu* edition, 1853.

Wu-tai Shih Pu 五代史補, in 5 ch., by T'ao Yüeh 陶岳, 1012, *Ch'an-hua An Ts'ung shu* edition, 1887.

Yü Hai 玉海, in 204 ch., by Wang Ying-lin 王應麟, thirteenth century, 1738.

Yüan-ho Chün-hsien T'u-chih 元和郡縣圖志, in 40 ch., by Li Chi-fu 李吉甫, completed 813-5, *Chi-fu Ts'ung-shu* edition, 1879-82.

General Collections

Ch'an-hua An Ts'ung-shu 懺花盦叢書.

Chi-fu Ts'ung-shu 畿輔叢書

Chih-pu-tsu Chai Ts'ung-shu 知不足齋叢書

Pai-hai 稗海

Shih-yüan Ts'ung-shu 適園叢書

Ssu-pu Pei-yao 四部備要

Ssu-pu Ts'ung-k'an 四部叢刊

Ts'ung-shu Chi-ch'êng 叢書集成

Yüeh-ya T'ang Ts'ung-shu 粤雅堂叢書

Yün-tzu-tsai-k'an Ts'ung-shu 雲自在龕叢書

b. *Recent Chinese and Japanese Works*

Ch'ên Yin-k'o 陳寅恪, *T'ang-tai Chêng-chih Shih Shu-lun Kao* 唐代政治史述論稿, Chunking 1944, reissued Shanghai, 1947.

—— "Ch'in-fu Yin Chiao-chien Chiu-kao Pu-chêng" 秦婦吟校箋舊稿補正, *Lingnan Journal*, 10/2, 1950, pp. 17-33.

Chou Lien-k'uan 周連寬, "T'ang Kao P'ien Chên-Huai Shih-chi K'ao" 唐高駢鎮淮事蹟考, *Lingnan Journal*, 11/2, 1951, pp. 11-45.

Ch'üan Han-shêng 全漢昇, *T'ang Sung Ti-kuo yü Yün-ho* 唐宋帝國與運河, Chungking 1944, reissued Shanghai, 1946.

Hinō, Kaizaburo 日野開三郎, "Gōdai Chinsō Ko 五代鎮將考 *Tōyō Gakuho*, 25/2, 1938, pp. 54-85.

—— "Tōdai Hanchin no Bakko to Chinsō" 唐代藩鎮の跋扈と鎮將, *Tōyō Gakuho*, 26, 1939, pp. 503-39 and 27, 1940, pp. 1-62, 153-212 and 311-350.

—— *Shina Chusei no Gumbatsu* 支那中世の軍閥 Tokyo, 1942.

——"Tōmatsu Konran Shiko" 唐末混亂史稿, *Tōyō Shigaku*, 10 (1954), pp. 1-94 and 11 (1954), pp. 1-18.

Hori, Toshikazu 堀敏一, "Gōdai Sōsho ni okeru Kingun no hatten" 五代宋初における禁軍の發展, *Tōyō Bunka Kenkyujo Kiyō*, 4, 1953, pp. 83-151.

—— "Tōmatsu Sho Hanran no Seikaku—Chūgoku ni okeru Kizoku-seiji no Botsuraku ni tsuite" 唐末諸叛亂の性格—中國における貴族政治の沒落について, *Tōyō Bunka*, 7, 1951, pp. 52-94.

Katō, Shigeshi 加藤繁, "Shina to Bushi Kaikyu" 支那と武士階級, *Shigaku Zasshi*, 50/1 (1939), pp. 1-19.

Kikuchi, Hideo 菊池英夫, "Gōdai Kingun ni okeru Jiei Shingun Shi no Seiritsu" 五代禁軍における侍衞親軍司の成立, *Shien*, 70, October 1956, pp. 51-77.

Ku Chieh-kang 顧頡剛 and Shih Nien-hai 史念海, *Chung-kuo Chiang-yü Yen-ko Shih* 中國疆域沿革史, Ch'ang-sha, 1938.

Kurihara, Masuo 栗原益男, "Tōmatsu Gōdai no Kafushi teki Ketsugo ni okeru Seimei to Nenrei" 唐末五代の假父子的結合における姓名と年齡, *Tōyō Gakuho*, 38/4, 1956, pp. 430-57.

Miyazaki, Ichisada 宮崎市定, *Gōdai Sōsho no Tsuka Mondai* 五代宋初の通貨問題, Kyoto, 1943.

Niida, Noboru 仁井田陞, *Tō Sō Hōritsu Bunsho no Kenkyu* 唐宋法律文書の研究, Tokyo, 1937.

— *Shina Mibunhō shi* 支那身分法史, Tokyo, 1942.

Sudō, Yoshiyuki 周藤吉之, *Chūgoku Tochi Seidoshi Kenkyu* 中國土地制度史研究, Tokyo, 1954.

—— "Gōdai Setsudoshi no Shihai Taisei" 五代節度使の支配體制, *Shigaku Zasshi*, 61, 1952, no. 4, pp. 289-329 and no. 6, pp. 521-39.

—— "Gōdai Setsudoshi no Yagun ni Kansuru ichi Kōsatsu—Bukyoku to no Kanren ni oite" 五代節度使の牙軍に關する一考察—部曲との關聯において, *Tōyō Bunka Kenkyujo Kiyō*, 2, 1951, pp. 3-72.

c. *Works in European languages*

Chi Ch'ao-ting, *Key Economic Areas in Chinese History*, London, 1936.

des Rotours, Robert, *Traité des Fonctionnaires et Traité de l'Armée, traduits de la Nouvelle Histoire des T'ang*, 2 vols. Leiden, 1947.

Eberhard, Wolfram, "The Composition of the leading political group, during the Five Dynasties", *Asiatische Studien*, vol. 1, no. 2, 1947, p. 19-28.

—— "Some sociological remarks on the system of provincial administration during the period of the Five Dynasties", *Studia Serica*, no. 7, 1948, pp. 1-18.

—— "The Formation of a new dynasty", *Beiträge zur Gesellungs- und Völkerwissenschaft* (Thurnwald Festschrift), Berlin, 1950, pp. 54-66.

—— "Remarks on the bureaucracy in North China during the tenth century", *Oriens*, no. 4, 1951, pp. 280-299.

—— *Conquerors and Rulers, Social Forces in Medieval China*, Leiden, 1952.

—— "Additional Notes on Chinese 'Gentry Society' ", *Bulletin of the School of Oriental and African Studies*, vol. 17, no. 2, 1955, pp. 371-377.

Levy, Howard S., *Biography of Huang Ch'ao* (translation from *Hsin T'ang Shu*), Berkeley and Los Angeles, 1955.

Pulleyblank, Edwin G., "A Sogdian Colony in Inner Mongolia", *T'oung Pao* vol. 41, 1952, pp. 317-356.

—— "Gentry Society: some remarks on recent work by W. Eberhard", *Bulletin of the School of Oriental and African Studies*, vol. 15, 1953, pp. 588-597.

—— *The Background of the Rebellion of An Lu-shan*, Oxford University Press, 1955.

Reischauer, E. O., *Ennin's Diary: the record of a pilgrimage to China in search of the law* (translation), New York, 1955.

—— *Ennin's Travels in T'ang China*, New York, 1955.

Waley, Arthur, *The Life and Times of Po Chü-i*, London, 1949.

Wang Gungwu, "The *Chiu Wu-tai Shih* and history-writing during the Five Dynasties", *Asia Major*, vol. VI, no. 1, 1957.

Wittfogel, K. A. and Feng Chia-sheng, *History of Chinese Society, Liao*, Transactions of the American Philosophical Society, Philadelphia, 1949.

Yang Lien-sheng, "A 'Posthumous Letter' from the Chin emperor to the Khitan emperor in 942", *Harvard Journal of Asiatic Studies*, vol. 10, 1947, pp. 418-428.

Index